CLUE BY CLUE, THE MYSTERIES
ARE UNRAVELING.
DON'T MISS—

- The shocking details found in the Ebla tablets about the people of Sodom and Gomorrah

- New facts that support the amazing life spans—*up to one thousand years*—reported in the Bible

- The mind-boggling discovery about technological advances known to the ancients

- The stunning real purpose of the Tower of Babel . . . and where it was built

- The fascinating long-lost tunnels uncovered beneath the streets of Jerusalem . . . and where they led

- The eyewitness accounts described in the Ipu-Wer papyrus . . . about the dark, deadly night of Passover

- What Napoleon first found about crossing the Red Sea

- The astounding discovery deep within a passageway *under* the Temple Mount.

SHARE THE MOST EXCITING DISCOVERIES
OF MODERN TIMES IN THE PAGES OF
OUR MOST ANCIENT BOOK—THE BIBLE!

ANCIENT SECRETS

OF THE

BIBLE

Charles E. Sellier
and Brian Russell

CHIEF RESEARCHER
David W. Balsiger

A DELL BOOK

Published by
Dell Publishing
a division of
Bantam Doubleday Dell Publishing Group, Inc.
1540 Broadway
New York, New York 10036

All scriptures are from the New International Version of the Bible and are used by permission.

ISBN: 0-440-21801-2

Printed in the United States of America
Published simultaneously in Canada

September 1994

10   9   8   7   6   5   4   3   2   1

OPM

ACKNOWLEDGMENT

The authors wish to express their appreciation to Leslie H. Stobbe for his editorial assistance on this book and to the numerous experts quoted herein who granted interviews for this book and the related television special.

FOOTNOTES

Experts who granted interviews for this book and the television special are usually not footnoted. All interviews were conducted during 1992.

CONTENTS

1

NEW ATTACKS
ON THE BIBLE

The idea that Moses with hundreds of thousands of Israelites passed through the Red Sea on dry ground is crazy.

No knowledgeable person believes in the account of the Tower of Babel.

We can all stop looking for the lost ark of the covenant and leave it to Hollywood, because that's where it belongs—in the realm of fantasy.

All the shouting and trumpet blowing in the world will not cause the fifteen-foot-thick walls of Jericho to collapse.

Why all the fuss over Sodom and Gomorrah? It's a mythological, moralistic story. The cities never existed.

THE BIBLE IS UNDER SIEGE! IT IS BEING ATTACKED from all sides—by the media, the academic world, credentialed experts, and by our society and governmental leaders. Even many who believe in the Bible often express doubts about the historical reliability of many biblical accounts. And as the critics have made stronger and stronger, well-documented arguments against the Bible, there have been fewer and fewer defenders of this great book coming forward.

Until now!

Hard-hitting critics argue for dumping the Bible into the trash can of antiquated legends and information useless for living in the modern world. These critics often center their attacks on the great unexplained mysteries of the Bible—the so-called "unbelievable" accounts of miraculous intervention by God.

Some of the world's greatest mysteries, and the world's greatest truths, lie hidden between the covers of the Bible. You will see, before you finish these pages, that in many cases they are one and the same.

It is indisputable, however, that these ancient accounts have generated more controversy and inspired more new books than ever could have been imagined by their writers. And until recently, neither those who love the Bible nor those who doubt its veracity have been able to settle the controversies with any degree of certainty.

Some of the "ancient secrets of the Bible" the critics love to question involve the mysterious disappearance of the world's original language and the emergence of five thousand new languages; the cataclysmic destruction of a whole group of cities in a fertile valley that is now a vast desert; the freeing of millions of slaves from Egypt; and the improbable destruction, by a band of wanderers, of an impregnable fortress city. These, and many more biblical stories the critics scorn, are not easily disposed of.

- How could upward of two million Israelites with animals and household items make it through the Red Sea, while Pharaoh's pursuing army drowned in it?
- What is the documentable evidence that all the races and languages of the world originated at the Tower of Babel?
- Is there any real evidence that the cities of Sodom and Gomorrah ever existed, and what was the "fire and brimstone" the Bible says fell on these cities?
- How could an army led by musicians blowing rams' horns bring down the walls of Jericho when there were two of them, each fifteen feet thick and over thirty feet high?
- What happened to Israel's most holy object, the

ark of the covenant? If it cannot be found,
maybe it never existed!

Certainly, critics of the Bible are justified in asking
tough questions about the more miraculous accounts in
the Bible. And those who believe in the Bible are justified in crediting God with the power to work miracles.
They are also justified in accepting these miraculous accounts on faith, because that is, after all, what God de-
mands. But does that mean we shouldn't face the critics
head on? Cannot we uncover the historical facts that lie
hidden in the Bible and present a reasoned response as
well as a faithful argument?

The answer is yes!

The Bible, in point of fact, stands on very solid scientific ground. As experts have learned more about the
sciences of archaeology, geology, climatology, anemol-
ogy, vulcanology, linguistics, sociology, and many other
disciplines not even known to some of the older and
more strident critics of the book, the feasibility, indeed
the probability, that the historicity of the Bible is accurate in every detail becomes more and more defensible.
Moreover, you will find in these pages evidence that
many scientific discoveries began with a careful reading
of the Bible.

It doesn't take away from God's amazing power to
perform miracles if we as intelligent, inquiring people
attempt to unravel the mystery of the forces He brought
to bear in causing such miraculous events. And until
we're able to explain the how and why behind these and
other miraculous biblical occurrences, the critics will
rage on and their voices will grow even louder.

This book will engage in that debate. We will present the biblical view and let the critics have their say. And we will present the case for the defense. Space limitations prohibit our being able to deal with all the miraculous events that take place in the Bible, but we will demonstrate that the children of Israel could have crossed the Red Sea on dry land while Pharaoh's soldiers perished; that the Tower of Babel did, indeed, exist; that the walls of Jericho did come tumbling down, just the way the Bible says; that the ark of the covenant was not only real but that it exists today; and that Sodom and Gomorrah were real cities that today lie buried under a layer of ash.

AN UNBELIEVABLE ESCAPE

Clouds of blowing dust stretched for miles. Men, women, and children, sheep and goats, donkeys and household pets walked, ran, and pushed each other in what seemed like an unending column. Already those in front were halfway across a ridge between two walls of water.

"Hurry, Ephraim, you don't have time to pick up anything," Bilhah exclaimed. "We've got two more miles to go before we get to the other side."

Seemingly oblivious to his mother's urging, Ephraim bent down to pick up a colored stone washed clean by the retreating waters of the Red Sea. Bilhah grabbed his arm and yanked him beside her.

"Ephraim, didn't you hear me? We've got too much to carry as it is. This is no time to add rocks to our load.

"I wish Dan were here to help me," she muttered,

looking around at the rest of her family trudging by her side. "He's always gone with Joshua and his soldiers when I need him most."

Her friend Sarah smiled at Bilhah.

"Don't be too hard on the boy. They want mementos of this trek through the Red Sea. After all, we are part of a miracle."

Bilhah nodded her head knowingly.

"I've never seen water pile up in two walls like this," she said, grabbing Ephraim again just as he was about to dart off.

Sarah smiled. "Were you there when Moses lifted up his hand over the water? I saw the waves get larger and larger until there were literally two walls of water, with dry land appearing between them," Sarah said, adjusting her load of personal belongings. "It was a true miracle of God."

"Dan said the Egyptian chariots will catch up with us and take us back or kill us all if we don't get to the other side quickly," Bilhah responded, keeping a firm grip on Ephraim's arm.

The long column's haste confirmed that all the people shared Bilhah's fear. Families were carrying all their belongings as they jostled each other for position in the line of march. Older men not suitable for battle under Joshua shifted heavy loads on their shoulders. Teenagers kept sheep and goats in formation, running about as they tried to keep the animals moving forward at the pace of the families.

Two million Israelites were being propelled forward by four words: "Pharaoh's army is coming." They knew their dreaded former taskmasters, the hated Egyptians, were on their way to return them to Egypt or kill every man, woman, and child.

"THE WHOLE IDEA IS CRAZY"

The idea that hundreds of thousands of Israelites passed through the Red Sea is crazy. The Bible says there were 600,000 males. That means over 2,000,000 people passed through those waters. It most likely would have taken several weeks for all those people just to cross. The whole idea is crazy.

That's a highly respected Jewish rabbi speaking, Rabbi Sherwin Wine of the Birmingham Temple, Farmington Hills, Michigan, founder of Humanistic Judaism.

Do you agree? Is it fact or fiction? Even General Norman Schwarzkopf, the hero of the Persian Gulf War, would find moving that many men, women, children, and animals a challenge! Alas, the crossing of the Red Sea, as the critics say, just doesn't seem possible!

Another story that is documented with some precision in the Bible has to do with a father and his two daughters in the center of another highly controversial series of events. In fact, virtually every aspect of the following events has been called into question.

THE DAY FIRE FELL
FROM HEAVEN

The evening sun's rays were slanting across a well-watered, grassy plain. On a treed hillside above the small city of Zoar, a father and his two daughters were resting under a tree, their eyes focused on clouds of dust rising amid the distant roar of thunder and flashes of lightning. Intermittently a new black column of smoke arose, seemingly lifted by the bright glow of a tower of fire.

"I am glad the angels let us stop at Zoar before God destroyed it, too," Lot said wearily. "I could not have gone another mile." Lot was trying to find something positive for his daughters to think about amongst the devastating events of the day. "We'll stay in this cave overlooking the plain," he added.

"But Father, what happened to our fiancés? And all our other friends?" asked the younger of the daughters, brushing back a wisp of hair from her eyes.

"I can't tell you," Lot said. "All I know is that the divine visitors said God would destroy our city with fire and brimstone. I hate to think of what is going on in Sodom and Gomorrah and the other cities of the plain."

"Why did Mother stay behind?" the other daughter asked. "She was with us for miles, and suddenly I did not hear her complaining voice anymore. And you would not let us look back."

Lot stroked his beard in obvious grief.

"Let's leave her to the mercies of a righteous God. I, too, miss her already, despite her complaints at our sudden departure from the home we loved so much. But the angels would not be denied . . . they insisted we leave immediately."

"IT'S A MYTHOLOGICAL STORY"

Why all the fuss over Sodom and Gomorrah? It's a mythological, moralistic story. The cities never existed. This story and similar stories were used by the high priest to instill fear and guilt among his followers.

Speaking for the skeptics is well-known television host and Bible critic Dr. Michael Chandler, founder of the International Research and Educational Society, headquartered in southern California.

Are you ready to accept Dr. Chandler's conclusion? Many do, because Bible scholars have failed to address the numerous questions surrounding the account of Sodom and Gomorrah—questions that have gone unanswered for nearly three thousand years.

Now let's drop in on a biblical account that's even harder to believe than the one concerning Sodom and Gomorrah.

A TOWERING ACHIEVEMENT

The plains of Shinar surrounding the city of Babel were truly a beehive of activity. As far as the eye could see, rich farmlands teemed with people harvesting exotic fruit trees, bushes loaded with a marvelous variety of berries, and gardens filled with an abundance of vegetables and grain.

On a farm near the city of Babel a father and son were starting the wine-making process.

"Have you heard the latest from King Nimrod?" Jared asked as he dumped grapes into the winepress.

"You mean about the tower?" his father responded as he stepped on the new grapes to press out the juice.

"Right. My friend is part of the work crew. They've discovered how to make a new burnt brick that will support a lot more pressure and last longer. Now they can add at least several hundred more feet to King Nimrod's tower," Jared said, picking up another container of grapes.

"Why are they trying to build an even higher tower? After all, we already have a high tower and many beautiful temples," Mahalaleel asked.

"King Nimrod is determined to reach into the heavens," Jared said. "His priest has assured him that the gods will visit with him personally if the tower reaches into the heavens."

"Maybe, but have you heard the old prophet of God who is walking the streets denouncing the tower and insisting God will judge King Nimrod for building it?"

"He's just a beggar looking for a handout," Jared scoffed. "Announcing judgment just gets him attention."

Out in the fields around Babel the talk was all about this astonishing new tower being erected in the city of Babel at a site selected by King Nimrod. Everyone marveled at the unusual architecture that displayed the extraordinary new burnt bricks developed specifically for the tower.

Those who came back from selling produce in the city's marketplace reported that the king had ordered a new addition to the height of the tower. It appeared he was defying the God of Noah's day by constructing a new ziggurat that would let him stand face-to-face with the gods of heaven.

"KNOWLEDGEABLE PEOPLE DON'T BELIEVE THE ACCOUNT"

No knowledgeable person believes in the account of the Tower of Babel as historical fact . . . or that the races and languages on the earth all sprang from this one little area in Mesopotamia.

That's the outspoken criticism of a renowned Assyrian biblical scholar, Dr. Rocco A. Errico, professor of Aramaic studies in southern California and author of the book *The Mysteries of Creation.*

Is the Bible's description of the Tower of Babel fact or fiction? Is it a description of a real event, or a fanciful reconstruction of a biblical fable? Dr. Errico certainly expresses the beliefs of millions of people, including an ever-growing number of Christians.

Now, sit back as we let another highly controversial scene from the Bible take place before your mind's eye.

A YELL AND A CRASH

"Rahab, Rahab, they've stopped marching."

Susannah was breathless from hurrying in off Jericho's city wall.

"I counted, and they have marched around the city seven times. I wonder what they are going to do now."

Rahab stopped her cooking and rushed to the city wall with her daughter.

"Are you sure the scarlet rope is still in our window?" she asked as they began the ascent to the outer city wall surrounding the inner wall protecting Jericho.

"Yes, I checked only an hour ago. I know something terrible is going to happen, but I don't know what."

Susannah stepped onto the roof with Rahab.

"I've done what the Israeli spies told me to do," Rahab said breathlessly. "I have no idea what is going to happen next either. But their god has helped them defeat every army that has met them on their way to Jericho. And our spies reported that the Jordan River had literally stopped flowing and let them walk through on dry land." Rahab surveyed the line of Israeli warriors around the city. "Jericho's leaders are truly afraid of what their god is going to do for them next," she added.

Just then they saw rams' horns being raised. The sound of a fanfare of rams' horns split the air, joined by the fierce yell of thousands of voices from all the Israelites encircling the city of Jericho. At that moment the whole city began to heave and shake. At regular intervals along the wall, bricks started falling down.

"Hurry, let's get back to our house. If we can trust the word of the Israeli spies, we should be safe," Rahab said as she rushed off an already shaking wall and ran to her house.

The region's oldest and most fortified city was clearly under siege by more than a motley crew of Israelite soldiers. A mighty force was shaking the foundations of the city, and the walls were beginning to collapse.

"JUST A RELIGIOUS LEGEND"

All the shouting and trumpet blowing in the world will not cause fifteen-foot-thick walls to collapse. The whole Joshua/Jericho account is just a religious legend. While Jericho is one of the oldest cities of the world, there is nothing on the site that relates it to the story of Joshua's conquest.

Pointed criticism indeed from Dr. Gerald Larue, emeritus professor of biblical history at the University of Southern California at Los Angeles and author of *Old Testament Life and Literature*.

But is the story of the destruction of the walls of Jericho make-believe, or is it based on a true story? Is it a miracle of God's intervention for his people or an over-dramatized version of an attack on an insignificant fortress? Today many people side with Dr. Larue's opinion, since the evidence seems to support his view.

Let's visit one more hard-to-believe scene in biblical history, this one from the time of everyone's hero, King David.

IT WAS A WRONG MOVE!

The procession had begun early in the morning. King David was bringing the ark of the covenant, the most holy possession of the Israelites, into the city.

"I'm so glad King David decided to bring the ark of the covenant to the tabernacle." Zadok turned to his fellow priest Ahimelech. "That's where it belongs, according to our ancestor Aaron. Yet it's been fifteen years since it was brought back by the Philistines and placed in the home of Abinadab."

The music of the orchestra accompanying the procession almost drowned out his words. Musicians ahead of them with harps, lyres, tambourines, drums, and cymbals seemed in ecstasy as they played their hearts out.

Ahimelech looked back. "This looks like a military procession," he muttered. "All I can see are his warriors. The ark certainly didn't need an army to protect it when it was captured by the Philistines."

"That is true," Zadok replied, "and they did not keep the ark very long after their god Dagon mysteriously fell over on his face in front of the ark without any help from anyone."

Ahimelech listened to the music for a minute. He could see David playing his harp with the best of them.

"No wonder David is bringing the ark to the tabernacle on a new wagon pulled by oxen. That's how the Philistines brought it back safely," he added, almost as an afterthought. Turning to Zadok, he said, "But if he had asked me, I would have told him that the law says it must be carried on poles by priests."

Zadok's arm shot out. "Look, the ark is going to fall

off the cart," he almost shouted. Ahimelech and Zadok could see Uzzah, one of the sons of Abinadab who had been appointed by his father to accompany the ark, reach out to steady it. In that frozen moment of time between the cart starting to tip and Uzzah reaching to steady it, a streak of blazing light hit the son of Abinadab and knocked him to the ground.

The sound of music stopped instantly. . . .

King David then instructed the Levites to transport the ark in the manner prescribed by God! It was moved to the tabernacle, where it remained during his lifetime. Later it rested in the temple built by King Solomon.

It is now about four hundred years, and many kings later, and Jerusalem has been under siege by the armed might of King Nebuchadnezzar of Babylon for over two years.

"Will their battering rams ever stop pounding?" Jephthah, the priest, wailed. "King Zedekiah insists our walls will hold, but I'm beginning to wonder. There is no more food, and people are dying on the street." He turned to the others in the room and added, "Jeremiah the prophet has predicted the city will fall to the Babylonians. Maybe he is right after all."

The small circle of gray-bearded priests nodded their heads in agreement.

"What happens to our holy objects if the wall is breached?" asked one of the priests.

"Jeremiah the prophet says the city will be totally destroyed and everyone taken to Babylon. He says we'll be captives for seventy years and then return. We've got to hide our most holy objects for the day of repentance when God lets the people return," Jephthah said.

"But where will they be safe if Nebuchadnezzar's troops destroy the temple and burn it with fire?" asked one of the priests.

Everyone sat silent for several minutes. Then one of the priests spoke up.

"There's a secret passage under the temple leading to a vault. If we hide the ark of the covenant and other holy objects there, we can seal the entrance to the secret passage. Then we can give the secret to one of our young priests who still worships Jehovah and pray that he survives," he said.

At that point another priest burst into the room.

"The wall has been breached. Nebuchadnezzar's men are entering the city. King Zedekiah is trying to escape."

"The time has come," Jephthah announced. The priests left hurriedly on their secret mission.

"LEAVE IT TO HOLLYWOOD"

As serious scholars, we can all stop looking for the lost ark of the covenant and leave it to Hollywood. Because that's where it belongs, in the realm of fantasy. The fact of the matter is that, if the ark ever existed, and that is doubtful, it would have been lost during Solomon's reign.

That's the frank opinion of religious researcher and Bible critic Jordan Maxwell, author and guest lecturer at the University of California. Millions share his view that the ark of the covenant is fantasy, because there is little nonbiblical evidence that would support what's described in the Bible regarding the ark.

And why is there no word of the ark's whereabouts after the death of Solomon? Should we believe the statements of Jewish rabbis who insist they know where it is today? Too many questions without good answers, say the critics!

THE STAGE IS SET

Five of the ancient mysteries of the Bible have now been identified. The critics have submitted their first round of opinions, and they'll be back with more hard-to-refute criticisms.

In our journey to find the ancient secrets behind these mysteries, we're going to go head to head with these critics. Ours is a scientific and archaeological quest to discover, identify, and report the truth as it unfolds through a close examination of facts and claims by both critics and proponents of this amazing book, the Bible.

These new findings will challenge your understanding of the Bible and strengthen your faith in what is unquestionably the bestselling book of all time . . . because you are about to discover that although it was written two thousand years ago, the Bible's universal relevance is even more astonishing today.

2

A BATTLE FOR CITIES THAT NEVER EXISTED

No scholar, no historian, takes any of these stories as historical facts.

Dr. Rocco A. Errico
Professor of Aramaic Studies

SODOM AND GOMORRAH. ABRAHAM AND LOT. Mesopotamian kings. The cities and people in the first few chapters of the Bible. Are they real cities and real people?

"Only the gullible can accept these stories as historically accurate," insists eminent critic Professor Rocco Errico, a man well versed in the ancient Aramaic language. According to him, the stories are all myths and legends.

Yet if you take away the historical reliability of the story of Abraham, this pivotal figure in the history of Arabs, Jews, and Christians simply disappears. It's like telling the millions of people who have venerated him for over four millennia that their great man of faith, their literal progenitor, is a fraud. That is not an easy pill to swallow. Perhaps we shouldn't be trying to swallow it. We'll see shortly.

But before we examine both the case made by the critics and the evidence for relying on the stories of and about Abraham, let's get acquainted with the two men introduced in the Bible as Abraham and Lot. To do that we have to turn the clock back more than four thousand years.

AN ANCIENT CIVILIZATION

Let's start with the region in which these two men lived; historians refer to it as Mesopotamia. It was the area between the Tigris and Euphrates rivers where, it is generally believed, civilization began. Abraham was born in Ur of the Chaldees, an important city in Mesopotamia. It was located north and east of Canaan. Today the area is included in Iraq's territory.

Chedorlaomer, the king of Elam, the Bible tells us, allied himself with three other kings from Mesopotamia to raid the five cities in the Dead Sea region. The coalition may have plundered other cities along the trade route from Mesopotamia to the Dead Sea as well.

Canaan, which later became Palestine and then Israel, lies on the route between Egypt, Assyria, and Babylon, so it was frequently invaded, both from the north and the south.

This then, generally speaking, was the area in which Abraham and Lot were caring for their herds and flocks and families at the time that our story begins.

AN ARMY DEFEATED
BY SERVANTS

The slanting rays of the setting sun cast long shadows on the fertile Jordan Valley. On an incline leading to the forested slopes of the hills above it, a collection of tents of goats' hair was dominated by a multi-roomed "mansion" set up under a large tree. Herds of sheep and goats milled about to one side. Shepherds on the lookout for stragglers or predators patrolled the perimeter.

In the shade under the awning of the spacious, multi-roomed tent, Abraham and his nephew, Lot, reclined on couches made of sheepskin. They were enjoying a relaxed evening meal. Women served them with choice morsels.

"I'm certainly thankful to the Lord and to you and your men for saving my life," Lot said as he reached for a piece of lamb. "Two weeks ago when we were led away as captives by Chedorlaomer's triumphant soldiers, I didn't think I'd ever see you again or eat food like this. In fact, I thought we'd be slaves in Mesopotamia for the rest of our lives."

Lot instinctively began to rub his wrists gently. "I can still feel the iron shackles on my arms and legs," he said. "It will be weeks before the bruises from the guards' beatings will heal. My wife and daughters are still having nightmares from their abuse by lustful soldiers."

"Yes, that certainly was a close call," Abraham confessed. "I was shocked when an escapee told me that all of the cities of the plain had been plundered by Chedorlaomer's army." Abraham stroked his beard and added pensively, "I thought the city's armed forces were stronger than they obviously were." He looked up at Lot. "When your man escaped and came here to tell me that you and your family were among those taken captive, I had to do something."

"Clearly, the kings of Sodom and Gomorrah, and of the three cities who were allied with them, chose a poor place to stand and fight," Lot said. "They were no match for the highly trained and well-equipped army of Chedorlaomer and his allies. In a matter of minutes they fled, with many losing their lives in the tar pits behind them. Those who escaped the sword and the tar pits fled into the surrounding hills, leaving us helpless as the soldiers ransacked the cities. They took everything of value as the victor's spoils."

"I'm glad my trained servants were equal to the task. If we had met Chedorlaomer in formal battle lines on a plain, we would have had no chance."

"But the idea of splitting your men," Lot interjected, "and attacking them at night from opposite sides while they were celebrating worked very well."

"If it hadn't, you'd be a slave by now," Abraham observed, "close to where you were born."

Lot's gaze locked onto his uncle's. "I am indeed grateful that you risked your life on my behalf. You have rescued me twice, first when my father Haran died and now this. I owe you so much."

TRUE STORY OR HEROIC LEGEND?

Is this episode from the life of Abraham and Lot a true story or a heroic legend? Are stories about the rapid deployment force used in the rescue of Lot, told in Genesis 14, historical truth or myth built on legend? Did the story of Abraham simply grow as it was told and retold?

Perhaps the most commonly held view is that expressed at the beginning of this chapter by Dr. Rocco Errico, professor of Aramaic studies at a California university. "No scholar," he says, "and no historian takes any of these stories as historical facts."

Dr. Errico appears to have one thing on his side.

Even though Abraham looms extra-large in biblical history, for years he was nowhere to be found in the historical records found in ruins of the region.

It seems now, however, that Abraham may have been there all along. Earlier archaeologists just didn't know what to look for.

Dr. Bryant G. Wood is an atomic energy engineer turned archaeologist and biblical scholar. With a doctorate in Syro-Palestinian archaeology from the University of Toronto, Canada, Dr. Wood has been either a volunteer or supervisor on three major archaeological digs in Egypt and Israel. A specialist in Canaanite pottery of the Late Bronze Age, Dr. Wood has received major international acclaim for his research on ancient Jericho, and he is quick to respond to Dr. Errico.

Dr. Wood reports that those digging in the ruins of Numeira, an ancient city next to the Dead Sea, "found a stone tower with evidence of warfare and destruction." In fact, the scholars found two destructions. One happened just shortly before the final destruction of the city by a massive firestorm (more about that later). The earlier attack, according to Dr. Wood, could be related to the accounts in Genesis of the kings of Mesopotamia coming against the kings of Sodom and Gomorrah and the cities of the plain.

Circumstantial evidence? True, and the kind that critics quickly dismiss as inconsequential. But there is much more to come.

BORN A CITY DWELLER

The biblical story itself is clear enough when it comes to Abraham. It identifies his birthplace as Ur of the Chaldees in the region of Haran to which his father moved the family. The Bible also indicates the areas in Canaan in which Abraham eventually lived. But again, neither Ur or Haran were found in archaeological excavations during the flurry of digs in Mesopotamia in the last century. Critics had a field day mocking the biblical record for its inaccuracies.

Then, in the 1920s, excavations revealed a truly magnificent city and advanced civilization clearly identified as Ur of the Chaldees. Ten years later cuneiform tablets found in another newly excavated city, Mari, the capital of the northern Mesopotamian kingdom of Mari, revealed a whole series of familiar-sounding biblical names, including Peleg, Serug, Nahor, and Terah. The tablets even named the city of Haran, where, the Bible says, Abraham lived until his father, Terah, died.

Biblical scholars took the offensive. After all, if the place names in biblical stories had been found, couldn't the other details in the stories be accurate as well?

So, what might life have been like for Abraham in the city and country he grew up in before leaving for Canaan? Let's drop in once again on our very likely conversation between Abraham and Lot. After all, it's not unlike conversations that go on between an uncle and a nephew almost every day.

AN AMAZINGLY ADVANCED CIVILIZATION

Nibbling at a fig, Abraham was clearly ready to talk, so Lot seized the opportunity.

"Let me ask you a question," Lot said eagerly. "I wasn't yet born when you and grandfather Terah left Ur. What was life like in Ur?"

"Ah, yes, Ur! Ur of the Chaldees." Abraham obviously relished the recollection. "I was in my late teens when we left that marvelous city, but I remember it well. Ur had developed on the delta between the great rivers, the Euphrates and the Tigris. It was a magnificent city, flourishing as a center of trade and commerce.

"Merchants from all over the world brought their spices, gold and silver, precious stones and ivory. We loaded them down with woolen goods for the return trip. Temple workshops turned out the finest wool wall hangings, carpeting, garments, and accessories made in the world.

"Ur was a great place to live. Whatever my father and mother wanted could be purchased from the merchants in Ur."

Lot shifted his position to get more comfortable. "What were the houses like? I've seen Ebla and Damascus. Were they anything like that?" he asked.

"Hardly." Abraham smiled. "You remember that almost all Damascus homes were single-story. But in Ur the majority of houses were two stories high, with the lower section built with burnt brick and the upper walls with mud-brick.

"When you came into the house, the entrance hall

contained a basin with water to wash the dust off your hands and feet. Then you walked into an inner court paved with smooth stones. Around this room were the reception area, the kitchen, living rooms, and private rooms."

Lot could not imagine a house that size. "What was on the second story?" he asked.

"Up a stone staircase you reached a hallway, off which branched the rooms for the various members of the family, as well as the guest rooms. As children we ran up and down those stairs constantly between our room and the living area on the main floor." Abraham was clearly remembering some very good times as a child.

"Did you worship the Lord God there?" asked Lot.

"No," Abraham replied, a tone of reverence in his voice. "The Lord became my God when he spoke to me directly." He paused for a moment and added, "But the city had large temples for numerous other gods, and the temples were far more than places of sacrifice to the god of that temple. That's where my father went to deliver his taxes, which were paid in oil, fruit, wool, and cattle. These were stored in great warehouses. Of course my father also brought animals for the sacrifices required by the priests. My father was a wealthy man, so we made many trips to the temple each year."

Abraham poured Lot and himself another mug of wine.

"Why did you move to Haran?" Lot asked. "That was a long trip for your family, wasn't it?"

"Indeed it was, but opportunity beckoned and my

father packed up and moved the whole clan," said Abraham, shifting position as he relaxed with a cooling drink.

"Was Haran like Ur?"

"No, for even though it was the capital of the Plain of Aram, it was still not nearly as well developed as Ur. Culturally it represented a big step down for our family, but we did very well at Haran until my father died." Abraham sat back, a faraway look in his eyes.

Lot grew reflective as well. "It must have been hard for you to pull up stakes and move a second time, and to take me along after my father died."

"Yes, especially since Sarah was most comfortable there and had all her friends and family in Haran. But when God spoke to me so clearly, telling me to move on, I knew we had to obey."

"Yes, I remember. What a trip that was!" Now Lot's eyes had that faraway look as he thought back on the six-hundred-mile journey. "All those caravans of camels meeting us, loaded down with a wide assortment of goods from Egypt, of purple cloth from Phoenicia. Even as a boy I could see that merchants considered this the main trading route between Mesopotamia, Egypt, and Phoenicia.

"And those evenings together on the oases along the way! As young people we had so much fun sharing our experiences as we watered the sheep and goats at the wells."

"Do you remember Damascus?" asked Abraham.

"Who could forget it?" Lot was getting quite animated. "I remember the huge increase in traffic, coming from both directions, as we approached the city. What a prosperous place that was.

"I loved the apricot and almond trees in full bloom as they lined the streets, turning the city into a pink wonderland. And the shops . . . amazing. There seemed to be everything you could imagine available in the shops, a lot of which we had not seen in Haran."

"But there was not a lot we could take with us," Abraham interjected. "After all, we had no idea how much farther we had to travel."

"What a disappointment that was for me as a young man," Lot said, smiling. "But the trip through the region by the Lake of Galilee almost made up for it. The memory of snow-capped Mount Hermon in the distance and Lake Galilee sparkling below us has not faded with the passing years."

"I remember your reaction when we first entered the Jordan Valley," said Abraham. "You could not get over the forests of trees on the hillsides, the carpet of green grass on the plains in the valley. And our shepherds could not wait to get to the lush carpeting of grass either."

"But it also did not take us long to run into some of the Canaanites and Perizzites who considered the Jordan Valley their own," said Lot, his face turning serious. "The Perizzites had the choice pasture lands to themselves for many years, backed up by the Canaanites in their cities."

WHEN WEALTH MEANT
GREAT HERDS

We'll leave Abraham and Lot to their reminiscing for a moment.

In terms of degree of difficulty, you could compare their move to a trek from New York State to Colorado in covered wagons, stopping at Chicago and St. Louis on the way. But after their years in Canaan, they had both become wealthy men.

Yet, what was wealth in those days? We have an account of another ancient wealthy man to help us visualize Abraham's riches. In Job 42:12 we read that Job "had 14,000 sheep, and 6,000 camels, and 1,000 yoke of oxen, and 1,000 female donkeys."

The Bible does not give us any count of Abraham's possessions, but we do have an indication of the number on his "payroll." Remember the story of King Chedorlaomer joining forces with three other kings to defeat the kings of the five cities in the area, including Sodom and Gomorrah?

The Bible tells us Abraham received the news of the capture of Lot, along with the other prisoners taken by Chedorlaomer, as he was hobnobbing with two Amorite kings who were his allies.

The retreating army was in no hurry, for they were bringing back large quantities of booty and thousands of sheep and cattle. Knowing that Chedorlaomer and his allies would be moving slowly and not expecting any attack, Abraham quickly marshaled his security force. He had 318 armed men trained specifically for this kind of action. They rushed after the retreating four kings, probably riding camels. When Abraham and his men caught up with them, he split his small force into two groups, and under cover of darkness, ambushed Chedorlaomer and his allies, putting them to flight. Lot and his family were released and all the prisoners returned to Sodom,

Gomorrah, and the three other cities of the plains, Admah, Zeboiim, and Bela (later called Zoar).

If, as the Bible reports, Abraham had a personal security force of 318 armed men, and they were strong enough to defeat the joint army of four kings, then he clearly was a powerful man in his area. He probably had more than a thousand employed as shepherds and cattle and camel herdsmen.

The Bible reports that the increase in the herds of both Abraham and Lot resulted in too many sheep, goats, and cattle for the available pasturelands. To see how they resolved this problem, let's rejoin Abraham and Lot in an even earlier time as they met to try to resolve the problem of increasingly bitter skirmishes between their respective shepherds.

TIME TO NEGOTIATE FOR PEACE

"Abraham, Abraham, come quickly. There's a group of people arriving," Joel shouted, breathing hard after his sprint to find his master. "The size of the dust cloud tells me this is more than just one or two men."

Abraham hurried to the area in front of his large tent. He stopped long enough to alert Sarah to begin preparing refreshments. By the time he had done that, he could identify that there were possibly a dozen men in the approaching party. As they came closer he recognized his nephew Lot on the lead camel.

The great animals swayed to a halt in front of Abraham. Lot and his men dismounted. Abraham and Lot greeted each other warmly with a kiss on both cheeks.

"It's so good of you to come at my bidding," began Abraham as they headed for the shade. "I'm sure you are hungry after your ride, so let's relax under this tree while the food is prepared.

"The Lord has been too good to both of us," began Abraham after they had settled down under the tree. "My herds have multiplied incredibly the last few years. Yours, too, have increased dramatically in number."

"Yes, but the pasturelands have not increased in size, nor has the supply of water," Lot replied. "Our shepherds have begun to fight over the right to water their sheep, goats, cattle, and camels at the same wells. Some of my men were wounded in a pitched battle over a section of grazing land."

At that point the women brought the food prepared hastily for the honored guest. Serving dishes were piled high with roast lamb, a form of pita bread, and fruit.

"If it were only the two of us, it would be enough," said Abraham as he reached for a piece of lamb, "but the Canaanites living in the fortified cities want water to irrigate their gardens. And the Perizzites want water from the wells for their herds of sheep and goats, as well as access to the available pasture. We must do something, and soon."

Lot's hand was poised over the food as he turned to Abraham. "You are right, Uncle. There's just no way to stop the ewes having lambs and the goats having kids. At this point the competition between your shepherds and mine to see who can get the biggest increase in their herd is costing us both dearly."

"I have a suggestion to make," Abraham replied, "but let's finish the meal first. I feel we need to take the time to look over the land God has given us to make the right decision."

After the meal the two men wandered away from the tent and climbed a promontory overlooking the Jordan Valley to the east. To both sides and behind them lay the hills, southwest, west, and east of the valley, many covered with trees above the lowlands between them.

"Isn't this a marvelous sight?" asked Abraham, sweeping his hand over the hills and the valley. "I'm so thankful God brought us here. But the beauty of this valley and our relationship could be shattered if we don't do something about the strife between our shepherds."

"I agree. What do you suggest?" asked Lot.

"First let me assure you that I care about you as if you were my own son. More than that, we are brothers in the love of God. I cannot bear the thought of strife coming between us, between your herdsmen and my herdsmen.

"At our feet lies a beautiful valley. Behind us are the lowland pastures of the hill areas. There is really enough space for both of us. So I'm suggesting that you decide which area you would like as your homeland, your territory, whether it is the valley of the Jordan or the hills with their lowlands. Whatever you choose, the area to the left or to the right, I'll take what remains."

"As always, Uncle, I bow to your wisdom." Lot turned to look over the area. He pivoted from the left to the right, taking in the features of the plains, mentally evaluating the special benefits of the hill country. He lingered over the beautiful valley of the Jordan, carpeted with luxuriant green meadows, with large flocks of sheep, goats, and an occasional group of camels.

A FATEFUL CHOICE

Lot knew that in the distance lay five cities, including Sodom, which was known for its temples and special religious festivals. He had visited Sodom on more than one occasion on business, and the idea of settling near there was most attractive. He knew his wife would enjoy getting out of the tent and into a real house someday, no matter how comfortable the tents were.

Abraham waited patiently, for he could see Lot was lost in thought. Suddenly Lot turned to Abraham.

"I've made up my mind. I'll take the valley," he said. "There'll be lots of pasture for my herds, and I know my wife will enjoy going into Sodom more often."

"If that is your choice, may the Lord bless your decision, may He increase your herds and bless your family richly. I will take the hills and lowlands between them," said Abraham.

They embraced and turned to go back to the encampment.

A MORALISTIC STORY?

The Bible comments on Lot's decision:

> Abram, whose name was later changed by God to Abraham, lived in the land of Canaan, while Lot lived among the cities of the plain and pitched his tents near Sodom. Now the men of Sodom were wicked and were sinning greatly against the Lord. [Genesis 13:11,12]

There's a clear forewarning of impending trouble in that statement, leaving us wondering if Lot made a bad decision. That's a good mystery fiction technique, but is it a contrived tale written by ancient priest storytellers to serve as a warning to their listeners?

Dr. Michael Chandler, a specialist in mythological theology, educated at Stanford University and founder of the International Research and Educational Society, agrees with the last suggestion. He asks, "Why all the fuss over Sodom and Gomorrah? It's a mythological, moralistic story. The cities never existed. This story and similar stories were used by the high priests to instill fear and guilt among their followers. The priests, having knowledge of science and astronomy, still used these mythological stories to control the people."

But remember Dr. Wood, our atomic scientist turned archaeologist? His group found evidence of two destructions in the plains cities, which definitely did exist. Nor is Dr. Wood alone in his findings.

Let's examine what another scholar specializing in the history of that region has to say. Dr. William H. Shea, a medical doctor and medical school professor who then gained a second academic doctorate to become a professor of Near Eastern studies at Andrews University, reveals some startling new evidence that Sodom and Gomorrah really did exist.

Now a research associate with the Biblical Research Institute in Washington, D.C., and author of more than one hundred articles on Near Eastern archaeology, Dr. Shea states emphatically, "Sodom and Gomorrah certainly did exist, and we have an ancient cuneiform tablet from the city of Ebla in Syria which mentions them."

Since this is our second mention of cuneiform tablets, perhaps we should take a moment and discuss exactly what a cuneiform tablet is. That term will come up many times as we examine the findings in the ruins of ancient cities.

"Cuneiform" is the word used to describe wedge-shaped ancient writing. It appears inscribed into clay tablets and on round cylinders and prisms. These clay tablets with the funny-looking symbols contained the records of shopkeepers, travelers, and lawyers of the day, as well as the history of the kings. First attempts at reading the symbols proved futile, but word by word, specialists in ancient languages were able to decipher them. Even then, they discovered they had to constantly learn either new languages or variations of existing ones as they dug up new ruins of ancient cities in order to interpret them.

The Ebla tablets referred to by Dr. Shea were an incredible archaeological find. Something like twenty thousand clay tablets were unearthed in northern Syria. These ancient tablets, found by two professors from the University of Rome, Dr. Paolo Matthiae, an archaeologist, and Dr. Giovanni Pettinato, an epigrapher, contain significant information for Bible students.

Based on the information in these tablets, we know that the city of Ebla was at its height of power in 2300 B.C., with a population of probably 260,000 people. It was destroyed in about 2250 B.C., but in the ruins this treasure trove of tablets describing the activity of daily life in the ancient world was discovered. Once scholars unlocked the secrets in these tablets, historians were able to have a much clearer picture of what life was like during the time of Abraham. In fact, it has become clear that Abraham must have visited the city when he moved from Haran, even farther north, to the Jordan Valley.

Bible scholars are also intrigued by the references to place names and to male and female names we see in the Bible. But most important, Dr. Shea's studies revealed details of a merchant's trip taken before 2300 B.C., probably even before Gomorrah was developed as a city. Dr. Shea comments:

> When the Ebla tablet discovery was first announced in 1976, there was some debate and discussion over whether the names of Sodom and Gomorrah were mentioned in those tablets. The tablets discussed at that time were relatively minor and not important for our purpose.
>
> We have a more important tablet now to study. It's known as the *Eblaite Geographic Atlas*. It contains a list of 290 place names. I have studied about 80 of these place names in two different segments.
>
> These two segments of the list give names that run through the land of Canaan, where the ancient biblical patriarchs lived. The second segment cuts from the central hill country of Canaan east towards the Dead Sea, around the south end of the Dead Sea, and then up to the plateau of Jordan, and finally south to the Gulf of Aqabah.
>
> Of particular interest is name number 210, Admah in the old Canaanite form. That's Admah from the biblical list of the cities of the plain from Genesis 14. The next name, number 211, is very interesting because it is written with signs that are unmistakably clear . . . Sadam, or Sodom, the biblical Sodom.
>
> But the debate is whether Sadam is really south of the

Jordan, or somewhere else, like in Syria. It's the final name on the list of this merchant's travels. Aqabah is obviously the Gulf of Aqabah, and that confirms that he had traveled through Sadam south of the Dead Sea. That's where the biblical Sodom was located.

Yet why is this list of names from the *Eblaite Geographic Atlas* so important? One reason is that it is a diary of cities visited by a well-traveled merchant from the great city of Ebla of the Early Bronze Age just before the time of Abraham. Suddenly the cities of the Bible gain recognition as real cities during a period of ancient history also described in the Bible.

A REWARD FOR SELFLESSNESS

But wait, there's more. Like any good whodunit, the good guy has to be rewarded. The Bible gives us another description of scenery that has become a major target for critics.

Obviously a softy, Abraham got the raw end of the deal by letting Lot have first choice and moving to the highlands, the mountainous terrain. Or did he? This is the biblical report:

> The Lord said to Abram after Lot had parted from him, "Lift up your eyes from where you are and look north and south, east and west. All the land that you see I will give to you and your offspring forever. I will make your offspring like the dust of the earth, so that if anyone could count the dust, then your offspring could be counted." [Genesis 13:14–16]

It certainly sounds like Abraham is going to get his reward. In fact, the promise seems to imply his descendants will inhabit even the valley and the grassy plain selected by Lot. But there's no dire prediction of a terrible fate for Lot in these words.

One final encouragement from God for Abraham: "Go, walk through the length and breadth of the land, for I am giving it to you." [Genesis 13:17]

And here's where we get a hint of what we just had not expected to find in Canaan, based on today's barren hills (until the modern Israelis began planting trees): "So Abram moved his tents and went to live near the great trees of Mamre at Hebron, where he built an altar to the Lord." [Genesis 13:18]

Great trees of Mamre? A primeval forest of giant trees in what for the last two to three thousand years was a dry and barren landscape? We know trees existed in Lebanon, up in Mount Hermon territory, for they were used as timber in many parts of the Near East.

But "great trees" at Hebron? South of Jerusalem in the hills baked by the hot Canaanite sun?

Here is yet another unbelievable description that set critics of the Bible chortling and Bible believers reeling. Is there evidence that the hills of southern Canaan were forested more than four thousand years ago? And if there is such evidence, is it reliable? But we're getting ahead of our story.

To many, an even greater mystery is the role of divine messengers in Abraham's life. In the next chapter we'll explore their mysterious appearance and their astounding messages.

3

A HARSH LAND
OR A FERTILE VALLEY?

*This is a harsh, hard land . . . certainly not a
land where a pair of Bedouin stockmen could
become rich inside of a generation.*

Austin Miles, Author
Don't Call Me Brother

Is there any way to really tell what it was like to live in Canaan in the area around the Dead Sea around 1900 B.C.? Did Abraham and Lot live like the bedouin in Jordan and Israel today, as our author critic implies? Or were they the equivalent of nomadic millionaires, as the Bible indicates?

Scholarly critics attack the biblical story as impossible in light of the barren hills and plain in the region around the Dead Sea. But is there genuine evidence that in the Early Bronze Age, Abraham's day, Sodom and Gomorrah and the other cities of the plain were surrounded by a fertile valley?

If the critics are right, then Abraham becomes another mythical figure in religious history, and we cannot trust any part of his story . . . nor the Bible as a historically accurate document.

You'll recall that according to the Bible, Abraham settled by the great trees of Mamre, near Hebron, after Lot chose the lush plains around the city of Sodom. Then one day divine visitors came to Abraham. They brought a message of an upcoming miraculous birth, as well as a foreboding message that meant extreme danger for Lot and his family. Let's join Abraham as he welcomes the visitors.

A GUEST WITH A SPECIAL MESSAGE

In a large opening in the forest on a gently sloping hill near Hebron stood a large tent, more like the pavilion of a Near Eastern potentate or the general of a large Assyrian army. All the flaps were tied back to let what little breeze there was flow through the tent.

In the doorway sat Abraham, the most powerful man in the region. That morning a series of key men on his staff of shepherds, herdsmen, and camel drivers had come by for consultation. Now it was time to relax and catch some of the shade provided by the pavilion.

What an incredible month it had been, Abraham reflected. God had appeared to him in person and promised that he, at age one hundred, would be the father of a boy to be named Isaac. He had had a good laugh at the idea, since Sarah was ninety. But God had overlooked his laughter and said that, yes, indeed, in less than a year he would hear the cry of a son.

God had also asked that, as evidence of their commitment to each other, Abraham circumcise all of the males of his company. What an undertaking that had been, he mused. Not every shepherd or herdsman had jumped to attention when the idea was first presented to them. But it was done.

The bleating of goats interrupted Abraham's musings. He looked around and saw three men standing nearby. How did they get by his guards? He jumped up and hurried to meet the men, bowing low to the ground in Near Eastern fashion.

"Peace be with you, brothers, and welcome to my humble tent. Will you not rest and refresh yourselves?"

"We are not really in need of refreshment at this time, but we welcome your hospitality," said one of the men, obviously the leader from the way he spoke.

"I look forward to serving you, even though it be but a poor meal. I'm sure your feet are hot and dusty and will feel refreshed after being washed," Abraham said. "Let me provide a resting place in the shade of that great tree there. It has provided refreshing shade for many a weary traveler."

Abraham was famous for his warm hospitality, and his servants were well trained to go into action immediately when a stranger arrived. They appeared seemingly out of nowhere carrying rugs and clean water in jugs and clay basins in which to wash feet.

Abraham left his guests in the capable hands of his servants and rushed to find Sarah.

"Quick, get some flour and mix some bread dough. Your fresh pita bread is so good, and these guests deserve the best," he ordered.

Sarah gave him a look and said, "Oh, no, not another of your *important* guests. The way you keep interrupting me, I'll never get my work done."

But Abraham hardly heard her. As he rushed off he thought, *That's Sarah. She complains but she is a most gracious hostess.* On his way to a corral where they kept some ewes with lambs, he was joined by another servant. He was very particular about the meat served, so he selected his own animals for the meals for special guests. He pointed out a good-looking lamb and ordered the assistant to have it prepared for roasting. Now he could relax and take time for his guests.

Abraham approached his guests under the tree at a more leisurely pace, not at all aware of the astonishing news he was to receive. As he joined his guests, servants were already bringing dried fruits to munch on. He kept a sharp eye open for the progress of the food preparation while entering into conversation with his guests.

A MESSAGE FOR SARAH

"Where is Sarah?" asked the leader of the trio of guests.

"She's in the tent helping to prepare the meal," Abraham replied, surprised by the question.

"I will be returning in a year," said the visitor. "And when I return, Sarah will be nursing a son."

The light wind had carried the conversation to the tent, where Sarah was making final preparations to deliver the food. At his pronouncement she began laughing inwardly, catching herself in time to prevent an audible sound so as not to appear impudent.

What a ludicrous prediction, she thought. *Here I am, old and worn out, and my husband is well beyond his best years, and we are to have a child?*

As she emerged from the tent with the servants to set the food before the guests and Abraham, the leader looked at Abraham.

"Why did Sarah laugh and say, 'How ridiculous that I am to have a child, since I am old'?"

Knowing that no one had heard her laugh or could read her thoughts, Sarah said, "I didn't laugh."

The leader watched her set out the food and then said gently, "Oh, but you did. No need to deny it."

After enjoying a hearty meal, the leader signaled his companions that it was time to leave. They stopped to raise their hands in blessing over the household of Abraham.

"Let me accompany you for a while," Abraham suggested, falling in step with them. It appeared they were headed for Sodom.

"Abraham," the leader said, "because of their total disregard of human decency and their outrageous self-indulgence, the outcry against Sodom and Gomorrah is so great that I am on my way to see if it is really as bad as the reports. Maybe the news I have been receiving is exaggerated. If it is not, I will destroy the city."

A MYTH CREATED BY THE CHURCH?

What is it about Sodom and Gomorrah that upsets the God of Abraham so much? Here's what the Bible says about these cities: "Now the men of Sodom were wicked and were sinning greatly against the Lord." [Genesis 13:13]

It's this kind of gratuitous comment that sets the critics on edge. One of them is Austin Miles, a former minister in the Assemblies of God churches and currently an author and speaker. His most recent book is entitled *Don't Call Me Brother*. Here's what he has to say about the cities of Sodom and Gomorrah:

Sodom and Gomorrah is a myth created by the church, and that illustration is used as a constant threat against the disobedient. Nor were Sodom and Gomorrah destroyed by fire and brimstone. This was invented by the same minds that invented hellfire.

For millions today that criticism rings true. They have had more than enough condemnation, they tell us, from Bible believers referring to Sodom and Gomorrah.

Nevertheless, the criticism of the Sodom and Gomorrah story by Austin Miles also brings a strong rebuttal from many who are convinced of the historical accuracy of the Bible.

One of the experts who comes down on the side of biblical accuracy regarding Sodom and Gomorrah is Dr. Marvin A. Luckerman. Dr. Luckerman is the publisher of the *Catastrophes of Ancient History Journal*, and a scholar specializing in the Middle East. Dr. Luckerman studied history at the University of Southern California, received an M.A. in Islamic Studies from the University of California at Los Angeles, and completed post-graduate studies in the history of the Middle East at the same university. For a year he studied Hebrew, Arabic, and the history of Egypt at the Hebrew University in Jerusalem. For three seasons he did field excavation as an archaeologist.

Dr. Luckerman's studies have convinced him that Sodom and Gomorrah certainly did exist, but were destroyed by a massive fire and brimstone explosion, as described in the Bible.

It is my belief that Sodom and Gomorrah were located on a fault that runs from Turkey to Central Africa, and that this fault was very active seismically. Also in the same area was pitch and oil that even today bubbles up to the surface of the water.

I believe that this combination of factors, the earthquakes, the petroleum in the area, creates the possibility for a disaster that could have destroyed all five cities of the plain. I believe that it is very real and very possible.

The evidence that Sodom and Gomorrah existed and were destroyed during the Early Bronze Age is mounting. Let's summarize what we have learned thus far.

- An ancient merchant traveled a route that included Sodom and Admah, another of the five cities on the plain.
- Archaeologists digging at the ancient city of Numeira (Gomorrah) near the Dead Sea found evidence of two destructions, close together. The second one terminated all life at the site.
- The cities of Sodom and Gomorrah lie on a fault that has been seismically active at regular intervals in history.
- There is clear evidence of incendiary materials like pitch bubbling up in the Dead Sea.

With that evidence in mind, let's rejoin Abraham and the divine messengers.

AN ATTEMPT TO AVERT DESTRUCTION

By now Abraham knew he was dealing with no ordinary visitors. God had, after all, visited him in human form before this, in Haran and again at the terebinth-tree of Moreh. As the reality of what might be on God's mind exploded in his head, Abraham stopped the leader of the group.

"Sir, are you really thinking of sweeping away the righteous with the unrighteous? Suppose there were fifty righteous persons in Sodom and Gomorrah, would you still destroy the cities? I know you are a righteous God and must bring judgment, but why destroy those who are living righteously as well?"

"Abraham, I understand your concern. If there are fifty who worship God, I will not destroy the city."

"But what if there are only forty-five?"

"Not even if there are forty-five."

"Well, maybe there are only forty. Would you still destroy it?"

"No, that's enough to hold off my judgment."

They had resumed their walk toward Sodom as the exchange continued. Eventually Abraham got down to what he thought might be the number of righteous people in Lot's household . . . ten people.

"And if there are ten, O Lord, will you destroy the cities?"

"Abraham, if there are ten people who worship the true God, I will not destroy Sodom and Gomorrah."

At that Abraham reluctantly bade farewell to his guest and returned to his encampment, still deeply troubled. He was hoping against hope that Lot and his family had won over at least six or seven to serve the Lord.

"HE COULD MAKE A GRAND LIVING"

Abraham's negotiation with God on behalf of Lot and his family has also been a sore point with many critics. Why would God bother to haggle with a mere man? The whole story, they say, is contrived just to make a point.

I suppose it depends somewhat on whether or not you have already accepted the story of Abraham, the way he lived, and his dealings with God as credible.

If you have not, count on author Austin Miles to agree with you. He not only objects to accepting Sodom and Gomorrah as real cities, he also refuses to accept the Bible's depiction of Abraham and Lot's lifestyle in the Jordan Valley. Says Mr. Miles:

My main objection to this is the depiction of the area as a well-watered, fertile land that could sustain giant herds of cattle. In reality, this is a harsh, hard land . . . certainly not a land where a pair of bedouin stockmen could become rich inside of a generation.

Additionally, the Bible describes the area as watered by "five rivers" and supporting five cities. Yet there are no traces of agriculture ever having been an extensive enterprise. Certainly the history of neighboring towns and the country around it does not support the fact that there were five rivers and five cities on the plain.

That kind of challenge to the Bible's truthfulness is worth considering and investigating, especially if we consider the landscape of this area today. Around the Dead Sea the land is indeed barren, with the exception of a strip of agricultural land with a stream on the southeast coastline of the Dead Sea.

As Dr. Bryant G. Wood, the Syro-Palestinian archaeologist, puts it: "The landscape today is like a lunar landscape. It is very dry."

Enter a critic of the critic! Dr. Steven Collins, a professor of cultural anthropology, has done research in Europe and the Near East, including studies at the prestigious International Institute for Human Rights at the University of Strasbourg, France. He specializes in ancient climates. Dr. Collins says:

It is terribly naive to assume that the climatological aspects and other features of the land in Palestine have remained the same over the course of several thousand years. We know that in the American Southwest we have had a great deal of climatological change over historical periods. It is the same in the Middle East.

As we look back to periods prior to 1000 B.C., we find much evidence that the region of Palestine, at least at higher elevations, was heavily forested. There were very large trees, and the rainfall that would have resulted from such forests would have been much greater than it is today. The grasslands which would have been around Sodom and Gomorrah would have been able to support a wide range of domesticated animals. In addition, there is much evidence that the land supported a wild animal population that is not unlike North Africa. Elephant herds even roamed northern

Syria, with the demand for their tusks being so great that the elephants became extinct by the eighth century B.C.

Through the centuries, beginning around 3000 B.C., deforestation was in process. The great empires of the day took the trees and used them to construct their buildings and build their cultures. By 1000 B.C. the climate had changed dramatically as a result.

As part of our research we have compiled a great deal of the world's weather patterns over the years and created a data bank. By factoring in what we know about an area, we can combine this data to produce computer projections concerning annual rainfall and the climate. Based on our readings, I would have to say that the Bible is accurate.

Thus in Abraham's time, as the Bible states, this particular part of the world was capable of supporting his flocks. He could make a grand living in this part of the world.

Then perhaps the Bible is right, after all, when it reports: "Lot looked up and saw that the whole plain of the Jordan was well watered, like the garden of the Lord, like the land of Egypt, toward Zoar." [Genesis 13:10]

Dr. Bryant G. Wood agrees with that assessment, but on the basis of archaeological evidence:

In Abraham's day, this was a lush region. There were tens of thousands of people living there then. We know this from the cemetery at the ruins at Bab edh-Dhra (Sodom), and the four other cities to the southeast of the Dead Sea, all with very large cemeteries, with tens of thousands buried in them. And the people in the cities depended on the plain for their livelihood, for their food.

We can tell something about the life of these people from the burial places. Anthropologists have studied the skeletal remains and have determined that these people were very, very prosperous. They had a very good diet, for they were clearly healthy.

In fact, these people were quite a bit taller than the average height for that time. Some of these people were over six feet tall. In those days anyone over six feet tall would have been considered a giant, for the average height was about five feet and two inches. Evidently the plain produced a lot of food, so they had all they would need.

DID SOMEONE SAY ELEPHANTS IN SYRIA?

Archaeological evidence also supports the position that climates, and thus animal and plant life, changed in the centuries after Abraham lived. For example, we now know that up to the eighth century B.C. a major source of ivory from elephants was a region in northern Syria. Syrian and Phoenician craftsmen provided a variety of beautiful ivory carvings from the tusks provided by these elephants. King Solomon was one of the key buyers of this ivory. Yet the elephants totally disappeared after the eighth century B.C.

The critics dismiss Abraham as a fictional figure because they say the region could not have supported the herds of sheep and cattle the Bible says he had. Their judgment is based on the way things are in the region today. On the other hand, there are those whose study of climate and archaeological remains has convinced them that the region definitely could support the lifestyle described in the Bible.

In fact, the more we learn, the more convincing the evidence seems to be that Abraham could indeed have been grazing thousands of sheep, goats, and camels in south Canaan. The case for Abraham as a genuine historical figure is growing stronger!

In light of that, what do you think went through his mind as he conversed with God and watched the two angels walk toward Sodom? Would Lot and his family survive? Would the cities of Sodom and Gomorrah survive?

We know, of course, that the Bible reports that Sodom and Gomorrah did not survive; that they were destroyed by fire and brimstone..

But what is the evidence of "fire and brimstone"? Are the critics right when they insist this is just a "mythological and moralistic" story concocted by priests to scare people?

Dr. Luckerman, remember, says there is ample evidence that fire consumed the five cities on the plain. But just what is "brimstone"?

Keep these questions in mind as we join the divine messengers during their visit with Lot in Sodom.

4

DIVINE VISITORS BRING A WARNING OF DOOM

Why all the fuss over Sodom and Gomorrah? The cities never existed.

Dr. Michael Chandler
Professor of Astrotheology

TIME TO TAKE OUR EYES OFF ABRAHAM AND FOCUS ON the Early Bronze Age city of Sodom.

The divine visitors, who had left Abraham with the commitment that if ten righteous remained in Sodom they would spare it, were now approaching the city. Inside the walls they could hear the sounds of a great celebration, like Mardi Gras in New Orleans. The city was rocking with what seemed like nonstop revelry. After all, they were rich, abundantly supplied with everything needed to enjoy the good life.

Is this what Sodom was really like?

Combining biblical and archaeological information, we see that the city may well have been everything the biblical record suggests and more. When the two divine messengers appeared at the gates, they may have walked into the following scene.

AN ASTARTE REVEL

Shutters were removed from windows. Tables appeared in the street. First, a few people here and there emerged from houses, but they were soon joined by a swelling multitude of men and women beginning the celebration of the monthly festival know as the "Astarte Revels," two days of drunken revelry, licentiousness, and general abandonment of moral principles.

Following the afternoon heat, the streets of Sodom were awash with people dressed in festive garments, seemingly bent on making every moment a moment of pleasure. No one bothered with even the briefest courtesy.

Carts loaded with merchandise and donkeys laden with goods and led by businessmen competed for space to move around. Almost hidden by the mass of humanity were the beggars with outstretched hands or the occasional musician playing for coins to be dropped into clay containers.

Shopkeepers set out tables in the street to capture the attention of passersby. They knew that men drunk with celebrating spent more freely.

Live music floated from eating places, entertaining revelers determined to drink themselves into oblivion to satisfy the gods of the festival. Occasionally, a group of young men singing bawdy songs marched down a street, looking for sexual prey. Male and female prostitutes solicited at key intersections.

As the evening progressed, the intensity of the celebrations increased. Wine and beer released inhibitions, and men engaged freely in public displays of sexual acts. No one seemed concerned, going about their business as though this were normal.

Crowds gathered around games of chance, captivated by the risk-takers and occasionally joining them. The higher the risk, the bigger the crowd. Young and old alike collected together, and neither gave any deference to the other.

A MISSING ELEMENT

Archaeology has uncovered a major mystery about life in the cities of the plains during the Early Bronze Age when Abraham and Lot apparently lived there. It may explain why the divine messengers were sent to Sodom.

Though the archaeologists have determined that life was indeed prosperous in the cities of the plains during the time of Abraham and Lot, there is no archaeological evidence of clearly formed families. According to Dr. Bryant G. Wood, the Syro-Palestinian archaeologist, an examination of the cemeteries in Bab edh-Dhra (Sodom) and four other plains cities reveals no evidence of normal family life.

Dr. Wood says, "Anthropologists have concluded from the burial sites that it was a communal type of life. They did not have families, for we have no evidence for any sort of family burials. It's as though they were a wide open society, with homosexuality and all kinds of other things going on there."

This is a strong assessment, and anthropologists make their claims only on the strongest evidence.

There are two kinds of cemeteries, or burial sites, in the ruins of Bab edh-Dhra and the adjoining cities of the plains on the southeast end of the Dead Sea. According to Professor Randall Younker, director of the Horn Archaeological Museum, Amman, Jordan:

These cemeteries of the Early Bronze Age at Bab edh-Dhra consist basically of a shaft into the ground. After two meters, they would dig sideways, creating five chambers for the burial of bodies to be laid out in these side chambers. With 50,000 bodies located in the area, a large number of these shafts exist in the region.

Another type of burial is in the charnel houses. These are basically large rooms on the surface. The bodies were laid out inside these large burial houses.

The skeletal remains in these burial sites indicate no family groupings, as they do in cemeteries in other parts of the world. Could the Bible be right after all when it reports, "Now the men of Sodom were wicked and were sinning greatly against the Lord"?

DIVINE VISITORS MEET LOT

Just inside the main gate, the leading businessmen of the city seemed a world apart from the revelers. Real estate brokers concluded transactions. Grain and produce buyers haggled with farmers for the large quantities of grain, sheep, and cattle needed to feed a growing population. Builders dealt for the bricks and other products needed to erect new structures.

The leading businessmen also represented the governing elite of the city, so between deals they negotiated with people from the food and entertainment world for licenses granting special privileges. Special interests fought for positions on government councils. The under-the-table money was often as substantial as the business income that had brought them their status as power brokers in the city.

Facing the gate in a privileged location sat Lot, the nephew of Abraham. He was busy negotiating for the sale of a new crop of lambs when he glanced up and saw two men coming through the gate.

Lot knew immediately that there was something different about these men, for their appearance set them apart. They simply did not "look" like residents of Sodom.

"Joshua, take over," he said as he turned to his assistant. "I'll be back in a few minutes. Don't complete the deal on the lambs until I return."

Lot knew that strangers were always received with suspicion in Sodom. This was particularly true during festival times, since it was easy for spies and ne'er-do-wells to mingle with the crowds. Lot determined to intercept the two visitors before the celebrating Sodomites approached them. As a well-known resident of Sodom, he felt he could prevent the visitors from being harmed.

Pushing aside the clay tablets on which he was doing business, Lot got up and headed for the visitors. As he did so a small mob of howling, singing revelers in masks and costumes rolled by. He glanced at them apprehensively and hurried to the visitors.

Bowing low to the ground he said, "Gentlemen, I perceive that you are visitors to our city. May I know your names and whether you have friends in Sodom who can provide hospitality for you?"

The visitors glanced at each other with knowing looks.

"I am Raphael," said the taller of the two men, "and

this is my companion, Jaliel. We are unknown in this city."

"We shall spend the night in the streets," his companion added. "After all, you seem to have a festival going on."

Looking around to make sure no one could overhear him, Lot said quietly, "That would not be wise, gentlemen. This is the first night of Astarte Revels. Strangers are not welcome in the city of Sodom, particularly during the celebration."

"We appreciate the warning," said Raphael, "but we thought we could mingle with the crowds and be quite inconspicuous."

Lot looked them over and smiled. "Unless you wore masks and costumes you would be perceived as strangers," he said. "We have gangs of young men who just love to overtake strangers and amuse themselves by sexually molesting and beating them."

Jaliel asked, "What do you propose we do?"

"I have a good and secure house," said Lot quietly so as not to be overheard. Receiving a visitor was almost as dangerous as being a visitor in Sodom. "My family and I will be happy to entertain you for the night. My wife and daughters will prepare a fine meal, and I know you will enjoy their company as well."

Lot felt Raphael's eyes upon him and felt the power in his voice.

"You clearly follow God's ways," the stranger said, "for it is clear that few, if any, would extend hospitality as you have. We will accept your offer."

"Come with me and I will close my business for the

day," said Lot. The men joined him as they walked toward his tables.

"Hazor, can we complete our negotiations on the lambs tomorrow? I have unexpected company that I must see to."

Lot then turned to his servant and said, "Joshua, give me the tablets. I'll take them home with me. You take care of the tables so we will be ready for Hazor in the morning."

Lot and his guests made their way through the crowds as quickly as possible, hoping to avoid attracting the revelers' attention.

REAL CITY OR GOOD STORY?

Does the above bear some resemblance to fact or is it just another small fiction? Could this scene, based on the biblical account, be a true reflection of what went on in a real city more than four thousand years ago? Or is it just another in the accumulation of priestly stories designed to hold the faithful in line?

Some scholars suggest that the excavations in the cities of the plains reveal a rather prosperous community around the time the Bible says Abraham and Lot lived in the area.

In an article titled "The Antiquities of the Jordan Rift Valley" in the *Biblical Archaeology Review,* Rami G. Khouri, a reporter for the *Jordan Times,* offers an interesting revelation about that particular area around the Dead Sea:

Before starting the first of four seasons of excavations between 1975 and 1981, Dr. Walter Rast and Dr. R. Thomas Schaub in 1973 surveyed the area in the vicinity and south of Bab edh-Dhra, to place the large site within its proper historical and geographical context.

They discovered that Bab edh-Dhra was not an isolated urban phenomenon in an otherwise sparsely populated area. Rather, it was the largest and northernmost of a line of Early Bronze Age town sites along the southeast shore of the Dead Sea, that were also adjacent to fertile agricultural lands and had good sources of fresh water nearby. . . .

During the Byzantine period, the area was once again densely inhabited and extensively cultivated—indicating that the growing population and more extensive agricultural activity taking place today in the Southern Ghors and northern Wadi el 'Araba are only a contemporary repeat of historical development patterns dating back thousands of years.

Regarding the agricultural activity in the area during the time of Abraham and Lot, Rami G. Khouri writes:

Flotation of plant remains from Bab edh-Dhra indicates the people were growing and harvesting wheat, barley, grapes, olives, figs, lentils, chickpeas, flax, pistachio, almond and assorted wild plants, with strong evidence that irrigated agriculture was practiced. . . .

Bone remains show that animal species that existed at Bab edh-Dhra, whether to be eaten, used as beasts of burden or for other reasons, included sheep and goats, donkeys, camels, gazelles, cats, dogs, hyenas, rodents, lizards or turtles, and possibly some fish and birds.

With many scholars now convinced that Bab edh-Dhra is indeed the actual site of Sodom, this archaeological evidence of a rich and diversified agriculture and animal life would seem to confirm that the lifestyle of Abraham and Lot, and of the residents of Sodom and Gomorrah, was indeed comfortable if not sumptuous.

STRANGERS COME TO DINNER

Lot glanced up and down the street as they approached his residence in a quiet neighborhood of Sodom. The noise of the revelers could be heard, but was now too distant to be bothersome. Yet Lot knew he had to be careful, for revelers were known to wander outside the downtown area. So he swept the street with one last glance before he opened the door and entered with his guests.

"Belilah," Lot said to his wife, as he entered the living area. "I'd like you to meet two guests I intercepted entering the city, Raphael and Jaliel." He turned to his two girls and said to his guests, "And there are my daughters, Rachel and Sarah, who will wash the dust from your feet."

As the men sat down to relax for this common gesture of hospitality, Lot joined his wife in the kitchen.

"I've tried to find out why these men have come to Sodom, but they have not told me. Yet I am sure these are not ordinary visitors. Perhaps by the time dinner is ready they will learn to confide in us."

"Dinner will be ready in half an hour," she replied.

Lot faced his family at the dinner table.

"It is God's blessing to have guests at dinner with us

tonight. But just the same, I was most careful to make sure no one in the neighborhood was aware of them entering our home. You never can tell who might come down our street during the Astarte Revels."

The face of Lot's wife wore a stricken expression. The daughters looked at each other almost hopelessly. Lot could see he had struck a nerve.

"Belilah . . . ?"

"I needed salt because of our guests. I borrowed from Ismeth, our neighbor. I'm certain she will say nothing."

The visitors seemed unconcerned, but Lot gave his wife a strongly disapproving look.

Later that night the table had been put back against the wall, with the benches placed on top. The daughters were spreading sleeping rugs on the floor for the guests, and Belilah was tending the lamp.

Every head turned to the door as the sounds of revelers suddenly ricocheted down their street. Lot and his wife looked at each other again in concern, but the visitors remained calm.

Meanwhile, a raucous mob of masked revelers rounded the corner into Lot's street. People popped out of doors to see what was going on, and some of the young men of the neighborhood joined the crowd. As they approached Lot's house, a tiny woman hurried up to the mob leader and cupped her hand to his ear to share some news. The leader let out a wild howl. He raised his torch and cried for the mob to follow him.

THE ATTACK BEGINS

Inside the house the approaching din continued to raise Lot's fears. Suddenly the house reverberated with the sound of heavy pounding on the front door. Everyone turned instinctively to see if the door had given way. They were relieved it had not broken.

The pounding continued as a rough voice, slightly intoxicated, was heard: "Ho in there! You son of a camel! If you abide in our city, live as we do. Send those strangers out."

The first voice was joined by a second. "Because you are rich and your uncle is Abraham, you think you can scorn us! Send those men out, or we will knock your house down brick by brick, with you in it."

On the street, more torches joined the mob as word of strangers in the home of Lot was passed from person to person. The derisive shouts, demanding the strangers be put in the street, grew in volume.

Lot's concern now was not only the fate of the strangers, but that of his wife and daughters as well. He had heard many stories of drunken mobs attacking a house, breaking in, and sexually molesting both male and female inhabitants. Now they were the target, and they were clearly outmanned by the intoxicated mob.

Rachel and Sarah were cowering in a corner, crying silently. Lot's wife gestured to him to help her move the heavy table against the door, when Raphael stepped to the door. Lot and his wife stepped forward as though to stop him, but he waved them off.

Raphael slid back the bolt on the door as Jaliel joined him. As the door opened, the mob surged forward to enter the dwelling. Raphael lifted his hand as though in a blessing. In that moment everyone in the mob was blinded and their shouts turned to grumbling and fear as they groped foolishly in the dark.

Lot and his family heard the frenzy of the crowd change to curses and occasional screams of pain as they stumbled into each other and trampled those hapless few unlucky enough to stumble and fall.

Raphael and Jaliel kept their hands raised, and as each new group entered the street they were stricken with the same lack of sight. Several fell writhing in the streets, clutching their eyes. Others groped about, whimpering and calling for help. Those left unaffected took off on the run.

The divine visitors closed the door, sliding the bolt to secure it.

"Who . . . who are you, sirs?" Lot asked, still frozen in utter astonishment at what he had seen.

"We are angels of the Lord, good Lot. We have come on His mission to destroy this evil place and the other cities of abomination," Raphael said.

"Do you have any family not under this roof?" Jaliel asked.

Still reeling from the events of the past minutes, Lot had to think a few seconds before he replied. "There are the men who will become the husbands of my daughters. They are the only ones."

"Try to get in touch with them tonight, for tomorrow morning at the first light of dawn you must all leave the city," Jaliel told them.

"This is no idle threat," Raphael said sternly. "Tomorrow we will destroy this city with fire and brimstone.

You and your family must leave at the break of day so you can get far enough away not to be destroyed yourselves."

The manner of his two guests was gentle but firm. There could be no doubt they meant every word they said.

WHAT ARE FIRE
AND BRIMSTONE?

Here's that phrase again, "fire and brimstone." What could that refer to? One of the critics of the Bible, Dr. Michael Chandler, founder of the International Research and Education Society, states emphatically:

> Our atmosphere is largely composed of nitrogen and oxygen. Brimstone is not stones. It is sulphur. When oxygen mixes with sulphur under moderate heat, it unites, dissolves, and converts into oil of vitriol. Rather than being pelted with fire and brimstone, the cities would have experienced liquid coming down that would have hurt no one because it would have been a very cool substance.

"That's certainly not what happened when the cities of the plains were destroyed," writes editor Hershel Shenks in the September/October 1980 issue of the prestigious *Biblical Archaeology Review*. He comments further: "Beneath the rubble [of Bab edh-Dhra] there is clear evidence of a fiery conflagration." Referring to Numeira, a city near Bab edh-Dhra and possibly Gomorrah, Shenks writes, "Even without excavation, the archaeologists [Rast and Schaub] could see that the site had been burned. Spongy charcoal was all over the ground and could be scooped up by hand."

Scooped up by hand. Imagine. Here are respected archaeologists suggesting that the residue of the very wrath of God can today be scooped up like a handful of sand.

This will require a more in-depth investigation in the next chapter. But for now, let's return to the home of Lot in Sodom.

A MISSION WITH EXTREME URGENCY

Lot looked at his wife, who was still cowering in a corner from the impact of the mob's attack on the divine visitors and the angels' response. He went to her and helped her to their bedroom, where the daughters could hear them in conversation that grew more animated by the minute.

"I can't believe you are going to leave behind your years of work just because of the words of a couple of strangers. I certainly don't intend to leave in the morning," Belilah said defiantly. "They may have cowed the mob, but I don't believe they have the power to bring fire and brimstone on the city."

"These men are different from any I have ever met. They are clearly messengers from God," Lot said, standing his ground. "We would be foolish indeed not to heed their warning. If nothing happens, we can always come back."

"Well, you can forget inviting our daughters' future husbands to join us on this escapade. They'll laugh you out of their houses. And you'll have to drag me out of bed and out of the city if you think I'll follow you on this harebrained idea." Lot sighed and left the bedroom. His two guests were making themselves comfortable for the night as he hurried out of the house. The street was quiet now, and he was able to get to the homes of his future sons-in-law without being noticed. Once safely inside, he repeated the angels' warning.

"Men," he told them, with all the conviction he could muster, "this evening divine messengers came to our home to warn us that tomorrow God will destroy this city with fire and brimstone. They told me that I may alert you so you can escape with us in the morning."

Their reaction was both a surprise and a disappointment.

"Tell us, Lot," they said, "do you really believe two strangers can destroy this city? Surely you can't expect us to leave our homes and our possessions just because these men say God is displeased." Lot could not persuade them, and he returned to his home burdened with a feeling of great sadness.

As the crowds celebrating the Astarte Revels in Sodom partied into the night, as mobs roamed the streets looking for likely sexual victims, they gave no thought to whether or not this would be their last festival. The divine visitors, meanwhile, bedded down in Lot's home. They had seen enough to know that everything they had heard was true. Sodom was ripe for God's judgment.

During the night Lot awakened frequently, his mind churning with the events of the evening. He was alternately convinced they had to leave the city with the divine visitors . . . and then worried whether this was all a delusion. Were the visitors right, or was his wife right?

When dawn broke, Lot was still wrestling with the reality of what had happened the night before. Then, suddenly, rumblings began deep in the earth . . . the shock waves of which would bring devastation to five cities.

But we are getting ahead of ourselves.

WHY ALL THE FUSS?

What of the story so far? Given the evidence to this point, pro and con, can you make an informed judgment? Over the years many critics of the Bible have attacked the credibility of the Bible because of stories like this.

Remember the comment by Michael Chandler, host of the TV program "The Naked Truth," whom we quoted at the beginning of this chapter: "Why all the fuss over Sodom and Gomorrah? The cities never existed."

And what of those who accept the biblical record as accurate? Do they speak out as forcefully? Indeed they do. For example, the publisher-editor of *Catastrophism in Ancient History*, Marvin Luckerman, says, "Sodom and Gomorrah certainly did exist, and they were destroyed by a massive fire and brimstone explosion, as described in the Bible."

Perhaps we will discover the solution to the mystery of Sodom and Gomorrah in the chapter just ahead.

5

WHAT DESTROYED TWO ANCIENT CITIES?

It is possible by comparing biblical chronology with secular chronology and astronomical data to determine the exact day on which Sodom and Gomorrah were destroyed.

Gene Faulstich
Chronology-History Research Institute

THE DIVINE VISITORS BROUGHT LOT AND HIS FAMILY the message that God would destroy the cities of Sodom and Gomorrah, and the Bible supplies very specific details on how this destruction took place. For many people, however, that biblical record is not enough evidence.

Before we visit with the scholars and their evidence for and against the destruction of Sodom and Gomorrah, let's return to the dilemma faced by Lot, his wife, and their daughters.

AN UNUSUAL ALARM CLOCK

The first streaks of dawn were breaking over the Moabite mountains to the east of Sodom and Gomorrah. City dwellers were still asleep after the Astarte Revels, many sprawled where they had fallen in a drunken stupor earlier that morning.

In the house of Abraham's nephew Lot, the two divine visitors became the family's alarm clock. Lot had just fallen asleep, after tossing and turning most of the night, when Raphael shook him awake.

"We must be going," he said firmly. "There is no

time to waste. You've got too far to go to get away from the destruction that will envelop this city. You cannot stay in bed another minute."

A groggy Lot awakened his wife and daughters, who felt put upon by an emergency they did not feel.

"I thought you'd sleep off your infatuation with last night's strangers," Belilah grumbled as she tried to catch a few more moments of rest. "I can't believe you accept their dire predictions. Have you *ever* heard of a whole city going up in fire and brimstone?"

"I'm too tired to argue with you," Lot said, adding, "Our visitors are insistent that we leave the city immediately. They revealed to me that Abraham interceded for us with the Lord God, himself. Can we be so foolish as to disobey? We must leave now."

"Well, you've got to give me time to get some breakfast. I'm no good on the road to nowhere without something in my stomach," Belilah grumbled.

Raphael turned to Belilah as she shuffled into the kitchen. "No time for breakfast today. Just take what you can carry. Your lives depend on getting far enough away to escape the awful heat that will surely be generated."

Lot's wife seemed determined to stall as long as she could, but the visitors grabbed her hands, those of Lot and their daughters, and led them out of their home toward the city gate. No one was on the street yet, except the guard who opened the gate for them to leave.

Once all were outside the city, the divine visitors released them and said, "Flee for your lives. Don't look back, and don't stop anywhere in the plain! Flee to the mountains, or you will be swept away."

THE ESCAPE ROUTE DEFINED

"No, my lords," Lot responded. "Please! We found favor with you, and you have shown great kindness to us in sparing our lives. But I cannot flee to the mountains, for the disaster will overtake us before we get there, and we will die. I cannot run like a young man anymore. Look, over there on the slope is a town small enough to run to. Let us escape to it, for it is really so small it does not need to be destroyed."

Raphael turned to Lot and conceded, "Very well, I will grant your request. I will not destroy the city of Zoar because of your intervention. But hurry, for I cannot do anything until you get there."

IDENTIFYING ZOAR

Zoar, according to the Bible, is another name for a city in the plains of the Jordan Valley. Is it a real city or a nice human touch added by the storyteller? I mean, it's great to be able to show the angels willing to make accommodations for human weakness. After all, that's the way God is supposed to act . . . to show mercy . . . is He not?

For information on Zoar, we turn again to Dr. Bryant G. Wood, the Syro-Palestinian archaeologist, who says:

We know about the site of Zoar from the Madaba Map. This map is a mosaic on the floor of a church in Madaba, Jordan. It dates from about the fifth century A.D., and it shows us the land as it was at that time. On it you can see the Dead Sea, the Jordan River flowing into the Dead Sea.

In the center is the city of Jerusalem, and also on the map is Jericho, the city of palms. Zoar is shown just at the southern end of the Dead Sea.

Zoar was the city Lot fled to. The angel said that "I will spare Zoar." In the Old Testament we see that, indeed, people continued to live in Zoar. It is referred to a number of times, and apparently was occupied right up to the period of this mosaic map.

The church housing this unique mosaic map is only an hour's drive from the spot it identifies as Zoar. Archaeologists say the ruins of Safi may well be the site for Zoar.

This then was where Lot and his family were headed.

AN UNHAPPY FAMILY

Suddenly the divine visitors disappeared, leaving Lot, his wife, and his daughters to make their way to Zoar. They had not taken many steps when Belilah began complaining again.

"My dear husband, I still consider this great foolishness. Here we are out on the road at the crack of dawn, turned out of our home by two insistent visitors with dire predictions of disaster. I cannot believe you accepted their strange ideas about the wickedness of Sodom."

Lot kept on walking, carrying the few belongings thrown together in haste. "Belilah, I'd rather believe them and escape than not believe them and die. Understand me, wife, these were not men. They were messengers from God. Didn't you notice how they just disappeared after we talked to them?"

"I still cannot believe you let perfect strangers herd us out of our home on a cold morning," Belilah grumbled, trying to keep up with her husband's rapid pace. "Our daughters were to be married next month and I was looking forward to that. Now it seems everything is going wrong."

"Just keep moving, my dear wife," Lot said as he reached out his hand to help her along. "You'll soon thank me for getting us out before God destroys everything in these cities."

"But why are you so sure it will happen?" Belilah questioned.

"Because those men were angels sent by God. Abraham has been visited by angels many times, and he has spoken with God, even as one man speaks to another. He has told me of these things, and I know he speaks the truth. These angels went to see Abraham first, and only then did they come to visit us. I know by their very mannerisms, by their voices and the way they act, that they are divine messengers. We should thank God they intervened in our behalf," Lot explained patiently.

They were nearing Zoar when they felt the ground begin to roll and shake under them. The sky darkened significantly. Lot looked up to see the moon begin to move in front of the sun. Angry clouds scudded across the sky as well, occasionally hiding what, hundreds of years later, would be known as a solar eclipse. To Lot and his family, it was another setting and rising of the sun.

A SOLAR ECLIPSE?

It is safe to say that no one knows all of the forces that were brought to bear in the destruction of Sodom and Gomorrah, but the evidence clearly points to an earthquake as one element in the destruction. Both cities, indeed all five cities of the plain, lie on a seismically active fault line.

Corroborating evidence comes from a unique scientific discipline that identifies the time frame in which ancient events may have happened through a combination of astronomical observations and the historical chronology in ancient writings.

A specialist in astronomical-based historical chronology is Gene Faulstich, founder of the Chronology-History Research Institute. Mr. Faulstich says:

> It is possible by comparing biblical chronology with secular chronology and astronomical data to determine the exact day on which Sodom and Gomorrah were destroyed. Through data gained from astronomy, computers can identify exactly when events like eclipses occurred all the way back to the beginning of human history.
>
> Now it is interesting that in that particular biblical text it talks about the double rising and setting of the sun. It inspired our curiosity, so we checked to see if in that particular year there had been a solar eclipse. And, in fact, we found one—Friday, October 29, 1952 B.C. During a

solar eclipse, an event like an earthquake is more likely to occur.

The extra gravitational pull exerted on that October twenty-ninth, during an eclipse, could have possibly contributed to the kind of earthquake scholars think destroyed Sodom and Gomorrah.

THE DESTRUCTION BEGINS

The darkening sky suddenly brightened as lightning flashed from the dark cloud masses. As it struck in and around the city of Sodom, the city's thick wall developed large cracks, and brick cascaded to the ground. Explosions, like those when natural gas is ignited, threw huge rocks into the air. Flames began to shoot into the air.

"What in the world is going on there? It's stupid not to be able to turn around and see what is happening to our city!" Belilah exclaimed, as she turned to look.

"Don't!" Lot exploded, but it was too late.

To the horror of Lot and his daughters, Belilah suddenly turned into a white statue. With renewed energy, they hurried on, scared to even look back at what had happened to Belilah. They recognized that the shifting earth underfoot and the sound of explosions behind them meant the total destruction of the city.

As they entered Zoar they began to hear a new pattern of explosions. Safe at last, they looked back as a massive earthquake shook and rolled through the plain. Chunks of flaming debris shot into the air, arcing back to earth, only to seemingly start another explosion and fire.

Lot's daughters clung to him in despair as they saw

their beloved home and city go up in fire and smoke. Lot tried to console them, but the tears were now flowing freely as they thought of their fiancés dying under crumbling brick and rock, of their mother left on the plain.

DID IT REALLY HAPPEN?

The major controversy over the destruction of Sodom and Gomorrah, as described in Chapter 19 of Genesis, really boils down to one issue: Did it really happen? The explanation will, of course, have to include how it might have happened.

Let's now examine comments by scientists and scholars on whether and how the destruction of Sodom and Gomorrah can be explained in physical terms.

Our first response comes from Dr. Revell Phillips, professor of geology at Brigham Young University, who is convinced that "the events of Sodom and Gomorrah can easily be explained in terms of normal scientific behavior. Volcanic activity and earthquakes are perfectly adequate to explain the biblical account of Sodom and Gomorrah."

The following description of earthquake and volcanic activity by Dr. Phillips provides the scientific explanation behind his assertion:

The biblical account of Sodom and Gomorrah speaks of raining fire and brimstone. It speaks of land rising with the smoke of the furnace. A typical volcanic eruption would include the fire of molten rock, as well as the smoke of the gases and ash. Actually, more gas is given off during an eruption than molten rock.

The destruction of Sodom and Gomorrah is a very typical picture of a volcanic eruption. The brimstone, of course, is sulphur, and the sulphur gases one smells at a volcanic eruption. They may become toxic to the point where people suffocate and die.

Perhaps we can imagine Lot and his family fleeing from the destruction of Sodom and Gomorrah. The smoke and volcanic ash form the sulphur smog. Now imagine the family fleeing across the shallow water at the southern end of the Dead Sea. Lot's wife, perhaps overcome by the volcanic gases, simply drops into the shallow water. In a matter of a few days, or even a few hours, she would be encrusted with salt. One may well speak of a pillar of salt.

THE RIFT VALLEY FAULT LINE

Yet what would cause this type of volcanic activity? Again we turn to Dr. Phillips, who says:

The earth's crust is divided into a number of rigid plates that interact with each other in three ways. . . . The Middle East is an active area in which the plates are spreading apart in a V kind of action.

The Rift Valley, which extends from Syria down through the Sea of Galilee, the Jordan Valley, the Dead Sea, and ultimately into the Gulf of Aqaba and the Red Sea, is a spreading center. As the plates spread apart, a block of rock called the Graben Valley drops between the two plates. This is the Jordan Valley, the Dead Sea region. As the plates jostle and separate, there is considerable earthquake activity. The destruction of Sodom and Gomorrah, located at the southern tip of the Dead Sea, fits the description of typical earthquake and volcanic activity combined.

A similar perspective is provided by Dr. Philip C. Hammond, whose doctoral studies at Yale University were in Middle Eastern archaeology. He spent two seasons doing field archaeology at the ancient site of Jericho with the American School of Oriental Research. Currently a professor of anthropology at the University of Utah, Dr. Hammond has been the referee for the National Geographic Society's Research and Exploration Committee.

Dr. Hammond explains:

The Dead Sea Valley is very much like it was up to 4,000 years ago. The area is full of sulphur, salt, asphalt and bitumen coming out of the surface of the water. I've seen pictures of people standing on blocks of asphalt in the Dead Sea. There are vapors all over the place. It is an accident waiting to happen.

Is that why, when the patriarch Abraham "looked down toward Sodom and Gomorrah, toward all the land of the plain, he saw dense smoke rising from the land, like smoke from a furnace"? [Genesis 19:28]

And was this destruction localized to Sodom and Gomorrah, or is there any evidence that the destruction extended to all of the cities of that plain?

We turn again to Professor Randall Younker, director of the Horn Archaeological Museum, Amman, Jordan, who reports:

Archaeologists have excavated at least three of the five sites along the Dead Sea, and they have discovered that all three of them were apparently terminated abruptly before the end of the Early Bronze Age, at approximately the same time. Some scholars who believe in the historicity of the patriarch Abraham have suggested that this Early Bronze period was the background for the biblical story of Abraham and the occupation of Sodom and Gomorrah by his nephew, Lot.

But the abrupt and complete destruction has intrigued scholars because it is not just a termination. There is actually an ash layer on top of the city ruins, and this suggests that the city was destroyed by fire.

Dr. Bryant G. Wood, Syro-Palestinian archaeologist, helps unravel the mystery regarding the destruction of the cities of Bab edh-Dhra (biblical Sodom) and Numeira (Gomorrah) when he explains:

At the end of the life of the city, they buried their dead in buildings right on the surface. These are called charnel houses, and they are simply a rectangular building made of mud-brick. Inside they would place the bones of the deceased, along with their pottery, much as they would in the underground burial sites.

The scholars had a problem here. They found that these charnel houses were all burned. Now the city itself was destroyed by fire at the end of its life. But they found that these charnel houses also had been burned at the end of the time of occupation there. Some wondered if it had something to do with hygiene. Perhaps these people would intentionally burn out the interior of these buildings to occasionally eradicate any kind of disease.

That was probably the most popular theory. But when they completed a very detailed study of a cross section cut through one of these charnel houses, they found that the fire did not originate in the building itself, but rather on the roof of the building. The fire began on the roof and then the roof collapsed inside of the building, and then the fire spread through the interior of the structure.

This still posed a question. How would a fire start on the roof? The scholars had a couple of ideas. One is that whoever destroyed the town came into the cemetery and set fire to all the charnel houses. Well, I don't know of any conqueror who would have the time or the interest to do such a thing. They also suggested that an earthquake caused the destruction, but I cannot see how it could do that. I think we have the answer in the Bible. Fire rained down from heaven and destroyed these wicked cities.

DID PETROLEUM DEPOSITS LEAD TO FIRE?

Yet not all scholars accept the theory of volcanic activity, because of a lack of evidence. Dr. Bryant G. Wood analyzes the alternative:

A geologist, Frederick Clapp, investigated the whole region looking for evidence of volcanic activity but found none. However, Clapp did find evidence of the deposit of petroleum products in the area around the southern end of the Dead Sea. In fact, often within the Dead Sea great chunks of bitumen, which is basically asphalt, will come floating to the surface, particularly in times of an earthquake. There are bitumen deposits around the southern end of the Dead Sea.

This led Clapp to the theory that when the Rift Valley settled down, this movement or earthquake put pressure on the petroleum deposits, the gas, the oil, and bitumen, forcing them up through the fault line and into the air. Through a spark or fire on the surface, they became a flaming mass of material that then fell back onto the cities of the plain, destroying them. Now that we know where those cities were located, that theory makes a lot of sense, since they are located exactly on this fault line.

The earth's crust does not change much in such a short time. What you must imagine is that this entire area was like a vast sponge, hundreds of feet thick, but not full of air holes. Instead, it was full of asphalt, natural gas, sulfur, phosphates, and several other minerals located very close to the surface.

In fact, in the same part of the Bible you will find a description of a battle fought in this area that mentions pools of asphalt covering the valley floor and even floating in the water.

Petroleum, natural gas, asphalt, sulfur . . . all flammable materials found near the surface along a fault line that history reveals has had a whole series of major earthquakes. Not surprising, then, that earth scientists consider the "fire and brimstone" described in the Bible as perfectly natural.

That leaves one more small mystery still nagging at us.

A PILLAR OF SALT?

The biblical account of Lot's wife turning into a pillar of salt is a strange oddity in this story.

Earlier in this chapter we presented Dr. Revell Phillips's theory that Lot's wife may have been overcome by volcanic gases and fallen in the shallow part of the Dead Sea, where she became encrusted with salt within a short period of time.

Another perspective that examines Mount Sodom at the southern end of the Dead Sea is provided by Shlomo Goren, director of information for the Dead Sea Industries:

> The mountain of Sodom, which is a piece of salt, is about eight miles long. But what can be seen is only the tip of the iceberg, for this mountain is two miles deep and almost entirely composed of salt. In the mountain you can see strange layers and caves created by the penetration of water, which suggests an outlet to the top.

Erosion has cut this mountain into pinnacles and strange shapes. One of these is locally identified as "Lot's wife."

Yet another theory is that Lot's wife may have been buried by a mass of salt thrown into the air by the tremendous explosions in the earth.

The mystery of Lot's wife clearly cannot be solved. That there is an abundance of salt in the area is clear. That it could have been thrown into the air is possible. That she may have fallen in crossing a shallow part of the Dead Sea is an interesting possibility. Until new information is developed, however, the biblical record stands in its stark simplicity: "But Lot's wife looked back, and she became a pillar of salt." [Genesis 19:26]

We've discussed Sodom, with archaeologists identifying the ruins at Bab edh-Dhra as the probable site of that city. But what about Gomorrah, which some have identified with the ruins at Numeira, but which is not mentioned in the *Eblaite Geographic Atlas*?

IDENTIFYING BIBLICAL GOMORRAH

Dr. Wood, the Syro-Palestinian archaeologist, presents a fascinating perspective:

> We can perhaps identify the site of Numeira as Gomorrah based on its Arabic name. The name Numeira is made up of the consonants NMR. Ancient Canaanite and ancient Hebrew were made up of only consonants, with no vowels. These were added later, but when these ancient languages were no longer living languages, it wasn't clear what the vowels should be.
>
> When we look at the consonants for Numeira, NMR, we find they are almost the same as the consonants for Gomorrah. In the case of Gomorrah, the first letter is not a G but a later transliteration. The initial consonant, or Ion, is a guttural sound, then MR, compared to NMR. The only difference is in the first letter. So over time the name Gomorrah could very well have changed to NMR. I feel quite confident in identifying Numeira as Gomorrah.

So why is Gomorrah not mentioned in the Ebla tablets? Numeira lasted only about 100 years. The Ebla tablets date back well before that time, to about 2250 or 2300 B.C., before Gomorrah was established. So when they established the itinerary, they only encountered Sodom and Admah.

Since it was first written, there has been controversy over the Bible and its interpretation. This is particularly true of the ancient patriarchs and the story of Sodom and Gomorrah. Yet as more and more ancient sites give up their secrets, the Bible's accuracy is validated more and more.

Let's summarize, then, the evidence favoring the biblical account of Abraham and Lot, and Sodom and Gomorrah:

- There is strong evidence for the existence of Abraham in the Ebla tablets. The cities mentioned in the Bible in connection with Abraham and his family are listed on clay tablets found at Ebla.
- There is strong archaeological evidence in the ruins of Bab edh-Dhra and Numeira that this was a lush region with a wide variety of agriculture during the Early Bronze Age. During the latter part of that period, the Bible says that Abraham and Lot herded their sheep, goats, and cattle in an area with large forests, rich grazing lands, and abundant animal life.
- Two of the five cities mentioned in the Dead Sea region in the Bible in connection with Abraham and Lot are clearly identifiable on the *Eblaite Geographic Atlas.* This contains the travel itinerary of a merchant who visited Sodom

and Admah, cities of the plains in the Dead Sea region. Zoar has also been found on a mosaic map on the floor of a church in Jordan dating back to the fifth century A.D.

- Sodom and Gomorrah have been identified with Bab edh-Dhra and Numeira by archaeologists and anthropologists. The destruction of these two cities by fire and earthquake, along with that of three others on the plains, is clear from the layers of ash and evidence of burned stone segments visible even today. The fact that all of these cities were destroyed at the same time during the Early Bronze Age and were never rebuilt validates the Bible's story of the destruction of the cities of the plains by fire and brimstone.

- The discovery of burial sites with a minimum of fifty thousand bodies in Bab edh-Dhra alone, identified as the biblical Sodom, indicates the area was heavily populated. The large numbers buried at the other four sites also validates this conclusion.

Abraham and Lot. Sodom and Gomorrah. Stories of wealth and power, of faith and failure. Yet the Bible's telling of those stories is so uncannily accurate, there is no doubt the people and the cities existed. The evidence that the cities were destroyed by an area-wide upheaval that ignited the gases, asphalt, and other petroleum products so plentiful in the region is also substantial.

It's time now to turn our attention to another of the great mysteries of the Bible. For centuries critics have scoffed at the idea of the construction of the ancient Tower of Babel and the dispersal of the people because of confusion over the sudden appearance of hundreds of new languages. Even firm believers in the Bible began to wonder if the story was true. There didn't seem to be any answers that could counter the attacks leveled by linguistic scholars and others who saw in the story nothing but pure fantasy.

There may be more to the story, however, than meets the critical eye. We are about to discover that the legacy of King Nimrod stretches out worldwide and that the "cradle of civilization" may be better named than we ever dreamed.

6

THE MYSTERY OF
THE TOWER OF BABEL

*The Tower of Babel could not have been
destroyed by God, because it never existed.*

Tim C. Leedom
Publisher, *Ancient Myths*

THE TIME IS MORE THAN FIVE THOUSAND YEARS AGO. Everyone speaks one language, what linguists call the proto-language. Then in one of the Bible's most baffling mysteries, God delivered a knockout punch to the ancients' attempt to build a tower that would reach into the heavens. He brought utter confusion to the tower builders by instantly creating multiple languages, making communication with each other impossible.

Truth or fiction? An accurate description of the event that launched streams of migrations, taking people to the ends of the earth? Or merely an early scribe's teaching tale?

We'll let both critics and defenders of the story have their say, but first let's examine an earlier event that will help explain why God was so angry with the men building the Tower of Babel.

The Bible tells us that in the centuries between Adam and Eve and Noah, people on earth not only multiplied prolifically, but they also developed culturally and technologically. Here's how the writer of Genesis puts it:

Adah gave birth to Jabal; he was the father of all those who live in tents and raise livestock. His brother's name was

Jubal; he was the father of all who play the harp and flute. Zillah also had a son, Tubal-Cain, who forged all kinds of tools out of bronze and iron. [Genesis 4:20–22]

Because of the longevity of those who lived before the flood (the Bible records that Methuselah lived 969 years, and other, nonbiblical records indicate kings lived to be 600 years old), the knowledge of basic skills appears to have multiplied exponentially. This explosion of knowledge and skills created an environment that the Bible says caused God great concern. The Bible reports that man no longer felt a need for God.

In fact we are told:

The Lord saw how great man's wickedness on the earth had become, and that every inclination of the thoughts of his heart was only evil all the time. The Lord was grieved that he had made man on the earth, and his heart was filled with pain. So the Lord said, "I will wipe mankind, whom I have created, from the face of the earth." . . . But Noah found favor in the eyes of the Lord. [Genesis 6:5–7]

God had an assignment for one family—Noah and his three sons, Ham, Shem, and Japheth:

Make yourself an ark of cypress wood; make rooms in it and coat it with pitch inside and out. . . . I am going to bring floodwaters on the earth to destroy all life under the heavens. [Genesis 6:14, 17]

If we remember that Noah began building his giant boat at age five hundred, it is probably not too surprising that his family had already accumulated the technology for such a mammoth construction project.

WHY THE LONG LIFE OF EARLY MAN?

The Bible records some amazing life spans for those living between Adam and the flood of Noah, with Noah and his family still demonstrating that longevity as well. The Bible reports Adam lived 930 years, Enosh 905 years, Jared 962 years, Methuselah 969 years—an amazingly consistent life span.

Why did these ancients live that long? Many scientists believe that a water-vapor canopy encircled the earth before Noah's flood. This provided a universally tropical climate, with literally a greenhouse effect, which in turn afforded life the maximum environmental compatibility. The canopy also filtered out ultraviolet and cosmic radiation, which are major factors in the acceleration of the aging process.

The pre-flood atmosphere also contained 30 percent oxygen, compared to today's 21 percent oxygen. Additionally, the atmospheric pressure was about 27 pounds per square inch compared to today's 14.7 pounds per square inch. These conditions contributed to greater growth in both plants and animals and also facilitated more rapid healing from wounds or illness. With the precipitation of the canopy at the time of Noah's flood, these protective features and the different atmospheric conditions encouraging long life spans ended, resulting in today's drastically decreased life expectancy for both man and animals.

The flood also changed man's diet in a way that, according to some scientists, further contributed to a shorter life. Before the flood he ate only vegetables, fruits, and nuts, but after the flood meat was added to the diet. In analyzing this change, Dr. Ethel R. Nelson, a hospital-based pathologist in Tennessee, says that vegetarian diets seem to support the idea of longer life spans. She writes:

> So we see that not only Adam and Eve, but their descendants for ten generations, were to be complete vegetarians. Was this an adequate diet? Apparently, for most of these antediluvians [pre-flood people] had life spans approaching one thousand years.[1]

After the flood God told Noah that "every living thing" would be food for him. Diseases from animals and the effects of cholesterol added to the aging process. Writes Dr. Nelson:

> After the flood, not only man's diet, but life spans changed radically. Because of the added flesh, the protein and fat components of their diet were markedly elevated over that of their pre-flood food. Was this an improvement? It's interesting that the life spans of the antediluvians and postdiluvians are recorded for comparison in Genesis 5 and 11 . . . showing postdiluvian shortened life spans and decreased generation times [more rapid sexual development].[2]

[1] Ethel R. Nelson, "The Eden Diet and Modern Nutritional Research," a paper presented at the 1992 Twin Cities Creation Research Conference.
[2] Ibid., pp. 57, 60.

Dr. Jacob D. Liedmann, a neurosurgeon living in Israel, tells us:

> The human body is capable of living about one thousand years if certain glands were to continue functioning . . . the pineal gland, located close to the third ventricle of the brain, just before the corpus callosum, has never functioned in modern man. The thymus gland, located in the breastbone area, stops functioning at puberty. A third group of glands, known as the parathyroids . . . undergoes functioning adjustments in puberty that can directly relate to the proper or improper action of organs.
>
> The functioning changes in these three glands are most likely the major reason for our life span's reduction to about seventy years. The key to life spans like those mentioned in the Bible is within these glands.[3]

Even though Noah lived 350 years after the flood, by the time of King David and King Solomon normal life expectancy had declined to about seventy years as a result of the changes produced by the harsher new environment on earth.

But let's stay with Noah and his family for the moment, and the application of a highly developed technology as a result of their long life spans. Consider the possibility of the following scenario involving Noah and his sons. We don't know what terms Noah might have used back then, but if he were managing a project of

---

[3] *David Balsiger and Charles Sellier, Jr.,* In Search of Noah's Ark *(Los Angeles: Sun Classic Books, 1976), p. 144.*

that size and scope today, what follows might be a fair representation of the dialogue.

A FAMILY CONSTRUCTION PROJECT

Monday morning dawned bright and comfortably warm. The rays of the sun filtered through a vapor canopy that lessened the ultraviolet rays. The night's mist had refreshed plants and animals.

"Ham, we need to get started on our monthly team meeting," Noah said as he examined plans for yet another area of the giant boat. "Get Shem and Japheth. We'll need progress reports from the leaders of the various trades groups."

"I'll call them together, Dad," Ham said as he started off toward the ark.

"We're ready to move to the hull of the boat," Noah announced when his sons and their assistants had gathered. "We'll need curved timbers, flat iron strips to strengthen the pegged joints, and timbers of various lengths to use as bracing."

"We're ready to heat up the forge and produce the iron bars needed," reported Tubal-Cain, who turned to one of the supervisors and added, "Dad may be getting on in years, but he and I have perfected the art of producing quality iron bars."

"We can use the skills developed in making bows to produce the curved timbers," reported Jared. "Our woodsmen are bringing us quality logs from the forests to use both as curved timbers and for the bracing."

"You'll be pleased to know that we have found a new

source for pitch to waterproof the hull," reported Ham. "We've contracted for a steady supply in the coming months and years."

Noah explained the next step in the building project, providing each team with specifics for its area of responsibility. After the men dispersed, Noah huddled with his sons, giving each his supervisory instructions for the month.

A MIND-BOGGLING NEW DISCOVERY

Is that an impossible scenario, or closer to the truth than we might have imagined? Were the men and women populating the towns and cities five thousand to six thousand years ago cavemen? Or were they capable of astonishing technological feats like the 450-foot-long, 75-foot-wide, and 45-foot-high ark described in the Bible?

Proof that the biblical record may be truer than modern scientists would like to admit comes from an unusual source. In 1991 a tourist on a walking trip in the Austrian Alps made a mind-boggling discovery when he stumbled onto a corpse sticking out of the ice of a glacier.

This "Stone Age Wanderer" was chopped out of the ice and described in the October 26, 1992, issue of *Time* magazine in an article entitled "Iceman." The article quoted Markus Egg, a German archaeologist, as saying that the Iceman "was snatched from life completely outfitted with the implements of everyday existence."

Time magazine further comments: "Scientists . . . have been stunned by the sophisticated design of his arrows, which reflect a basic grasp of ballistics, and by the ingenuity of his clothing," despite the fact that radio-carbon dating places the Iceman at 3300 B.C.

Again according to *Time,* "his discovery has already upset some long-held notions about the Late Stone Age."

One reason was the sophistication of his metallurgy. His copper ax was initially mistaken by Konrad Spindler as evidence that the find dated from the Bronze rather than the Neolithic Age. But the blade turned out to be nearly pure copper, not bronze.

"The neolithic climber was also armed with a tiny flint dagger with a wooden handle . . . and a pencil-size stone-and-linden tool that was possibly used to sharpen arrowheads and blades," said the *Time* report.

The period when the Iceman appears to have roamed the earth, 3300 B.C., may well have been during the days Noah was called by God to build an ark. Upon further analysis the "Iceman" may prove an even greater "find" for those who accept the Bible's account of early history than for evolutionary scientists. He certainly reveals a high enough level of technological sophistication to make both Noah's ark and the Tower of Babel possible.

No doubt Noah and his sons carried this advanced technology with them as they built new homes and cities after the ark.

Let's imagine a scene that might have happened after the vegetation had reestablished itself following the flood, and after communities of families had begun to spring up.

THE BRAVE NEW WORLD
AFTER THE FLOOD

"Shelah, I'm so glad you came to visit your grandfather," Shem said as he relaxed in the cool of the evening in front of his tent. "I cannot keep up with you kids anymore. Every time I turn around I have another grandchild or great-grandchild."

"I'm glad I could come, too. You've got so many stories about building the ark that I can listen to you for days," Shelah said admiringly. "My father Arphaxad was born after the flood, so all his stories are hand-me-downs, but you were really there."

"Yes, but you've got to remember it's a hundred years since the flood. My memory is not as sharp as it once was," Shem confessed. "But you've reminded me. I think we should have a hundred-year anniversary of the flood. After all, we now have several generations who have been born on the plains of Shinar since the ark settled on Mount Ararat."

"That would be great fun, Grandpa," Shelah replied. "I haven't seen some of my cousins in years. And I cannot remember when I last saw Great-Uncle Japheth."

"That's because they have been so busy building boats on the Tigris and Euphrates rivers. They've been copying some of the design features from the ark," Shem said, as he sipped orange juice. "They should soon be ready to sail out into the ocean with the experience they are gaining on the rivers."

"Have you heard what my father's cousin, Nimrod, is up to?" Shelah asked. It was clearly a rhetorical question, for he immediately continued. "One of his cousins lives near us and says he is the greatest hunter of them all. He's developed the bow and arrow beyond everyone else, and now can kill a deer at a hundred feet."

"As long as he doesn't turn his arrows against other family members, I wish him well," said Shem. "But you've again revealed why we need to celebrate the hundredth anniversary of the flood—even I had not heard of Nimrod's successes. There's nothing like a reunion to remind us that we are one big family and need each other."

A TOWER TO END ALL TOWERS

If the Bible's genealogical list can be trusted, Shem would have been able to participate in four more hundred-year anniversaries. In fact, he may well have been alive when Nimrod marshaled the people on the plain of Shinar for his most ambitious project ever, the Tower of Babel.

According to the biblical record, Nimrod "grew to be a mighty warrior on the earth. . . . The first centers of his kingdom were Babylon, Erech, Akkad, and Calneh, in Shinar. From that land he went to Assyria, where he built Nineveh, Rehoboth-Ir, Calah, and Resen." [Genesis 10:8–11]

Nimrod was not, apparently, satisfied with being the mightiest hunter of his day and founder of numerous population centers. He may well have been the one who announced one day: "Come, let us build ourselves a city, with a tower that reaches to the heavens, so that we may make a name for ourselves and not be scattered over the face of the whole earth." [Genesis 11:4]

Skeptics, and there are many of them, have a real problem with the historical accuracy of that biblical statement. One of them is archaeologist J. David Davis, author of several books, including *Jesus, the One God of Israel: Rescuing Jesus from Idolatry.* He says, "We cannot prove that the Tower of Babel existed. If it did exist, it was an astronomical observation platform."

Even more emphatic is Tim C. Leedom, publisher of *Ancient Myths,* who says, "The Tower of Babel could not have been destroyed by God because it never existed."

Indeed!

SHINAR DISCOVERED

For many years critics attacked the Bible vigorously because of the biblical statement that the Tower of Babel was built on the "plains of Shinar." The name Shinar had not appeared on any of the material unearthed in the ruins of Near Eastern city-states.

Then came the breakthrough that defenders of the Bible had been waiting for.

David C. Duell is an associate professor of the Old Testament at Masters University in southern California. His studies at Dropsie College and Cornell University have involved him in extensive investigations of important archaeological discoveries with Aramaic inscriptions, as well as the Nuzi tablets and Eblaite documents. He taught in the Ancient Near Eastern Studies Department at Cornell University from 1983 to 1987. Mr. Duell tells us:

> For many years scholars and students of the Bible questioned the location, even the existence, of the ancient land of Shinar. They knew that the great city of Babylon existed. Ancient eyewitness historians such as Herodotus and Strabo claimed to have seen the city. The scholars had no proof, however, that Shinar existed apart from the Bible.
>
> Then in the early part of the last century archaeologists began to dig their spades into the soil of the ancient Near East, soon discovering thousands of cuneiform tablets. On these tablets from Egypt, Syria, and the Hittite kingdoms was the name of Shinar in various pronunciations. Archaeology had confirmed not only the existence, but also the general location of the land of Shinar.

That location is Mesopotamia, the area around and between the Tigris and the Euphrates rivers, which most scholars identify as the "cradle of civilization." And that is where, the Bible reports, descendants of Noah began to fulfill God's command to "be fruitful and increase in number; multiply on the earth and increase upon it." [Genesis 9:7]

Ancient Mesopotamia proved so productive that apparently few, if any, ventured into other areas of the world. Nimrod, the Bible says, founded a whole series of cities. And there can be little doubt that their common language facilitated the development of new technology that created new ambitions to "make a name for ourselves and not be scattered over the face of the whole earth."

Yet why should God have been displeased with their prosperity? Why was the tower such an affront to God? What was wrong with everyone speaking the same language?

Good questions, but for the present, let's join the crowd in the marketplace in Babel.

A NUISANCE REMOVED

"I know I should not have come shopping on festival day," said Bilcah dejectedly. "I simply don't get the same quality, because everything has been picked over."

"You're right. Look at those cucumbers. They look wilted already," said Sarai. "I cannot believe some of the stuff they are putting in the marketplace today."

An apparent disturbance prompted both to look down the street. Rounding the corner came a blind beggar. His tattered clothes revealed he had been unable to spend money on his appearance for some time. As he tried to make his way up the street, he was bumped by shopkeepers' helpers rushing to fulfill customer requests, by men who seemed to deliberately step in his way. A crowd of children jeered and mocked as they followed him. Bilcah and Sarai noticed he seemed to be saying something, but it could hardly be heard above the noise surrounding the beggar. The haggling of customers over prices and the din of shopkeepers yelling out their wares to attract customers all but drowned him out.

As the blind beggar drew nearer, they heard him shout, "O mighty King Nimrod! Hearken to the word of the Lord! You set yourself and your captains to turn the people away from the Lord of all. Take warning! Your days of glory are numbered."

Bilcah and Sarai looked at each other as he passed.

"I wonder who set him up. He'll be arrested soon and will end up dead," Bilcah said, turning to the vegetable selection again.

"King Nimrod will have his head soon enough. Then he'll be done with his mumbo jumbo about the warning of 'the Lord of all,'" Sarai said sarcastically as she picked up a head of cabbage.

King Nimrod was in his council room overlooking the main street of Babel when the insistent cry of the blind beggar broke through the noise of the festival.

"O great King Nimrod, your days are numbered, for you have forgotten the God of our forefathers. You have set yourself up as the king of heaven. But the God of heaven shall destroy your tall tower and scatter your people. There will come a day when your tower will be dust and your memory will be no more."

"Will no one set me free from that buzzing fly?" King Nimrod asked disdainfully, looking around the room. "Must I hear that old dog's whining every day?"

The captain of the guard whipped off his woven girdle and held it up like a choke cord. "I live to serve, Your Majesty," he said with pride.

The king glanced in his direction and said, offhandedly, "Whatever you want to do is fine with me, as long as you leave his old bones in the street for the dogs."

The captain hurried off while the king turned to his vizier.

"What was your complaint, vizier?"

"Not a complaint, Your Majesty! But," he hesitated,

"what the old beggar cries in the street is whispered in some quarters."

Now King Nimrod came alive. "Who is this god they talk about? What is his name? Because of some of the tales of sick, old people about a god who made the world, we should give up the power and the riches we have here? Who is this god that says this to me?"

He turned in rage to a priest with a breastplate studded with crystals.

"Priest, can you tell me who this god is, and why I should listen to him?"

The priest stuttered, bowing low, "I know of no god mightier than you, Your Majesty. It's the old fools who talk about a god who sent the great flood in the time of our ancestors. They say the flood was God's punishment because the people had forgotten Him."

King Nimrod roared, "Well, He shall send no flood against me or my city! You see that tower? We will build that tower to reach the heavens. No floodwaters will ever wash it away." The king turned to his craftsmen. "What do you say about that, builders?"

The chief architect stepped forward and replied, with an imperious look on his face, "The tower, O mighty lord, will prevail against any god the old people yammer about. You shall be the equal of any in heaven."

The sound of a crowd roaring in approval drifted into the room through the open window. The vizier walked to the window and looked down.

"The captain knows his trade well," he said, smiling. "He's strangling the old one slowly to amuse the crowd."

"Good! I hope that teaches all fools like him a lesson. King Nimrod will not share his glory with another."

With that he stepped down from his throne and examined the model of the tower on display in the center of the room. He looked at it from every angle. "Builder, what makes you think we can build into the heavens?" he asked, seeking confirmation of his earlier boast.

"Because we do not have soft stones. We have developed a new burnt brick that can take much more pressure. We now can build the highest tower in the world. You will certainly be able to reach into the heavens, my lord," the architect replied confidently, "and you will have your special temple rooms right at the top."

CAN THE SITE BE FOUND?

Assume for the moment that this scene could have taken place in ancient Shinar. What is the most likely site for the tower, based on excavations in the Middle East?

The answer comes from Dr. Charles Dyer, author of *The Rise of Babylon* and professor of biblical exposition at Dallas Theological Seminary. He says:

> The strongest body of archaeological evidence, combined with the biblical account, favors the ruins of Etemenanki as the likely spot for the Tower of Babel. This is located in the country of Iraq, in the city of Babylon, fifty miles south of today's Baghdad.
>
> This site was featured in a recent Reader's Digest reference book, which pinpoints it as the most probable location for the Tower of Babel. Today a model of this tower is featured in the Nebuchadnezzar Museum in the city of Babylon.

Yet do we know with any degree of certainty when this Tower of Babel was built, way back in antiquity? According to Gene Faulstich, founder of the Chronology-History Research Institute:

> The biblical account says the founding of Babylon occurred in 2242 B.C. It is interesting to note that when Alexander the Great captured Babylon in 331 B.C., a collection of star charts was found which stated Babylon was founded 1,903 years earlier—in the year 2234 B.C. This is eight years later than stated in the biblical account, but considered dead-on accuracy when tracing events back over 4,200 years.
>
> These star charts and biblical chronology also help us to fix the birth date and life span of Peleg. It was during his lifetime that the dispersal of the nation took place. And it was during his lifetime, from 2242 B.C. to 2003 B.C., that the Tower of Babel was not only built but also destroyed.

But building towers was a common practice in the ancient world. Or was it? We'll let a specialist answer that one—Henri-Paul Eydoux, who wrote about "The Men Who Built the Tower of Babel" in the book, *The World's Last Mysteries,* published by Reader's Digest.

> Some of the spectacular temple-monuments they erected to their gods—the soaring brick-built ziggurats—still tower over the ruined cities. The ziggurats were pyramid-like towers, consisting of a series of platforms, each decreasing in size as they climbed nearly three hundred feet towards the sky. At the top stood temples into which the gods were believed to step on their way to an earthly dwelling place; a second temple was at the pyramid's base.

The prolific city-states of Mesopotamia left some thirty known ziggurats dating to between 3000 and 500 B.C.! To the men of their day they were as impressive as the great pyramids of Egypt, but today most of them are mere rubble. The most remarkable of all can no longer be seen—the ziggurat of Etemenanki, thought to be the biblical Tower of Babel.

The Sumerians and their successors were artists who used all their skills to break up the monotony of the huge wall surfaces of the ziggurats. They built majestic sloping ramps, oblique stairways linking each stage to the one above, and decorative buttresses dividing the walls into sections.[4]

One of the most significant reasons to accept the story of the building of the Tower of Babel is in two sentences: "They said to each other, 'Come, let's make bricks and bake them thoroughly.' They used brick instead of stone, and tar for mortar." [Genesis 11:3]

A book written hundreds of years before Christ was born makes a point only a local would know—bricks were the only building material available on the plains of Shinar. The pyramids of Egypt were built of stone because it was available, but the stone available to the people of Nimrod crumbled under pressure. And there were no forests nearby to cut giant trees and build the structure of wood.

The builders of the Tower of Babel and the more

[4] Henri-Paul Eydoux, "The Men Who Built the Tower of Babel," in *Reader's Digest*, The World's Last Mysteries (*Pleasantville, NY: Reader's Digest, 1981*), pp. 169–170.

than thirty other towers in the adjacent city-states thus resorted to brick made of clay and straw. They used bitumen—tar—which they imported from the highlands of what we know today as Iran.

This attention to detail dramatically increases the credibility of the whole story! Chalk up one more bit of evidence for the historic reliability of the Bible.

Okay, but does acceptance of the events regarding the construction of the Tower of Babel, as they are written in the Bible, necessarily mean that God would zap the tower, virtually destroying everyone who worshiped there? That he would then instantly develop all kinds of new languages in people and send them packing so they would populate areas throughout the world?

If you have difficulty with that, you are not alone. Critics have long attacked the Bible for what they consider a totally unbelievable scenario. After all, it takes centuries to change a language. Even Bible scholars agree with the critics on that.

But when it comes to the Tower of Babel, that's just about all they agree on. You'll meet the critics and the defenders of the all-time "language barrier" as they square off regarding this ancient secret of the Bible in the next chapter.

7

COMMUNICATION TOWER OR WORSHIP CENTER?

Essentially, the story of the Tower of Babel is a legend. And the story of the confusion of languages is also a legend.

Dr. Rocco A. Errico
Professor of Aramaic Studies

GREAT KINGS HAVE BIG IDEAS, AND THE BIBLE REports that King Nimrod built one great city after another, cities whose names have been found on clay tablets in ancient ruins. Yet a great city was apparently not enough for King Nimrod. The Bible reports King Nimrod wanted to get as close to the gods as human construction would permit by building a great tower to reach the heavens.

Broadly accepted critics like Dr. Rocco A. Errico, quoted earlier, consider this particular biblical story fiction, with at best a glimmer of historical fact. And such attacks, which make sense to a majority of scholars, have been tough to deal with. Our investigations, however, demonstrate quite conclusively that the more we learn, the easier the task of validating the Bible story becomes.

Let's review the events as the Bible describes them.

The Bible reports that King Nimrod was constructing what was to become the tallest building ever constructed up to that time. Yet instead of using steel and glass, or even stone, he had to do it with bricks and mortar, or "slime" as the Bible puts it. The "slime" was a form of asphalt or tar that resisted water and wind erosion.

If the ruins of the tower of Etemenanki in ancient Babylon are the site of the Tower of Babel, as many defenders of the Bible believe, then we're talking about a structure 295 feet square and possibly 300 feet high. That's a lot of burnt bricks. Alexander the Great found that out when he tried to rebuild the ruins three hundred years before Christ was born!

Suppose for a moment we could just stop by the offices of the construction company.

CONSCRIPT LABOR

The offices of Murashu Construction Company represented a beehive of activity. People flowed in and out of various rooms, many of them carrying clay tablets.

At a table in what is clearly the manager's office sits a man with flowing robes, working on calculations on a clay tablet.

"Jared!" He clapped his hands as he called.

A well-built man entered the room, bowing.

"How many brick-makers are at work today?"

"Three thousand, sir," Jared answered, bowing again.

"We need two thousand more if we are to meet our schedule on the tower. Send out the king's soldiers to round up more laborers. King Nimrod is putting heavy pressure on me to keep the construction on schedule." Murashu added, "He is anxious to begin communicating with our god, Marduk, in the temple he has planned for the top of the tower."

"But where will we house them?" Jared asked.

"That's your problem. My job is to get the bricks made so the laborers can keep the construction on schedule," said Murashu. "Let them make their own mud huts the first day. But on the second day I want them making bricks."

"Yes, sir," Jared said, turning on his heel and leaving.

Murashu turned to his clay tablet again. Soon he clapped his hands again.

"Mahalel, we need to increase our production of bitumen for brick-making. I've just sent Jared to round up another two thousand laborers, and they will need a lot more bitumen than is now being mixed up," he said. "Have we received another shipment from the mountains?"

"Yes, sir," Mahalel replied, "the bitumen has arrived, but a lot of it is in big chunks. It will take awhile to heat it until it flows for the brick-makers."

"Make sure that by the time Jared gets the new crews making bricks, the bitumen is melted," Murashu said, turning back to his tablets.

Mahalel left quickly to allocate bitumen blocks from the storehouse and set up a crew to begin the slow process of heating it up. Just then a man rushed in, clearly out of breath. "We lost our fourteenth worker to an accident," he said. "He fell into a vat of bitumen. He's badly burned and barely breathing."

"Toss him onto the refuse heap," Murashu ordered. "We've got many more where he came from. We can't be bothered tending the injuries of nearly dead men."

The foreman started to say something, but thought better of it. It would do no good to protest.

THE PURPOSE OF THE TOWER?

The building of the Tower of Babel, with its grand design, put a heavy burden on both people and resources. Construction of the tower demanded more and more laborers and money. Nimrod clearly became a tyrant, for that is the only way he could have marshaled the resources needed to build the tower.

We know, for example, that when Alexander the Great set out to rebuild the tower at Etemenanki, he put twenty thousand men to work. Logic suggests the original tower must have required many more laborers than that.

Yet what was the real purpose of the Tower of Babel? Can we really trust the biblical record when we read of the tower's purpose? "Come, let us build ourselves a city, with a tower that reaches to the heavens, so that we may make a name for ourselves and not be scattered over the face of the whole earth." [Genesis 11:4]

A unique theory is advanced by Zechariah Sitchin, Near East linguist and author of *Genesis Revisited,* who says, "The temple towers of Mesopotamia were centers for communicating with ancient astronauts, the local gods."

A journalist and editor in Israel for many years, Sitchin believes that the advanced knowledge of the early Sumerian inhabitants of Mesopotamia can be attributed to extraterrestrial beings in contact with earthmen. He tells us:

> The Bible describes many events and phenomena in
> antiquity which can be explained only by the presence of

superior beings on earth with a high technology. Chapter 6 of Genesis, for example, talks of the Nephilim. They came to earth from heaven, married the daughters of men, and thus were distinct from them.

We know now that these tales were actually abbreviated versions of much earlier Sumerian texts. These spoke of the same beings, calling them Anunaki, meaning those who came from heaven to earth. The Sumerians were able to describe them, depicting them in statues.

One of these statues depicts the leader of the first wave of astronauts to touch down in the Persian Gulf. From the statues we can see they were really pilots who could fly in the skies of the earth. Some females wore the garb of astronauts, complete with helmets, earphones, a black box or piece of equipment on the neck, and a hole for breathing.

These then were the extraterrestrial beings the Bible describes as the ancient gods in whom the people believed.

That, I'm sure you'll agree, is pretty wild stuff. The question is fairly asked, is this scholar for real? His credentials certainly are! But that does not mean there isn't a large body of dissent.

One of those who disagrees with Zechariah Sitchin is Chuck Missler, a biblical scholar who has authored twenty books and publications on Bible-related topics and is a Bible commentator with seven million audio commentary tapes in circulation. He tells us:

Although the "Ancient Astronaut" theory is an interesting one . . . this is a total misreading of the Scriptures. If we look at the original Hebrew, the words "B'nai Elohim" mean angels, not astronauts or spacemen.

The Bible confirms in both the Old and New Testament that these "fallen angels" are supernatural beings who came to earth in physical form . . . in the period between creation and the time of Noah. They were the creatures who cohabited with human women. And it was this union that produced the so-called "Nephilim."

To take this further, it was this unnatural pollution of humanity by these creatures that brought the great flood upon the world. Personally, I wonder why people keep coming up with complex theories, like "Ancient Astronauts," when the real Bible story in Genesis is far more exciting and accurate.

Why indeed? But there are still other, even more exotic theories advanced as to the purpose of the tower. Let's return to the construction office for a moment.

BUILT-IN COMMUNICATION CRYSTALS?

Murashu had returned to his clay tablets when a form darkened the doorway. He looked up.

"Come in, come in. To what do I ascribe this honor?" he asked as a priestly figure entered the room.

"Just checking to see if the builders are making progress on plans for the top floor of the tower," the priest of Marduk said. He smiled. "Builders get so carried away with the task at hand, they sometimes forget the purpose of the tower."

"Not when you are building a tower for King Nimrod," Murashu replied almost grimly. "He is most impatient. But I sense his impatience stems from his desire to begin communicating with our god, Marduk."

"That's why I'm here. I'm curious whether any progress has been made in the experiments to develop a new material that will enhance our communication with other gods as well."

"There have been some exciting developments, but I am not ready to stick my neck out with King Nimrod about the results," Murashu said, his face clouding momentarily. Then he brightened. "But we have developed a new brick using a special sand brought in from the seashore," he said. "When we bake it, the sand crystallizes. If we place them correctly, we think we might have a new means of communicating with the gods."

The priest seemed pleased with that. "Good," he said, adding, "I won't steal your thunder and tell King Nimrod, but do keep me informed." The priest turned and disappeared through the door.

THE INTERNATIONALIZATION OF THE TOWER

This brings up the question of just how technologically advanced the ancient civilizations were. Recent archaeological work indicates that they knew far more about communication devices than we expected.

The idea that the Tower of Babel was a communication center to get in touch with the gods is also advanced by Roger Oakland, a science educator from Canada and co-author of *Understand the Times*. Oakland says:

The Tower of Babel was built for exactly the purpose stated in the Bible, for communication with the gods. Or as the Bible puts it, with fallen angels or spirits. For when the Bible says that the tower was to reach into the heavens, it was not in a physical sense, but rather as a communications system.

God was angered by what the people were doing, for they were attempting to communicate with the spirit dimension. So God confounded their languages, and they were spread around the world. You can go all over the world and see the evidence that the ancients of the past reconstructed what they were doing at Babel. They built ziggurats and temples associated with communicating with the spirit world, literally all over the world.

Some of the pyramids and ziggurats are identical. They can be found in both South America and in Central America. They are found in Cambodia, Indonesia, and in India. Worldwide there is evidence of ziggurats and towers associated with communicating with the spiritual dimension.

Yet how did they seek to communicate with the spirits? Oakland advances a unique theory:

I believe they were using quartz crystals. If you stack them in the right lengths, you can bring in radio waves. Chapter 11 of Genesis says that the Tower of Babel was constructed of thoroughly burnt bricks—"Come, let's make bricks and bake them thoroughly." [Genesis 11:4] They used bricks instead of stone, and tar instead of mortar. Combined with sand and baked under intense heat, these bricks would have acquired a quartz-like nature. This would make the tower achieve the qualities of a giant crystal radio set.

But this alone would not have allowed them to communicate. All ancient civilizations understood the power of crystal gems for communicating with the gods. Archaeology reveals that many of the ancient priests wore breastplates and headbands with crystals that were part of this communication device. A tuner such as a nine-square-inch breastplate and a turban with a golden band would have played a role. The ancient priests would actually be walking around with a form of portable radio. They were attempting to tune in to the spirit world. This idea is not particularly new. "New Agers" today attempt to communicate with the spirit world using crystals.

Even the construction angles were designed to facilitate communication with the heavens, Oakland reveals:

Archaeologists have found that these religious sites were purposefully constructed and aligned with specific points in the heavens. There was also an obsession with the solstice days [shortest and longest days of the year], which the ancients believed held particular spiritual significance.

According to this author, then, these towers and ziggurats were dedicated to specific gods.

The Tower of Babel and similar ziggurats were described in ancient accounts as "welcoming sanctuaries" for the gods. Some of the gods worshipped by the ancients were Marduk in Babylon, Nabu in Birs Nimrûd, and the moon-god Nanna at Ur.

Was that the reason God decided the tower should not continue to stand? Because the people were becoming too sophisticated in communicating with spirit entities?

Whatever the reason, one thing seems clear: The events that destroyed the tower came as a surprise to those who were there.

A person in Nimrod's court might have witnessed a scene similar to this.

UNNATURAL DELAYS

Jagged streaks of lightning illuminated the gathering dusk. Giant clouds pyramided into the sky, while at the surface, heavy rain drove everyone for cover. Shepherds hurried to guide their sheep into corrals. The brick-makers on the edge of the city rushed to cover just-formed bricks and piles of straw.

In the palace, King Nimrod strode back and forth in the throne room.

"This tower is taking forever. They've been at it for fifteen years and they still haven't started the temple room at the top. What's holding it up now?"

"The weather, sir," the somewhat graying architect said wearily. "We have had an unusual series of storms sweep across our city. At times it has washed away hundreds of bricks just newly formed. It's like we are taking three steps forward and two back. We have conscripted every able-bodied man not already in the military service for the tower . . . and we have even used army units to transport bricks up the tower, but still the delays come."

"Priest, can you tell me why we are having this

parade of dark clouds and thunderbolts? I've never seen anything like it. This weather is most depressing," fumed the king.

"We have always had storms this time of the year. I see no particular connection with thunderstorms and the tower," the architect interrupted.

The king looked darkly at the architect. "I have no memory of great dark clouds visiting us so often. Not only are we losing bricks, but I'm told we have lost some workers as well to lightning bolts."

King Nimrod turned to the priest. "Why can't you conjure the storms away? You're supposed to have special favor with the gods."

"I would not blaspheme the gods." The priest backed off respectfully as a thunderous clap signaled that the storm was upon them. "Perhaps the gods have heard us . . ."

A blast of wind whipped dust into the room. The king turned and ran for an inner chamber, shouting at his servants to stop up the openings. Obediently, they rushed to tie rugs over the holes, but with little success.

The vizier, the architect, and the priest followed the king.

"You see? Do you see, you fools? It is happening again. Why am I being destroyed?"

"Not so, Your Gracious Majesty. It is just the weather," the vizier said, trying to placate the king.

"Are not the gods and the weather one and the same?" The king turned in anger to the priest. "Priest! Priest! Why have you not placated the gods with a sacrifice? Are you anxious to see me dead?"

"Most powerful lord, I sacrificed an ox and two sheep this morning on the altar of Marduk."

"That's obviously not enough. Don't you see how they cry out at us? Burn more oxen, more sheep. A child . . . yes, a newborn infant. No, not one. Fifty," the king roared. "Throw fifty newborn infants into the sacrificial fire!"

An even more vicious gust of wind tore through the room, scattering rugs and furniture, pinning the king and his counselors against the wall. The king slid down the wall in terror, holding his robes about his face. Piteously he cried out, "Gods, why have you done this to me?" Suddenly his tone changed. "I curse you, spirits of the skies. I curse you."

The priest's face turned even whiter, while outside the wind tore huge chunks of brickwork off the wall, sending them flying. Ragged streaks of lightning exploded on the tower, precipitating a shower of bricks. Other lightning strikes split open buildings. One of the strikes hit the palace, tearing the roof open and raining bricks on the cowering king and his counselors, burying them in a living tomb.

A CATACLYSMIC EVENT

It may or may not have happened that way, but clearly there appears to have been a cataclysmic event that stopped the building of the Tower of Babel. Maybe the simple biblical statement is true after all:

But the Lord came down to see the city and the tower that the men were building. The Lord said, "If as one people speaking the same language they have begun to do this, then nothing they plan to do will be impossible for them. Come, let us go down and confuse their language so they will not understand each other." So the Lord scattered them from there over all the earth, and they stopped building the city. [Genesis 11:5–8]

This seems to suggest a scenario more like the following.

A BREAKDOWN OF COMMUNICATION

Murashu was busy at work at his table when a messenger burst into the room.

"They're starting to riot on the tower," he shouted between hurried breaths. "I couldn't make out what was going on, but I thought you ought to know right away."

"What seems to have started it?" Murashu asked as he hurriedly followed the messenger outside.

"I don't know, except men started screaming at each other all over the tower, as though they couldn't understand each other anymore," the messenger replied.

One of the foremen saw Murashu and ran up to him, spilling words in an outburst of anger.

"Stop," Murashu signaled with a wave of the hand. "I cannot understand a word you are saying. Tell me in plain words what is happening."

The foreman looked at him blankly as though he could not comprehend what Murashu was saying. At that point another foreman rushed up and, gesticulating wildly, spewed out a torrent of unintelligible words.

Murashu turned to his messenger. "What is going on here? I cannot understand either of them . . . nor do they seem to understand each other! Have they been drinking too much this afternoon?"

"No, sir, I know there's been no beer permitted on the tower, and I did not see anyone drinking today. I can't explain it. Look at those men. They're in a fistfight already," he said, pointing to a group attacking another group.

"I've never seen anything like it," Murashu muttered as he headed for the men yelling and throwing punches.

"Stop, stop, you fools. This is no time for a fight," he yelled. They stopped momentarily at the sound of his voice, but didn't seem to know what he was saying, so they resumed their fight. Murashu signaled a guard to stop the fight and walked off, confused.

That evening at supper he told his family, "I had the weirdest experience at closing time. Men were yelling at each other, others were already fighting, and foremen I've known for years talked gibberish to me. I just don't understand it."

His wife looked up in surprise.

"I was at the shop buying some fish. When I asked the shopkeeper for one of his fish, he looked totally puzzled, as though he had not understood me. I tried again, pointing at the fish I wanted. He picked it up and weighed it, but I couldn't understand how much it weighed. I finally held out some coins and he took what he wanted.

"On my way home I heard people talking strangely over and over again. It's as though we are not talking the same language anymore," she said.

The oldest boy stopped with food in midair. He looked at his father and mother.

"We were playing at the new construction site down the street. I was yelling at my friend to hide, but he couldn't seem to understand me. My other friend started talking a funny language that I could not understand either."

"Well, I'm glad we can understand each other," the mother said, putting more food on the table. "I hope everyone returns to normal tomorrow."

But that tomorrow never came. And for weeks people tried to come to terms with the strange languages their friends spoke. Eventually whole families packed up and started down the road to start over again, looking for a new land of opportunity.

This is a more likely scenario based on the information provided in the Bible, but is it defensible? Are there scientists or scholars who can provide a specific frame of reference that will lend credibility to the biblical account?

You be the judge.

LEGEND OR TRUE STORY?

If you are still skeptical, you have an ally in Dr. Rocco A. Errico, author and specialist in the Aramaic language. Dr. Errico says:

Essentially, the story of the Tower of Babel is a legend. And the story of the confusion of languages is also a legend. You see, this is a Hebrew worldview. The first eleven chapters of Genesis are all legendary. The stories do spring from northern Mesopotamian ideas, but they have been adapted by the Hebrew race to tell religiously the origins and the prehistory of Abraham. But no scholar, no historian takes any of these stories as historical facts.

The Hebrew legends take God out of the context of being one with nature. They place God above nature, rather than being in nature, like all the other Mesopotamian gods were.

This is the case with the Tower of Babel. It is a Hebrew explanation for the scattering of the people, of the division of languages, and the idea of building a great tower to enter the heavens.

Equally strong in his reaction to the idea that the biblical story of the Tower of Babel is factually accurate —and correctly presents the reason for the development of multiple languages—is J. David Davis, who has done extensive research into Christian origins for over twenty-five years, including archaeological work in Israel. He tells us:

Fundamentalist Christians have tried to teach that the confusion of the languages came as a result of the building of the Tower of Babel. This cannot be proven from either historical data or archaeological evidence. The word *Babel* has its origin in a Semitic word, which is actually two words, *ba* and *bel*, meaning "the gate to God."

Now where did they find this? It had to come from the Book of Enoch in which Enoch talked about the many portals or the gates to God. These people were trying to find a way back to God, or were looking into the heavens to discover God, so they built an observation tower.

Dr. Davis sounds convincing until you listen to Dr. Richard Bliss, author of twenty-five professional scientific articles and books, and the chairman of the science education department at a California graduate school. Here is Dr. Bliss's view:

> Actually, the Tower of Babel concept of racial and language generation is quite easily demonstrated through genetics, archaeology, and linguistics. Using the famous Punnett Square, a simple tool used by geneticists to explain the distribution of genetic information, I can demonstrate quite simply that it is theoretically possible for all the racial ethnic characteristics in the world today to have developed within a single generation after the Tower of Babel, as documented by the case of a family in Australia. This family, with a Nigerian black parent and one English white parent, produced twin boys who have completely different ethnic characteristics—one white son and one black son!

Since linguistics is the study of languages and language origins, let's consider the position taken by Dr. John Oller, professor of linguistics and educational foundations at the University of New Mexico, and author of *Language and Experience,* as well as nine other books in the field of linguistics. Dr. Oller says:

> Actually, as remarkable as it may seem, the biblical story of the Tower of Babel is completely consistent with all of the

evidence. Anyone who denies this fact is simply engaging in fantasy or speculation.

There are roughly five thousand languages in the world today, and fifty to sixty stocks. We can trace the best-known of those languages, the Indo-European system, back to about 3000 B.C., roughly the time of Babel. There is simply no evidence that existing stock can be traced back further.

Let me give you an example of how rapidly languages can change. Consider the following line from *Beowulf*, written in the eighth century A.D., and see how much you can understand. It is in Old English: "Wolde guman findan bone be him on sweote sare geteode." Translated into modern English this means, "He wanted to find the man who had harmed him while he slept."

Now if English could change that much in thirteen hundred years, there was ample time for Indo-Europeans to branch into a hundred different languages in approximately five thousand years. There is no reason to suppose it would take any longer for the other language families to have branched into their various denominations and derivatives.

Wrapping up the evidence for accepting the biblical story on the Tower of Babel and the confusion of languages is Dr. Steven Collins, who has done research in Europe and the Near East and is professor of biblical studies at Trinity Theological Seminary:

It is common knowledge in anthropology that the growth of world populations began in the Near East, primarily between the Black Sea and the Caspian Sea. And these populations dispersed out over the world. They went to Europe, into Africa, and over into India, into the Far East and, of course, over the Bering Strait into North and South America.

But it all started here in the Middle East. The interesting thing about this is that we have a document in the Book of Genesis that describes this ancient process as having begun right here, in and around the Tower of Babel. This is exactly what modern anthropology knows by way of the evidence.

Anthropologically and linguistically, then, the matter would seem to be resolved. One science says the biblical account could be true, the other says it definitely is. But there is even more evidence, and it has a surprisingly current origin.

THE ISSUE OF THE MOTHER TONGUE

In the November 5, 1990, issue of *U.S. News & World Report,* an article on page 60 focuses on "The Mother Tongue." According to this article:

> A few radical linguists have gone even further, claiming they have reconstructed pieces of the mother of them all: the original language spoken at the dawn of the human species.[5]

Two linguists from the former Soviet Union, Thomas Gamkredlidze and Vyacheslav Ivanov, according to the article:

[5] *"The Mother Tongue,"* U.S. News and World Report, *November 5, 1990,* p. 60.

. . . have offered new evidence that Indo-European originated in an area known as Anatolia, which is now part of Turkey, and from there spread throughout Europe and the subcontinent. Linguists had long thought that the Indo-European proto-language had originated in southern Russia. . . . But Gamkredlidze, Ivanov, and other Soviet scholars cite words in proto-Indo-European that appear to have been borrowed from the languages of Mesopotamia and the Near East, suggesting that the speakers of proto-Indo-European lived in close geographical proximity to these cultures.[6]

The article provides further confirmation of the possibility of languages spreading rapidly throughout the world. Colin Renfrew, a British archaeologist, suggests in the article that it was farmers, not warriors, who were responsible for the spread of the Indo-European language into Europe. He notes that even if a farmer's offspring had moved only ten miles from the family farm to set up farms of their own, the resulting wave of agriculture could have swept throughout Europe from Anatolia in about fifteen hundred years, carrying the Indo-European language with it.[7]

If farmers could spread a language that quickly, could they not also have developed new languages en route, as Dr. John Oller and Dr. Richard Bliss suggest?

Researchers have now also proved that the Bible is remarkably accurate in its description of the kind of tow-

[6] *Ibid.*, p. 62.
[7] *Ibid.*, p. 65.

ers, or ziggurats, built in ancient Mesopotamia, and specifically at the city we know as Babylon.

And there is more.

AN EXTRAORDINARY FEAT

An important discovery demonstrating the existence of the Tower of Babel is that the ziggurat as a tower for the worship of various gods was born about three thousand years before Christ, according to Henri-Paul Eydoux in *The World's Last Mysteries*. And the most impressive of all was the one in Babylon, according to Herodotus, the Greek historian, who saw it in about 460 B.C. He described it as having one central tower, with eight more levels added to that. All eight towers could be climbed by a spiral stairway running around it to the top.

The substantial dimensions of the Tower of Babel considerably exceeded those of other known ziggurats. The larger size was justified, for the monument belonged to Marduk, originally the local god of Babylon, who later became a national god as a result of Babylon's long preeminence over the other cities of Mesopotamia.[8]

This tower clearly provides nonbiblical affirmation of the significant size difference of the Tower of Babel, which the Bible describes as reaching to the sky.

We also have independent confirmation of the confu-

[8] Henri-Paul Eydoux, "The Men Who Built the Tower of Babel," in *Reader's Digest, The World's Last Mysteries (Pleasantville, NY: Reader's Digest, 1981), p. 177.

sion of tongues on a clay tablet written in Sumerian. The inscription reads:

Once upon a time, there was no snake,
there was no scorpion.
There was no hyena, there was no lion,
There was no wild dog, no wolf,
There was no fear, no terror.
Man had no rival. In those days, the Subur and Hamazi
Harmony-tongued Sumer, the great
land of the decrees of princeship,
Uri, the land having all that is appropriate.
The land Martu, resting in security.
The whole universe, the people in unison.
To Enlil in one tongue . . .
The A-da the Lord, a-da the prince, a-da the king.
Enki a-da the Lord, a-da the prince, a-da the king.
Enki, the Lord of abundance
whose commands are trustworthy,
The lord of wisdom who understands the laws,
The leader of the gods,
Endowed with wisdom, the lord of Eridu
Changed the speech in their mouths,
Brought contention into it,
Into the speech of man that had been one.[9]

S. N. Kramer, the translator, comments that it is "beyond all doubt that the Sumerians believed that there was a time when all mankind spoke one and the same

[9] *From a review of* The Babel of Tongues: A Sumerian Version (Journal of the American Oriental Society, *January 1968*).

language, and that it was Enki, the Sumerian god of wisdom, who confounded their speech."

Researchers have also discovered that all languages have their roots in one language spoken in Mesopotamia, or a nearby region, that is called the "proto-language."

No longer can critics call the biblical story a legend without being contradicted with striking, confirming evidence for the historical accuracy of the Bible's account of the Tower of Babel.

Have we heard the end of the controversy? Probably not. There are plans under way to rebuild the city of Babylon, and the Etemenanki Tower with it. What does this mean for the future of the Middle East and the entire world?

In the next chapter we will explore the answer to that question and consider some incredible new developments in the Middle East.

8

A MODERN KING NIMROD?

The end of the Tower of Babel story has not yet been reached. Even in the present day, still one more chapter is unfolding.

Dr. Charles H. Dyer
Author, *The Rise of Babylon*

CRITICS MAY SCOFF AT THE BIBLICAL STORY OF THE Tower of Babel, but an Iraqi ruler with ambitions as lofty as those of King Nimrod is not scoffing. Though in 1991 the modern version of fire and brimstone rained on Iraqi cities during the Persian Gulf War, it did not weaken Saddam Hussein's ambition to rebuild ancient Babylon and thereby restore its glory.

Construction is going on this very day at the site of ancient Babylon. Despite a temporary lull during and after the Persian Gulf War, construction soon began again. And another in a series of annual Babylon Festivals was held in September 1992, with invitations going out to leaders around the world, as well as to biblical scholars.

Saddam Hussein's ambitions remain clear: to control a modern Arab empire as its world-class leader, with a rebuilt Babylon as prime symbol of his own historical significance. Here's how Walter Laqueur put it in the *Washington Post*:

Saddam Hussein first appeared on the scene as a pan-Arab politician. His great hero is Nebuchadnezzar II, who was neither an Arab nor a Muslim, but the builder of a great empire [and the conqueror of Jerusalem].[10]

Wars aside, Saddam Hussein's ambition is expressing itself through what he has determined must be a world-class city. He is now rebuilding ancient Babylon, on its original site, just sixty-two miles south of Baghdad. He believes it will help him recapture the glory of Nebuchadnezzar's expansive empire, as well as give him the international status of the greatest ruler Babylon ever had.

WHY THE LOYALTY TO NEBUCHADNEZZAR?

Who was Nebuchadnezzar? And what accomplishments have made him such an emotional symbol for Saddam Hussein and his Baathist followers?

Nebuchadnezzar's father, Nabopolassar, was a tribal leader in the area we now know as Kuwait. In 627 B.C. he rallied the tribes and broke out of the Assyrian siege of the city of Erech, eventually freeing Babylon as well. The people of Babylon invited Nabopolassar to become their king. Is it surprising that Saddam Hussein, with his intense sense of history, wanted Kuwait as part of his empire?

Nebuchadnezzar initially served as his father's military commander. He used Babylon as a base for his many military campaigns into Syria and Canaan, as he

[10] *Walter Laqueur, "Like Hitler, but Different,"* Washington Post, *August 31, 1990, p. A25.*

systematically built an empire that eventually spanned all of today's Middle East.

First, Nebuchadnezzar led a coalition of Babylonians, Medes, and Scythians in the conquest and sacking of Nineveh, the capital of the millennium-long Assyrian empire. Then he met the Egyptians at Carchemish, defeating the forces of Pharaoh Necho in a climactic battle.

By 606 B.C. Nebuchadnezzar was at the entrance to Jerusalem, entering its gates and making Judah his vassal and initiating a seventy-year period of servitude. Daniel and his three friends were taken to Babylon during this conquest, as part of a remarkably enlightened policy of taking the best from the conquered cultures and absorbing it.

During this siege of Jerusalem, Nebuchadnezzar also heard of his father's death and he hurried home to ascend the throne. When he returned to do battle again with the Egyptians, he was defeated. This prompted Jehoiakim, the king of Judah, to rebel as well. Nebuchadnezzar besieged Jerusalem a second time and took the city. This time he took with him skilled craftsmen from Judah to assist him in the ambitious building program he had initiated in Babylon.

Nebuchadnezzar installed Zedekiah as king. Against the strong advice of the prophet Jeremiah, Zedekiah again rebelled. The city of Jerusalem fell to Nebuchadnezzar's forces for the third time in 587 B.C., with Zedekiah taken off to Babylon, along with a majority of the city's residents. In total, Nebuchadnezzar may have removed half of Judah's population, or an estimated

400,000 people, in his three campaigns against Judah and its capital city.

NEBUCHADNEZZAR'S ACHILLES' HEEL

His success went to Nebuchadnezzar's head. A Babylonian inscription reads:

I, Nebuchadnezzar, King of Babylon,
I am the son of Nabopolassar, King of Babylon.
I who erected the Ezida Temple,
I who built Procession Street,
The Street of Nebu,
And paved it with shimmering stones.
Nebu, you the divine minister,
Grant me immortality.

God, through Daniel, predicted a seven-year period of mental illness for the king. Daniel remained a close adviser throughout the king's illness, and after his recovery Nebuchadnezzar published his testimony, acknowledging the God of Daniel as supreme throughout his realm. It is the only chapter written by a Gentile king in the Old Testament.

Nebuchadnezzar's successors did not have his ability, and the Babylonian empire declined rapidly. But Nebuchadnezzar's star continued to shine brightly in history, encouraging Saddam Hussein to hitch his wagon to that star.

Shafqa Mohammed Jaafar, Babylon's chief archaeologist, has said, "Because Babylon was built in ancient times, and was a great city, it must be a great city again in the time of our great leader, Saddam Hussein."[11]

Saddam Hussein is undoubtedly aware of another factor—that "the strongest body of archaeological evidence . . . favors the location of Etemenanki . . . in Babylon." Today a model of this tower is featured in the Nebuchadnezzar Museum in the city of Babylon in Iraq.

WHY BE CONCERNED TODAY?

So why should the world care about an Iraqi ruler rebuilding an ancient city?

Consider the fact that the Tower of Babel and the city of Babylon are referred to repeatedly in the Bible as symbols of man's rebellion against God. It started with Nimrod building the Tower of Babel as the centerpiece of his rebellion against God. Babylon as a city picked up this reputation. God said the following about Babylon through the prophet Jeremiah:

> Summon archers against Babylon, all those who draw the
> bow. Encamp all around her; let no one escape. Repay her
> for her deeds; do to her as she has done. For she has
> defied the Lord, the Holy One of Israel. [Jeremiah 50:29]

Both of the prophets Isaiah and Jeremiah lash out repeatedly at Babylon for her wicked ways, prophesying dire judgments upon the city. God through Jeremiah

[11] John Burns, "New Babylon Is Stalled by a Modern Upheaval," The New York Times International, October 11, 1990, p. A13.

targets specifically the idols at the center of the city's worship:

> Babylon will be captured; Bel will be put to shame, Marduk filled with terror. Her images will be put to shame and her idols filled with terror. [Jeremiah 50:2]

According to authors Hal Lindsey and Chuck Missler in their book, *The Rise of Babylon and the Persian Gulf Crisis*:

> A review of ancient religious practices leads to the surprising discovery that virtually *all* forms of pagan idolatry and *all* forms of occult practices had their origins in the original city of Babylon. Isaiah, Chapter 47, notes that Babylon has labored with occult religions from its very origin: "[A] catastrophe you cannot foresee will suddenly come upon you. Keep on, then, with your magic spells and with your many sorceries, which you have labored at since childhood . . . let your astrologers come forward, those stargazers who make predictions month by month, let them save you from what is coming upon you." [Isaiah 47:11–13]
>
> As Babylon was conquered by subsequent empires, this entire religious system was transplanted, first to Pergamos and then to Rome.[12]

Though Babylon as a center of occult practices and idolatrous religious systems concerns Bible believers, it obviously does not disturb Saddam Hussein.

[12] *Hal Lindsey and Chuck Missler,* The Rise of Babylon and the Persian Gulf Crisis: A Special Report *(Wheaton, IL: Tyndale House, 1991), p. 39.*

BORROWING A SYMBOL OF SUPREMACY

Saddam Hussein realized early he needed some symbol of supremacy, a motivational project that would focus his people on the glory of Mesopotamia's past and the glory it could have among the nations. His personal "Tower of Babel" became the rebuilding of Babylon, started in 1979 and initially scheduled for completion in 1992.

A bloody and ruthless dictator, who personally killed one hundred generals when they refused to support his invasion of Kuwait and ordered the gassing of whole villages of rebellious Kurds, Saddam Hussein makes every effort to compare himself with that earlier blood-thirsty dictator, Nebuchadnezzar. He had a medallion made for the Babylon Festival of 1987 on which he put his picture beside that of Nebuchadnezzar in such a way they even looked alike. In 1982 Saddam Hussein's avowed purpose in rebuilding Babylon was to establish it as an archaeological park, to rebuild the monuments of the past. That purpose changed by 1987. The war with Iran had gone badly, and he needed a new focus.

MOTIVATING IRAQIS TO THEIR "MANIFEST DESTINY"

"Building Babylon became synonymous with rising to the Iranian threat and asserting Iraq's 'manifest destiny' to lead the Arab nations to glory. By rebuilding Nebuchadnezzar's city, Hussein has a natural opportunity to portray himself as Nebuchadnezzar's successor. Understandably, the rulers of Syria, Jordan, Israel, and Saudi

Arabia are nervous when Hussein extols Nebuchadnez-zar's kingdom and leadership, for the ancient king ruled the lands of the entire Arab world," writes Dr. Charles Dyer in his book, *The Rise of Babylon.*[13]

Ancient Persia, which is modern Iran, had con-quered Babylon under the Medo-Persian king Cyrus af-ter the death of Nebuchadnezzar. That historical note added to Saddam Hussein's desire to conquer Iran, for it would clearly symbolize a return to Babylon's glorious past.

Another enemy is now fueling Saddam Hussein's de-sire to rebuild Babylon: the United States of America. The results of the Persian Gulf War now constitute an additional major factor motivating the rebuilding of Bab-ylon as a symbol of Arab superiority and defiance, as the promotion for the 1992 Babylon Festival clearly shows.

Does the Bible portray a future for Babylon that even Saddam Hussein may not know about? One that should be of vital concern not only to Bible believers but also to anyone interested in the future of the world?

According to Dr. Charles H. Dyer, professor of bibli-cal exposition at Dallas Theological Seminary, "The end of the Tower of Babel story has not yet been reached. Even in the present day still one more chapter is un-folding."

[13] *Charles H. Dyer,* The Rise of Babylon *(Wheaton, IL: Tyndale House Publishers, 1991), pp. 40, 41.*

BABYLON AGAIN A WORLD CENTER?

It is the viewpoint of Lindsey and Missler that "the great prophecies concerning the city of Babylon in Isaiah Chapters 13 and 14 and Jeremiah 50 and 51 have never been fulfilled. Babylon, the city, has yet to rise to power, becoming again a key world center, and has yet to experience a destruction 'like Sodom and Gomorrah' at the 'Day of the Lord.' "[14]

The prophecies of Isaiah Chapters 13 and 14, written before Nebuchadnezzar's attack on Jerusalem, predict that Babylon will be destroyed like Sodom and Gomorrah: "Babylon, the jewel of kingdoms, the glory of the Babylonian's pride, will be overthrown by God like Sodom and Gomorrah." [Isaiah 13:19]

That did not happen even with the Medo-Persian conquest. Nor were the prophecies of Jeremiah fulfilled even under Alexander the Great, who actually began rebuilding Babylon. Jeremiah predicted: "A nation from the north will attack her and lay waste to her land. No one will live in it." [Jeremiah 50:3] At no time in history has Babylon been this deserted.

Couple these prophecies with Zedekiah's prophecy, made during the rebuilding of the temple after the Babylonian captivity. In that prophecy two women take a basket full of "iniquity" (the sins of Babylon) and fly it "to the country of Babylon to build a house for it. When it is ready, the basket will be set there in its place." [Zechariah 5:11]

---

[14] *Hal Lindsey and Chuck Missler,* The Rise of Babylon and the Persian Gulf Crisis: A Special Report, *pp. 31, 38.*

This prophecy clearly indicates that God will permit a time of extended wickedness, but that the "lid" will be lifted and punishment meted out upon Babylon.

The apostle John devotes two and a half chapters of the Book of Revelation to prophecies regarding Babylon. The punishment that is to be meted out to future Babylon is described as follows:

> With a mighty voice he shouted: "Fallen! Fallen is Babylon the Great! She has become a home for demons and a haunt for every unclean and detestable bird. For all the nations have drunk the maddening wine of her adulteries. The kings of the earth committed adultery with her, and the merchants of the earth grew rich from her excessive luxuries." When the kings of the earth who committed adultery with her and shared her luxury see the smoke of her burning, they will weep and mourn over her.
> [Revelation 18:2, 3, 9]

WILL BABYLON HAVE ITS OWN ARMAGEDDON?

Considering this trio of prophecies, Dr. Charles H. Dyer tells us, "The Bible says that just prior to the battle of Armageddon, Babylon, the wickedest, most powerful city in the ancient world, will again be rebuilt to play a major role in endtime events."

Apparently Saddam Hussein is not ready to accept these prophecies, nor is he determined to prove them wrong. In fact, what appears to be driving him is his worship of that great Babylonian king, Nebuchadnezzar II. With that in mind, it is not surprising to find Saddam

Hussein's archaeologists and architects researching the detailed description of Babylon at the zenith of its power and beauty under Nebuchadnezzar in the cuneiform writings found in the ruins.

By 1990, according to Dr. Dyer:

Sixty million bricks had been laid in the reconstruction of Nebuchadnezzar's fabled city. Saddam Hussein has ignored the objections of archaeologists who consider it a crime to build over ancient ruins. He has scrapped a plan to rebuild Babylon on a nearby site across the Euphrates River.

On the exact site of ancient Babylon, he has reconstructed the Southern Palace of Nebuchadnezzar, including the Procession Street, a Greek theater, many temples, what was once Nebuchadnezzar's throne room, and a half-scale model of the Ishtar Gate.

Hussein plans to rebuild the hanging gardens, once considered one of the seven wonders of the world; he has offered a $1.5 million prize to any Iraqi who can devise a plan to irrigate the gardens using only the technology available in ancient Babylon. Three artificial hills, each almost a hundred feet high, have been built on the plain and planted with palm trees and vines, and the ziggurat, or "Tower of Babel," may once again rear over the city.[15]

WHAT IS THE FUTURE OF BABYLON?

Saddam Hussein is clearly determined to continue the reconstruction, even though his people have to live in

---

[15] *Dyer,* The Rise of Babylon, *pp. 26, 27.*

primitive conditions as a result of the destruction from the Persian Gulf War. Not even the starvation of Iraqis seems to deter him from his grand vision.

What can be said about the future of Babylon? Will it again become a center of world commerce, as the Bible's prophecies indicate? Will world leaders someday come to Babylon to pay homage to a great leader of the nation, whether it be Saddam Hussein or a successor? Only time will tell.

In the meantime, let's all hope that Saddam Hussein's plan for the resurrection of once mighty Babylon is cultural and peaceful only. We can live with the mysteries surrounding the Tower of Babel, but the world can ill afford a modern, twentieth-century, nuclear-armed, Armageddon-minded Nebuchadnezzar.

With that, we leave the fate of Babylon to its rulers and the prophecies. There are other ancient secrets of the Bible still to be explored—each in its own way more fascinating than the one before. As always, our goal will be to answer that most elusive question: Can it be true?

9

THE BUSH
THAT WOULD NOT BURN

An episode like the burning bush, where Moses sees a fire in a bush and it is not consumed, goes back to ancient beliefs of animism.

Dr. Robert Eisenman
Professor of Middle East Religions

IF YOU WALKED INTO YOUR BACKYARD AND SAW A bush aflame, but it was not being burned up, you'd rightfully wonder who was pulling a trick on you. Now suppose a voice spoke directly to you out of that burning bush. Then you'd know for sure someone was perpetrating a hoax.

Yet the Bible reports that is exactly what happened to a shepherd named Moses nearly four thousand years ago. To this day, the story of Moses and the burning bush remains one of the great unsolved mysteries of Bible history.

Why is the story of Moses and the burning bush in the Book of Exodus so important? On what basis do critics debunk this episode in the desert of Midian? And why is it so difficult to defend this major event in Moses' life?

Larger questions that arise even among Bible believers are: Was Moses a real person? Were the Hebrews actually the downtrodden, abused people described in the Bible? Does the story of the crossing of the Red Sea bear any resemblance to what literally happened?

Given the scope of Moses' involvement with the Old Testament generally and the children of Israel specifically, it is perhaps not too surprising that those bent on destroying the credibility of the Bible would take dead aim at anything and everything attributed to Moses.

TRUE STORY OR PURE FICTION?

One critic, Dr. Robert Eisenman, chairman of the Department of Religious Studies and professor of Middle East religions at California State University, sharply attacks the credibility of the story of the burning bush. He says:

> On the face of it, the story of the burning bush is pure fiction or at least mythology. It smacks of pious enthusiasm. The idea that a bush can be burning and still exist is just not within the realm of probability.

Strong criticism indeed for an experience many believe was central to persuading Moses to tackle Pharaoh on behalf of his people.

On the other hand, an eminently qualified defender of the story is Dr. Amnon Shor, a dual citizen of the United States and Israel. Dr. Shor, Israeli born, speaks four languages, including ancient Aramaic, and is an educator in Old Testament studies at Vision Christian University in southern California. Dr. Shor tells us:

> The biblical story of the burning bush is completely true and provable. The Byzantine Emperor Justinian the Great erected a monastery in the sixth century as a fortress and

shrine on the traditional site of the burning bush, located in the central Sinai Peninsula.

Another major event in Moses' life that arouses the scorn of critics is Moses leading the Israelites through the Red Sea. Rabbi Sherwin Wine of the Birmingham Temple in Farmington Hills, Michigan, scoffs at the story:

> The Bible says there were 600,000 males. That means over two million people passed through those waters. It most likely would have taken several weeks for all those people just to cross. The whole idea is absolutely crazy.

Countering Rabbi Wine is Dr. Doron Nof, professor of oceanography at Florida State University in Tallahassee. He asserts confidently:

> Based on recent developments in physical oceanography and meteorology, we can prove today that the crossing of the Red Sea would have been possible.

But let's leave that battle for now to set the stage for an understanding of the episode involving the burning bush. For that we must go back to Moses' beginnings in Egypt.

BORN UNDER A DEATH SENTENCE

The amazing biblical saga of Moses begins when he is born to a Hebrew mother along the Nile in the land of

Goshen in Egypt. The high rate of births among the Hebrew population frightened proud Pharaoh Ramses II and his slave-masters, for as Semites they represented an exploding minority population. With no condoms or birth control pills to distribute, he ordered all male babies slain upon birth.

Moses' adoring mother knew she could not protect her son very long, so she prepared a waterproof basket and set Moses afloat on the Nile near the pharaoh's palace. Her ploy succeeded, and the baby was picked up by a princess of Pharaoh's court, who called him Moses, meaning "drawn out of the water." The princess raised him as her son.

Moses' ethnic consciousness awakened as an adult. He became acutely aware of his Hebrew heritage. He began to take a deeper, more sympathetic interest in his own people and as he went about his princely duties, he became increasingly aware of the constant mistreatment of Hebrews by their Egyptian taskmasters. His anger grew, until one day . . .

ETHNIC FEELINGS TRIGGER ATTACK

The Egyptian sun blazed hotter as noon approached. Hebrew slaves wearing only aprons mixed mud and straw and filled brick forms row upon row. Others lifted forms and piled the dried bricks for transport to building sites.

Egyptian supervisors sat with sticks ready in case a Hebrew slave even seemed to slow down his pace. Others cracked long whips on hot backs as reminders to work harder.

A cloud of dust announced the arrival of an Egyptian official on his horse. At the sight, a taskmaster supervising a Hebrew loading bricks onto a cart began beating the Hebrew slave. To the supervisor's amazement, the official stopped his horse next to him. "Stop! Stay your hand, pit-master! Why do you lash this man?" Moses barked.

"Man?" the pit-master exclaimed disdainfully. "These are not men, my lord. They are lazy dogs. The scourge is the only language they understand." He turned back to the Hebrew. "Get to it, dog!" and the lash fell once more.

At that moment Moses leaped off his horse and grabbed the lash with one hand. With the other he sent the pit-master sprawling with a quick punch to the abdomen. The falling man's head slammed against a rock and his body went limp.

Shocked at his own actions and dismayed at the results, Moses bent down to check the fallen pit-master. Several Hebrew slaves approached to see what had happened.

"I did not mean to kill him," Moses almost whispered as he bent over the man. He picked up the body and slung it on his horse in front of his saddle, mounted, and galloped off.

"They'll get him for that," one of the Hebrew slaves said quietly to his friends.

Once out of sight, Moses stopped his horse. He looked around to make sure no one could see him, then he dug a shallow grave in the sand and buried the Egyptian.

That night Moses did not sleep well. The enormity of his actions came crashing in on him. But since his actions had not been witnessed by any other Egyptians, he determined he could carry on as usual. The Hebrews would undoubtedly consider him a hero and keep quiet about it.

Approaching a Hebrew village the next day, Moses saw two men attacking each other with sticks. Moses galloped up and came to a halt beside them.

"What's going on here?" he asked the combatants, who stopped as he arrived.

"Oh, it's Moses." One of them taunted, "Are you going to kill us like you did the Egyptian?"

Moses pulled the rein sharply, turned his horse, and galloped off. He knew word of his previous day's action had spread quickly.

That night his trusted servant took Moses aside. "In return for special favors, one of the Hebrews has reported you killed a pit-master," he whispered. "My friend in Pharaoh's palace says that Pharaoh will call you into his presence tomorrow. Your life is in danger. You must leave before daybreak."

A FUGITIVE

The Bible reports that when Moses left Egypt, he traveled all the way to Midian—now in modern-day Saudi Arabia. There he married one of the daughters of Jethro and for forty years he herded sheep, convinced he would die a fugitive.

Let's join Moses in the desert of Midian. . . .

A STARTLING SIGHT

Shimmering heat waves danced across the desert floor. A recent rain had carpeted the valley with new green. Moses, a lonely shepherd, kept a wary eye out for impetuous sheep attempting to stray from the flock in search of desert specialties.

Suddenly Moses' attention shifted to the distance where a bush was burning brightly. Such huge flames spelled danger in the desert, so he temporarily left the flock to see if he needed to take steps to contain the fire. To his amazement the fire did not appear to even crisp the leaves.

And though he could see no one, the sound of a voice like no other he had ever heard thundered in his ears:

"Moses! Moses!"

He looked around him, since the voice seemed to be coming from everywhere at once.

"Here I am," Moses responded, stepping back in confusion. He suddenly realized the voice was coming from the bush.

"Don't come any closer," the voice commanded, and added, "Take off your sandals, for where you are standing is holy ground."

Still confused by the combination of a burning bush and the voice, Moses looked hesitantly at his feet, at the bush, and at his feet again. He slipped out of his sandals.

"I am the God of your father, the God of Abraham, the God of Isaac, and the God of Jacob."

Astounded and even more confused, Moses covered his face with a section of his head covering, for he felt totally unworthy of being addressed by the Almighty himself.

The voice continued. "I have indeed seen the misery of my people in Egypt. I have heard their prayers and I am going to rescue them and move them to a spacious new land with an abundance of food. I will give them the home of the Canaanites, Hittites, Amorites, Perizzites, Hivites, and Jebusites."

Moses' mind was in a whirl. His education in the court of Pharaoh had introduced him to all of these tribal peoples. He had met emissaries from the Hittites, since they had entered into an alliance with the Egyptians after the defeat of the Hyksos. And as God named the tribal groups, he realized the truth of God's description, "a spacious land," for the territory they occupied was large indeed.

"The voice of the oppressed has reached me, and I have seen the way the Egyptians are mistreating my people."

Moses was dumbfounded. He had left Egypt forty years ago and had severed his emotional connection with his heritage. His job was herding sheep, not dreaming up insurrections. The next words hit him like a sledgehammer.

"I am sending you to Pharaoh to bring my people, the Israelites, out of Egypt."

Moses couldn't believe his ears. Here he stood with a shepherd's staff in his hand. It was forty years since he had addressed anyone more important than his wife and her family. He began to backpedal furiously.

"But . . . but who am I, Lord, that I should go to Pharaoh to bring out the Israelites?"

The voice grew stronger. "I will be with you."

Moses was not comforted.

"Here's my commitment to you," the voice continued. "When you have brought out the Israelites from Egypt, you will come back to this mountain to worship God."

Still not convinced, Moses said, "Suppose I take your assignment. Suppose I go to the Israelite leaders and tell them about this meeting, and they ask, 'What is the name of the God who you say sent you?' What do I say to them?"

"I AM who I AM," the voice intoned, as though it were a formula. "You are to say to them, 'I AM has sent me.'"

Then the formula every religious Israelite already could identify echoed in his ears: "Say to the Israelites, 'The Lord, the God of your fathers—the God of Abraham, Isaac, and Jacob—has sent me.'"

Even though Moses knew that it was God speaking to him, that was not enough assurance. There was no way he was ready to make the commitment to go. Then God's voice continued: "Go and bring together the elders of Israel and tell them that the Lord, the God of their fathers Abraham, Isaac, and Jacob, appeared to you and said, 'I have watched and seen what has been done to you in Egypt. I am promising to take you out of your misery and bring you to the land of the Canaanites, Hittites, Amorites, Perizzites, Hivites, and Jebusites, a land flowing with milk and honey!' "

A BURNING BUSH, BUT NOT CONSUMED?

We'll leave Moses and his confrontation with God in the desert, for clearly the burning bush represents a problem to every thinking person. The bush not being consumed defies the laws of physics . . . and is contrary to common sense.

The critics clearly seem to have the high ground in this disagreement over whether the incident really could have happened.

Typical of the positions taken is that of Dr. Robert Eisenman, professor of Middle East religions at California State University in Long Beach, who strongly suggests the incident has its roots in primitive society:

> An episode like the burning bush, where Moses sees a fire in a bush and it is not consumed, goes back to ancient beliefs of animism. Primitive ideas that spirits dwelled in natural objects, such as brooks, streams, rocks in mountains, and in wells, are residues from early religious beliefs of man. I don't think they have anything to do with the Old Testament beliefs of one god. It's a perfect animistic story.

Defenders of the biblical story point out that the focus of Moses' experience in the desert is really not on the burning bush at all, but on God's revelation of himself to Moses as the "I AM," the one eternal God, the "God of Abraham, Isaac, and Jacob." Only that kind of personal revelation could propel a shepherd into leadership of a movement to free the Hebrews from Egyptian bondage.

Bible scholars and naturalists offer additional explanations for the burning bush. One of them comes from Dr. Amnon Shor, an Israeli Old Testament scholar, who suggests that a monastery in the Sinai may contain the original burning bush:

> At the foot of Mount Sinai on the Sinai Peninsula is the monastery of St. Catherine, famous for its ancient manuscripts and as the traditional site for the burning bush. . . . The local nomadic people, the bedouin, believe that the growing bush inside the monastery is the actual burning bush in which God appeared to the prophet Moses.

Providing additional insight is Phillip Haney, an Israeli naturalist, who says:

> I cannot confirm or reject whether the bush growing at the monastery is the actual burning bush, but it is a specific desert plant that fits the biblical description. The bush has also been described by the first-century historian Josephus.
> The bush is the *Fraxinella*, or gas plant, a sturdy perennial bush with white or purple flowers common in the Middle East. The bush produces an oil so volatile, it can be ignited by the sun. The oil quickly burns up, leaving the bush itself undamaged.

An alternative explanation is suggested by Nogah Hareuveni in the chapter, "The Secret of the Burning

Bush," in *Trees and Shrubs in Our Biblical Heritage.*[16]
After discussing the *Fraxinella*, the author suggests:

> In various regions of Sinai, as in other deserts and
> wilderness areas, mirages are well-known phenomena,
> caused by different density air layers refracting light waves.
> Images of lakes and trees which appear from a distance and
> disappear when approached are not the products of
> nomadic imagination.
>
> There are objects that do in fact exist in a distant place,
> and are transposed by the refracted light waves as images
> to the eye of the beholder who happens to be in the path
> of these light waves. It is therefore possible to imagine a
> situation in which the refracted light waves transmitted an
> image of a flame burning in some distant place and
> superimposed the image onto the bush that Moses
> saw. . . .
>
> The singularly low probability of such a coincidence puts
> it in the category of a miracle. It is reasonable to believe
> that although Moses must surely have seen mirages, he had
> never seen anything as astounding as this and so exclaimed:
> "I must turn aside to see this wonderful sight, why the
> bush is not burned."

Whatever the nature of the burning bush, clearly
something provided Moses with a powerful motivation
to leave his home and confront Pharaoh on behalf of the
enslaved Israelites.

A few moments ago we left Moses in the desert with

---

[16] *Nogah Hareuveni, "The Secret of the Burning Bush" in* Trees and
Shrubs in Our Biblical Heritage.

God's challenge. Now let's check on his response . . . and God's solution to the objections raised by Moses, since they will help us understand what happened next.

We suspect Moses would be wondering, "Me before Pharaoh? I haven't given a speech in forty years! Sheep don't need speeches. And whenever I get home, my wife is so glad to see me, I don't need to give any fancy speeches to delight her." Fortunately for Moses, God had some specific strategies ready.

THERE'S HELP ON THE WAY

"Don't worry, Moses," God's voice said. "The elders will listen to you. With them at your side you can then go to the king of Egypt and say, 'The Lord, the God of the Hebrews, has met with us. Please permit us to go on a three-day journey into the desert to offer sacrifices to Him.' "

Moses, having lived in the court of the pharaoh, did not believe such a request would be honored.

"I know what's on your mind," said the voice. "I agree, the king of Egypt will not let you go unless he is under extreme pressure. I will exert that pressure, Moses, by performing wonders that will force his hand.

"Furthermore, I will make the Egyptians so glad to get rid of you that you will not leave empty-handed. In fact, I suggest your women ask their neighbors for articles of gold and silver to take with you. When you leave, you'll be richer than they."

Moses was still backpedaling. "But what if they don't believe me and won't accept the fact that you have spoken to me?"

"What's that in your hand, Moses?"

Moses looked at the shepherd's staff in his hand. "A staff." What more could he say? After all, there was nothing fancy about it.

"Throw it on the ground!"

Moses tossed it on the ground. To his astonishment it became a moving snake.

"Take it by the tail," the voice said.

Moses grabbed it . . . and suddenly it was a staff again.

"Use that to prove to the people that I have sent you. Now put your hand inside your cloak."

Moses put his hand into his cloak, and when he took it out it was white as snow, like a leprous hand. He recoiled. Then the voice continued, "Put it back in again." Moses did, and when he pulled it out it was totally restored.

"Now you have two miraculous signs to validate that I have sent you. And if they won't believe those, just take some of the water from the Nile and spill it in front of them. It will turn to blood."

Feeling trapped, and still not convinced this assignment matched his skills, Moses said, "I'm just not a good speaker. Never have been. I tend to stutter, especially when I'm excited."

There was real gentleness in the reproof from God. "Moses, who gave man his voice? Who makes man deaf or blind? Is it not I? Stop worrying. I will help you speak!"

His face lowered, Moses still objected. "Lord, I cannot. Surely there is someone more capable than I."

Now there was a hard edge to the voice. "I will send

your brother, Aaron! He's a good speaker. In fact, he is already on his way to visit with you. He will take the challenge and speak for both of you. And don't forget your staff!"

Thoroughly chastened, Moses waited for more. Nothing came, so he turned, gathered his flock of sheep and started for home, his mind whirling with the implications of his assignment.

A STAFF THAT BECAME A SNAKE?

Rather incredible, isn't it? A piece of wood that becomes a snake, a hand that instantly changes texture. Who would believe that today?

Surprising information comes from a 1983 issue of *Biblical Archaeology Review,* in an article by Leon Shalit entitled, "How Moses Turned a Staff into a Snake and Back Again:"[17]

> Something happened to me here in Israel that may explain
> a bit of Moses' magic. . . . I was gardening at a friend's
> house in a seaside village. Opening the door of the
> toolshed, I saw a tail disappearing behind a sack lying in
> the back. Thinking it was a rat, I raised my spade to hit it
> as I picked up the sack. But when I picked up the sack, a
> snake reared up. I tried to cut its head off with the spade
> against the wall, but the wall was very rough and I could
> only trap and hold the snake. So I wedged the handle of
> the spade with a brick and went to get help from a

[17] *Leon Shalit, "How Moses Turned a Staff into a Snake and Back Again,"* Biblical Archaeology Review, *(May/June, 1983), p. 72.*

neighbor whose house, it happened, was being sprayed against mosquitoes. The man doing the spraying told me that he was also a snake expert, so I took him along. . . .

He caught the tail of the snake, released its head and swung it around his head a number of times, then he carried it to the lawn. In his hand it looked like a thick twig, a stick, quite lifeless. The snake was laid down and it looked more than ever like a stick, quite lifeless. . . .

This reminded me of the staffs that turned into snakes in Exodus, so I pursued the matter with the young man. He told me that as a boy he used to catch snakes this way. It was dangerous, however, because different snakes, even of the same species, took different times to regain consciousness. . . .

Thinking this over, I concluded that Moses and the Egyptians may have chosen particular snakes after some experimentation, finally selecting only those snakes that remained unconscious for a rather long and predictable time. By throwing the stiffened, unconscious snakes on the ground at the right time, Moses and Pharaoh's magicians were able to bring the snakes back to consciousness.

I found some confirmation for this theory in Exodus 4: "Then the Lord said to Moses, 'Put out your hand and grasp it *by the tail*' [emphasis added]. He put out his hand and seized it and it became a staff in his hand." [Exodus 4:3] Here is a clear suggestion that the snake became a staff when Moses grasped it *by the tail*—and probably swung it around his head. Here we have God explaining the trick to Moses.

Trick or not, it's a fascinating theory about an experience that clearly appeared to be a miracle to Moses, a miracle that drove home God's special provision if he would be obedient.

In any case we have discovered that there is, in fact, a bush that burns without being consumed, and snakes that can be made to look like a staff of wood. That may not solve the mystery to everyone's satisfaction, but stick with us. Just ahead is that incredible series of plagues in Egypt and the unbelievable crossing of the Red Sea by the Israelites *and* their animals. The critics don't have kind things to say about these miracles, either!

10

"LET MY PEOPLE GO"

The main purpose of the Exodus story is not to describe history. . . . What they used was a series of old legends and distorted memories which had no relationship to history.

Rabbi Sherwin Wine
Founder of Humanistic Judaism

I<small>F THE MIRACLE OF MOSES AND THE BURNING BUSH</small> has become a focal point of the critics of the Bible, what might they say about Moses' appearances before Pharaoh and about the ten plagues? And how should the defenders of the Bible respond?

Obviously there is no way of physically finding the bush in which Moses heard God. But a nation like Egypt suffering through the devastation of the plagues described in the Bible ought to be in social upheaval and economic disarray, recorded in detailed historical writing. However, lack of evidence for similar events during the years commonly accepted for the Exodus left the critics on the attack and defenders without answers. In fact, it is difficult to find anyone who will stand up and defend the biblical story of the Exodus.

A very common position among today's biblical scholars is that taken by Rabbi Sherwin Wine, founder of Humanistic Judaism and rabbi of the Birmingham Temple, Farmington Hills, Michigan, whom we heard from earlier. Rabbi Wine insists:

> The main purpose of the Exodus story is not to describe history. . . . As created by the priest scribes in Jerusalem,

it was to glorify their god. What they used was a series of old legends and distorted memories which had no relationship to history.

Fortunately for the defenders of the Bible, ancient ruins keep bringing new information to the surface. Old inscriptions are continually being reread and evaluated in the light of new information, and that information is regarded as more "friendly" to the Bible record.

Egyptologists (scholars studying the history of Egypt) are drawing some startling new conclusions from old information. But before we get to that, let's set the stage by visiting briefly with Moses in Egypt.

According to most scholars who place the Exodus from 1280 to 1270 B.C., the popular villain for the role of the pharaoh Moses had to approach was Ramses II—a builder of cities, great temples, and the first shipping canal between the Nile River and the Red Sea.

However, new scholarly evidence from both astronomical and archaeological dating moves the Exodus event back about two hundred years to the reign of Pharaoh Amenhotep II. Pharaoh Amenhotep was a large, athletic, muscular man who at eighteen was already an expert in all types of warfare. As an oarsman, he could outrow the best of his competitors. He was a great horseman who trained the finest steeds. As an archer his skill was said to be unmatched. Amenhotep II was indeed a formidable king to approach with a request as daring as what Moses and Aaron had in mind.

THE ANSWER IS NO, NO, AND NO!

The grand vizier entered the throne room and approached the pharaoh, bowing deeply as he arrived in front of the throne.

"Your Majesty, I have been approached by representatives of the Hebrews, who ask for an audience with you. They want to make a request to worship their god. Shall I bring them in?"

The pharaoh looked slightly amused. "I thought the Hebrews were gainfully employed making bricks for our great new city, Pithom," he said. "I don't see any need for them to worship their god. But to amuse ourselves this morning, bring them in." He looked at his counselors, who nodded approvingly.

"Yes, Your Majesty." The grand vizier bowed and left the room. He returned with a small group of older men. The two men in the lead were clearly in charge. They bowed respectfully as they approached the pharaoh.

"I'm told you have a request." The pharaoh smiled indulgently.

"Your Majesty, thank you for receiving us. We know you will listen to our request with great wisdom," said Aaron, stepping up to address Pharaoh. "The Lord God of Israel says to the mighty pharaoh, 'Let my people go, so that they may build a festival to me in the desert!' "

The pharaoh's face darkened in anger. His eyes flashed at this challenge to his authority as the god of Egypt. He exploded, "Who is the Lord, that I should obey him and let Israel go? I do not know this god, and I will not let the people go."

Aaron and Moses stood their ground, though the men with them started backing off.

"The God of the Hebrews has met with us. He has asked us to take a three-day journey into the desert to offer sacrifices to the Lord our God. If we do not do that, he may strike us with plagues or with the sword."

"Why do you want to take the people away from their work? Out! Out! Back to your work. You are stopping these men from doing their job!"

Moses and Aaron left, and Pharaoh turned to the grand vizier. "The Hebrews are now numerous. They are clearly a large problem. I want orders sent to all taskmasters that they are no longer to supply the straw for the Hebrews. Let them find their own straw. But don't let them slack off on their production quotas. Let's see if they'll find time to come up with more crazy ideas like this. Go into the desert and sacrifice to their god? Indeed! They have become lazy because we have not worked them hard enough."

The grand vizier hurried from the room to pass on the message to the taskmasters, who quickly implemented the new orders. Angry Hebrew foremen organized groups to spread throughout the countryside to find straw. Production slowed as those actually engaged in making bricks grew fewer. Taskmasters reprimanded the Hebrew foremen, insisting production quotas had to be met. Those who failed to produce were beaten.

A delegation of Hebrew foremen was sent to the pharaoh.

"Your Majesty, we do not understand. Why have you treated your servants this way? We are not being given straw anymore, yet we are forced to produce as many bricks as before. It's an impossibility, Your Majesty. Your taskmasters are making an unreasonable demand."

"Lazy, that's what you are, lazy!" the pharaoh thundered. "That is why you keep saying, 'Let us go and sacrifice to the Lord.' Now get to work. Nothing will change. You will not get straw and you must fill your quota of bricks!"

That night, crestfallen and angry foremen met with Moses and Aaron. "You and your great message from the Lord, the God of Israel! Instead of helping us, you have made us a stench to Pharaoh and his officials. You've given them the weapon they needed to oppress us even more!"

That night Moses approached his God. "Is this why you took me from looking after sheep?" he pleaded. "To bring even more trouble to my people? I just don't understand. You said you would help them, but all that's happened is greater oppression."

God responded, "I will redeem you with an outstretched arm and with mighty acts of judgment. And I will bring you to the land I swore to give Abraham, Isaac, and Jacob."

The next day Moses returned to the Hebrew leaders to reassure them, but they would have none of it. Then God insisted that Moses "go, tell Pharaoh, king of Egypt, to let my people go."

"If my people will not listen to me, how will Pharaoh

listen, since I am not an eloquent speaker?" Moses asked.

But God would not leave Moses and Aaron in peace, and they again approached the pharaoh with great trepidation.

WHAT'S THE EVIDENCE FOR HEBREWS IN EGYPT?

Critics dispute this whole episode of Moses and Aaron before Pharaoh because, they say, it is based on a premise discredited by most biblical scholars. The premise is that the biblical story of Joseph in Egypt, of the Hebrews occupying Goshen, of the oppression of the Hebrews by the pharaohs is not based on historical fact.

Most scholars insist there is no record in Egypt of the Hebrew presence. Since the Egyptians kept such meticulous records, they say, surely they would have interacted with such a large group of people, even if they were a minority.

We may not have direct references to Joseph in Egypt, says Werner Keller, author of *The Bible as History,* but we have substantial circumstantial evidence. Keller says:

> There is indirect proof of the authenticity of the Joseph story. The biblical description of the historical background is authentic; equally genuine is the colorful Egyptian detail. Egyptology confirms this from countless finds.[18]

[18] *Werner Keller,* The Bible as History *(New York: William Morrow and Company, 1956), p. 89.*

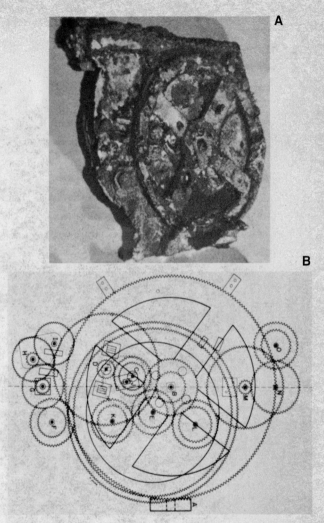

Ancient biblical man was thought to have little or no technological skills. This fairly sophisticated analog computer (photo A) recovered from a ship that was sunk in the Aegean Sea before the time of Christ was apparently used for navigation purposes. The second photo shows the technological engineering and components comprising this ancient computer.

COURTESY OF DR. DONALD E. CHITTICK

This small iron pot reveals ancient biblical man had smelting and manufacturing abilities. The iron pot was reportedly found in 1912 encased in a block of coal at the Municipal Electric Plant in Thomas, Oklahoma. The pot, with an affidavit from the pot finder, is now on display at the Miles Musical Museum in Eureka Springs, Arkansas. Some scientists believe this pot was from the biblical time of Tubal-Cain and buried sedimentarily in the worldwide flood of Noah's day. COURTESY OF MILES MUSICAL MUSEUM

About fifty years ago in West Virginia this pagan ceremonial brass bell with an iron clapper was reportedly found encased in a large lump of coal. A scanning electron elemental analysis performed on the bell determined that the elemental composition could not be reproduced by today's metallurgy technology. Many scientists believe the bell is an artifact from a highly advanced biblical civilization prior to Noah's Flood. COURTESY OF DAVID W. BALSIGER

The biblical story of Lot, his wife, and two daughters rushing to escape the cataclysmic destruction of Sodom and Gomorrah has been considered a 3,000-year-old myth by many scholars. However, new scientific and archaeological evidence indicates that this biblical account is historically true and factually accurate.

COURTESY OF HOLYLAND BIBLE KNOWLEDGE SOCIETY

This ancient cuneiform tablet from the city of Ebla in Syria mentions Sodom and Gomorrah as real cities. Another tablet known as the *Eblaite Geographic Atlas* contains 290 place names of geographic locations in the ancient biblical land of Canaan. Place name 211 on this diary of cities is "Sodom"—a city visited by a well-traveled merchant from Ebla just before Abraham moved to the region. COURTESY OF GIOVANNI PETTINATO

Two children stand on top of the defensive tower at Numeira in Jordan—said to be the archaeological site of biblical Gomorrah. In the second photo, a Jordanian family stands inside the remaining city wall of Gomorrah. COURTESY OF DR. BRYANT G. WOOD

This is a view to the north along the western city wall of Bab edh-Dhra, Jordan—said by archaeologists to be the remains of biblical Sodom. Today, the area is very desolate, although in biblical times it was more fertile. COURTESY OF DR. BRYANT G. WOOD

An excavated grain-grinding mill at Sodom, complete with several grinding stones, indicates the city was once a thriving community. Prisoners seated on the ground or a bench were the grinding laborers in these mills.

COURTESY OF DR. BRYANT G. WOOD

The large quantity of pottery recovered at Sodom reflects the usage of a wide variety of household pottery ware, diversity in pottery design, and excellent craftsmanship. This Sodom pottery collection is a part of a permanent display in the John Trever Museum Room at the Claremont School of Theology in California.

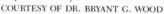

This display at the Smithsonian Institution in Washington, D.C., contains artifacts from an Early Bronze Age tomb at Sodom (Bab edh-Dhra) dating back to about 3000 B.C. Cemeteries at Sodom contain more than fifty thousand bodies, and charnel burial houses contain even more bodies, indicating Sodom was at one time a very sizable city.

There is no shortage of artistic works of Moses leading the Israelites through a parted Red Sea that drowns the pursuing Egyptians. Although many historians claim the Israelite Exodus and the Red Sea parting never happened, new evidence indicates that both events are historical fact. COURTESY OF HOLYLAND BIBLE KNOWLEDGE SOCIETY

According to the biblical account, Moses led the
Israelites out of Goshen, a fertile agricultural
region in Egypt. The Exodus moved from Egypt
into the Sinai Peninsula, a predominantly sun-
burnt landscape of rock and desert sand, as this
scene along the traditional Exodus route illus-
trates. COURTESY OF RICHARD EWING

St. Catherine's Monastery, located near the bottom of the Sinai Peninsula, is built at the foot of the traditional Mount Sinai, where Moses is said to have received the Ten Commandments. However, the monastery is most famous for its ancient religious manuscripts and as the traditional site of the "burning bush" in which God appeared to Moses, directing him to lead the Israelites out of Egypt. COURTESY OF RICHARD EWING

Local bedouin shepherds and some Old Testament scholars believe that the bush growing in a fenced area of St. Catherine's Monastery is the "original burning bush" in which God appeared to Moses. Although it's impossible to confirm this belief, the bush is a specific desert plant that fits the biblical description.

COURTESY OF DR. AMNON SHOR

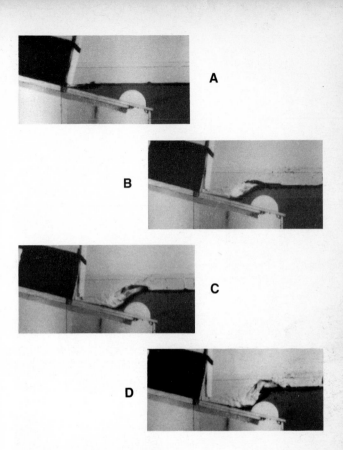

As the Bible seems to indicate, the parting of the Red Sea was probably due to a strong wind blowing all night that exposed a sandbar, allowing the Israelites to cross on dry ground. In 1992 oceanographer Dr. Doron Nof and meteorologist Dr. Nathan Paldor demonstrated scientifically the feasibility of a steady wind drying up a ridge through the top of the Gulf of Suez. In a lab experiment in which they duplicated the Red Sea with a submersed ridge (photo A), followed by applying appropriate wind conditions (B and C), they were able to expose a dry surface on the ridge, proving that specific wind conditions would result "in the parting of the Red Sea." They calculated that if the wind suddenly stopped, the water would flow back at a rate of fifteen feet per second over the ridge, destroying anything in its path. COURTESY OF DR. DORON NOF, FLORIDA STATE UNIVERSITY

For the Israelites, the ark of the covenant was their most sacred religious object and the center of all religious ceremonial practices. It was a wooden chest covered with beaten gold and inlaid with gold. Inside were the Ten Commandments tablets, Aaron's rod that had budded, and a pot of manna from the wilderness journey. From between the two cherubim on the top of the ark, God literally spoke to the Israelites through the high priest. The inset photo is a replica of the ark. COURTESY OF HOLYLAND BIBLE KNOWLEDGE SOCIETY AND GRANT JEFFREY

The ark of the covenant has been missing since the Babylonian king Nebuchadnezzar destroyed Jerusalem in 586 B.C. Several Israeli rabbis claim the ark is securely hidden in a secret chamber among the numerous underground tunnels beneath the Temple Mount in Jerusalem. They say it will be brought out when the holy temple (the third temple) is rebuilt on Temple Mount. Meanwhile, in preparation of rebuilding the temple, rabbinical groups are reproducing all the necessary temple vessels—except for the ark of the covenant. COURTESY OF DAVID W. BALSIGER, GRANT JEFFREY

There are several eyewitness accounts that the ark
of the covenant has been housed for nearly three
thousand years in a secret underground temple
beneath this Church of Zion of Mary in Aksum,
Ethiopia. Ethiopian historical records state that
King Solomon and the Queen of Sheba had a son
named Prince Menelik, who grew up in Jerusalem. At age nineteen, the records say, Prince
Menelik returned home with the real ark rather
than a replica made for him by King Solomon.
COURTESY OF GRANT JEFFREY

The idea that the Jordan River stopped flowing to let Joshua and the Israelites cross on dry land as this painting depicts, and that the walls of Jericho came tumbling down when the Israelites shouted, are two reasons skeptics question the Joshua account. However, modern science has determined that an earthquake could have been the moving force behind both of these seemingly unexplainable miracles. COURTESY OF HOLYLAND BIBLE KNOWLEDGE SOCIETY

This illustration is a reconstruction of Jericho. The outer sloped stone wall was about twelve feet high, and on top of this was a mud-brick wall about eighteen feet high. Behind these walls was a massive earthen embankment that surrounded the entire city. Jericho's poorer inhabitants lived in houses on this embankment. At the top of the embankment was another mud-brick wall about fifteen feet high. When archaeologists excavated at the base of the outer wall, they found piles of collapsed bricks, confirming the biblical account that the walls fell flat. The walls were probably brought down by earthquake activity.

ILLUSTRATION BY GENE FACKLER

There is ample evidence that an earthquake of magnitude 8.0 struck the Jericho region during the 1400 B.C. time frame. This quake temporarily dammed up the Jordan River and caused massive destruction in Jericho, including the collapsing of the defensive walls. The Bible says Joshua and his men walked up into the city after shouting and blowing their trumpets. The mud-brick wall fell in a heap at the base of the tell, creating a natural stairway for the Israelites to enter the city. ILLUSTRATION BY GENE FACKLER

This view is of the north end of the embankment level surrounding Jericho. It shows the housing foundations of Jericho's outcasts, like Rahab the prostitute, who provided Joshua's men with intelligence about the city. The death count from the earthquake is unknown, but archaeologists found victims trapped under walls and roofs that collapsed during the quake.

COURTESY OF DR. BRYANT G. WOOD

A man stands next to the excavated outer stone wall that surrounded ancient Jericho in Joshua's time. The wall is about twelve feet high, and on top of it was another eighteen-foot wall composed of mud-bricks. It was the uppermost wall that collapsed.

COURTESY OF THE BRITISH SCHOOL OF ARCHAEOLOGY

Nimrod is credited with being the instigator of the Tower of Babel in ancient Babylon. He was a mighty warrior and hunter whose empire included Babel in the biblical land of Shinar. His reign extended into Assyria, where he built the city of Nineveh and other settlements. Nimrod's grandfather was Ham and his great-grandfather was Noah. COURTESY OF HOLYLAND BIBLE KNOWLEDGE SOCIETY

According to the Bible, the Tower of Babel was to be a huge structure "with its top in the heavens." It was also a monument to human pride and mankind's continued disobedience to God. The tower was called *Babel*, meaning "confusion," because when God destroyed it, He confused the people's language, causing them to scatter by language groups throughout the world. COURTESY OF HOLYLAND BIBLE KNOWLEDGE SOCIETY

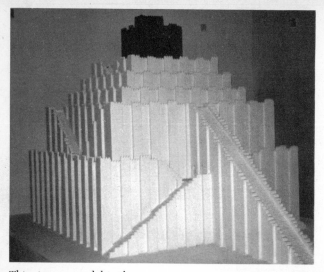

This ziggurat model in the Nebuchadnezzar Museum in Babylon is believed to be a close replica of the actual Tower of Babel. The tower was a monument to human engineering because fired clay bricks were used instead of mud-bricks or stone. Some experts believe these glasslike bricks functioned as a giant crystal radio set, allowing pagan high priests to communicate with the spirit world. The site of the original Tower of Babel can still be observed in ancient Babylon. COURTESY OF DR. CHARLES H. DYER

The vision of ancient Babylon conjured up by many is a city in total desolation. This view from the northern palace of Nebuchadnezzar shows that much of the ancient city is in total ruin. The piles of burnt brick in the foreground stand as solemn sentinels guarding the mound of dissolved mud-brick in the background. In the distance is a grove of date palms near the modern Arab village of Kweiresh.

COURTESY OF DR. CHARLES H. DYER

FROM **NABUKHADNEZZAR** TO **SADDAM HUSSEIN**

BABYLON UNDERGOES A RENAISSANCE

BABYLON INTERNATIONAL FESTIVAL

FROM SEPTEMBER 22 TO OCTOBER 22 1987

In this poster from the Babylon Festival, the two portraits on the medallion are those of Nebuchadnezzar (on the left) and Iraqi dictator Saddam Hussein. Emphasizing that Hussein is the logical heir to the Nebuchadnezzar legacy, the poster reads "From Nebuchadnezzar to Saddam Hussein—Babylon Undergoes a Renaissance." Hussein's ambition is to control a modern Arab empire, with a rebuilt Babylon as the prime symbol of his own historical significance.
COURTESY OF DR. CHARLES H. DYER

According to Bible prophecy, Babylon will be rebuilt to play a major role in end-time events prior to the battle of Armageddon. Saddam Hussein is rebuilding Babylon on the exact site of ancient Babylon. He has already reconstructed the Southern Palace of Nebuchadnezzar, a Greek theater, and many temples. In this photo, rising out of the ruins of the northern palace is the rebuilt western wall of the Procession Street—the famous entrance into Babylon. In the foreground, one can see more walls and foundations of ancient Babylon. COURTESY OF DR. CHARLES H. DYER

The rebuilt Ishtar Gate, which one must pass through to get into ancient Babylon, was flanked on either side by reliefs of bulls and dragons in alternating rows. Each bull and dragon is an exact duplicate and indicates that the brick molds must have been prepared for each section of the relief. The bull was the symbol of the Babylonian god Adad. COURTESY OF DR. CHARLES H. DYER

In the heart of ancient Babylon, the Iraqis have constructed the Saddam Hussein Guest House. This building contains guest rooms, dining facilities, and conference rooms. Iraqi President Saddam Hussein stays here when visiting ancient Babylon. COURTESY OF DR. CHARLES H. DYER

The idea that dinosaurs and man walked the earth contemporaneously may be confirmed by excavations in the Paluxy River bed near Glen Rose, Texas. Human footprints were found inside Tridactyl dinosaur prints, as if the person were following the dinosaur. Pictured is a fourteen-inch footprint found in Cretaceous limestone at Glen Rose. Excavations at Glen Rose have produced a nearly complete Acrocanthosaurus dinosaur, 203 dinosaur footprints, 57 human footprints among them, seven great-cat tracks, and various other fossil remains. COURTESY OF DON PATTON

The Bible's description of Joseph's elevation to viceroy of Egypt follows Egyptian protocol exactly, down to his traveling in the second chariot, insists Werner Keller.

An event identical to the patriarch Jacob's arrival in Goshen is described by a frontier official who wrote to his superior on papyrus:

> We have permitted the transit of the bedouin tribes from Edom via the Menephta fort in Zeku, to the fen-lands of the city of Per-Atum . . . so that they may preserve their own lives and the lives of their flocks on the estate of the king, the good Sun of every land. . . .[19]

Per-Atum is the biblical city of Pithom in the land of Goshen, later one of the cities where the Hebrews served as slaves to their Egyptian taskmasters.

AN EGYPTIAN RECORD OF JACOB'S FUNERAL CORTEGE?

An inscription found in Egypt also appears to be an eyewitness account of a participant in the procession taking Jacob's body to Canaan for burial, says Dr. William H. Shea, former associate professor of Old Testament studies at Andrews University, and research associate at the Biblical Research Institute in Washington, D.C. As part of his charge to his sons, especially Joseph, recorded in Genesis 49:30–33, Jacob requested they bury him in the Cave of Machpelah in the vicinity of Hebron in Canaan.

[19] *Ibid., p. 92.*

Pharaoh agreed, sending along some of his own servants and troops. (Genesis 50:6)

According to Dr. Shea, the pharaoh on the throne at that time was Sesostris III. In examining inscriptions in Egypt during that period, he found that "one record stands out as unusual—the mortuary stele of Khu-Sebek, an official who served under Sesostris III. On this stele, 'Khu-Sebek' tells of his participation in a campaign into Canaan, the only one known from the Middle Kingdom period."

Yet according to Egyptologists, Egypt did not have an empire in Canaan during this period. So why a campaign? Dr. Shea, after extensively evaluating the data for the reign of Pharaoh Sesostris III, comes to the conclusion that "exceptional as it is, I suggest that it was not the overtly military campaign that it may at first appear to be. I believe that this is an Egyptian record of the expedition to Canaan to bury Jacob."

The geographical details on the stele also confirm that conclusion:

> A geographical correlation arises from the mention of the town of Shechem as the place from which those who attacked the expedition came. That fits in well with the leg of the Israelite-Egyptian journey from Shechem to Hebron, after they crossed the Jordan River following events at the Threshing Floor of Atad. This geographical correlation reinforces the potential link between the two texts.

Dr. Shea concludes, "All in all, there is a strong correlation between the stele of Khu-Sebek and Genesis

50:4–14. Each records the burial of Jacob from a different perspective."[20]

Evidence that the Hebrews may well have been part of the work crews is also available. Werner Keller reports that on a painting from the patriarchal period, discovered in a rock tomb west of the Egyptian city of Thebes, a detail shows the manufacture of Egyptian bricks.

> The most notable feature being the light-skinned workmen, who are clad only in linen aprons. A comparison with the dark-skinned overseers shows that the fair-skinned men are probably Semites, but certainly not Egyptians. "The rod is in my hand," one of the Egyptian overseers is saying, according to the hieroglyphic inscription. "Be not idle."[21]

Though individually not conclusive, such archaeological evidence, when examined together, indicates that the stories of Joseph and Jacob have the ring of authenticity, that the Hebrews could well have been brick-making slaves.

With that as backdrop, let's go back to Moses and Aaron as they make their way reluctantly back to the pharaoh.

DIVINE INTERVENTION

The time for drastic action had come if Pharaoh was to budge from his entrenched opposition to the request

---

[20] *William H. Shea, "The Burial of Jacob,"* Archaeology and Biblical Research, 5, no. 2 (Spring 1992): pp. 33–44.
[21] *Keller,* The Bible as History, p. 105.

from Moses and Aaron. God let Moses and Aaron know that Pharaoh would repeatedly harden his heart despite a series of miraculous signs and wonders. But he assured them the Lord would be the eventual winner . . . and the Hebrews would be freed.

Then began a dramatic tug of war that lasted for weeks. At their next audience with Pharaoh, Aaron threw down his staff and it became a snake. Pharaoh's sorcerers threw down their staffs, and each turned into a snake. Though Aaron's snake swallowed those of the sorcerers, Pharaoh was not impressed.

At God's command, Moses and Aaron met the pharaoh at the Nile the next day. Aaron stretched out the staff and the *waters turned into blood.* The Bible records, "The fish died, and the river smelled so bad that the Egyptians could not drink its water. Blood was everywhere in Egypt." [Exodus 7:21]

But the Egyptian magicians "did the same things by their secret arts," and Pharaoh refused to listen to Moses and Aaron, while Egyptians dug wells for alternate sources of drinking water.

The next plague was that of frogs, with *swarms of frogs* occupying every nook and cranny, including baking ovens and bedrooms. The Egyptian magicians again duplicated the phenomenon, but it took Moses and Aaron to halt the plague. Though no new frogs appeared, the piles of dead frogs quickly decomposed, and a horrible stench filled the land. Still Pharaoh remained unmoved.

The pattern was set. God would send Moses and Aaron with the message of another plague. Pharaoh would reject the plea. The plague would begin. Pharaoh would "harden his heart." The plagues continued:

Swarms of gnats came. The magicians could not duplicate this and told Pharaoh that this was truly the finger of God. No response.

An *infestation of flies* was next . . . except that none showed up where the Hebrews lived.

A terrible *disease* that killed cattle in Egypt but none in Goshen followed.

Awful *boils* infested all humans and all the remaining animals, except in Goshen.

Then a devastating *hailstorm* came. By now Egyptian officials already believed that what Moses and Aaron predicted would come true. They hurried their families and animals into shelter. For the Egyptians, two of their main food crops were beaten down. "The flax and barley were destroyed, since the barley had headed and the flax was in bloom." [Exodus 9:31]

This brings to mind a biblical passage possibly overlooked by many. After seven plagues Pharaoh is still hard-hearted and committed to defying God's request. Not so his officials. The pharaoh may not be dealing with the reality of the destruction, but his officials are aware of the economic devastation caused by the succession of plagues. They implore him: "How long will this man be a snare to us? Let the people go, so that they may worship the Lord their God. Do you not yet realize that Egypt is ruined?" [Exodus 10:7]

A swarm of *locusts* was next. Everything that had been left green from the hail was eaten by the locusts.

Then came *total darkness for three days.*

Still Pharaoh hardened his heart, even though his officials pleaded with him to let the Hebrews go and perform their sacrifices.

The time had come for the final, decisive plague. God's words to Moses were:

> About midnight I will go throughout Egypt. Every firstborn son in Egypt will die, from the firstborn son of Pharaoh, who sits on the throne, to the firstborn son of the slave girl, who is at her hand mill, and all the firstborn of the cattle as well. . . . But among the Israelites not a dog will bark at any man or animal. [Exodus 11:4–7]

THE DEATH ANGEL MAKES AN EXCEPTION

Ohad hurried home from the meeting with the village leaders. "Timna, everything is set," he said to his wife. "We leave on the fifteenth. Moses and Aaron have said that God will finally force Pharaoh's hand. An angel will visit each Egyptian home the night of the fourteenth and kill the firstborn son."

"But where does that leave us?" she asked.

"You are to go to our neighbors and ask for silver and gold items to take along on our journey. I have to get a perfect lamb that must be roasted and eaten with special herbs on the evening of the fourteenth. We are to be dressed and ready to leave immediately the next day," Ohad said.

Their eldest son had overheard the conversation. "But how will the angel know which are Hebrew homes and pass over us?" he wanted to know.

"I have to take some of the blood from the lamb and with hyssop smear it on the sides and top of our door frames as a signal to the angel that ours is a Hebrew home," Ohad answered.

"May I come with you to select the lamb, Father?" the son asked.

"Certainly. You have better eyes than I and can make sure there is no blemish on the lamb."

That night "the Lord struck down all the *firstborn* in Egypt" [emphasis added] and Pharaoh summoned Moses and Aaron and said, "Up, leave my people, you and the Israelites! Go, worship the Lord as you have requested. Take your flocks and herds, as you have said, and go. And also bless me." [Exodus 12:31,32]

The Hebrews were told to ask their neighbors for articles of silver and gold. The Bible reports that "the Lord made the Egyptians favorably disposed toward the people, and Moses himself was highly regarded in Egypt by Pharaoh's officials and by the people." [Exodus 11:3]

Research into the gods of Egypt shows that every plague was designed to discredit a specific Egyptian deity:

1. Bloody water—against the god *Nilus*, the sacred river god, or against *Hapi*, the Nile River god.
2. Frogs—against *Heket*, the goddess of reproduction, who was represented by a frog.
3. Lice (gnats)—against *Seb*, the god of the earth.
4. Flies (beetles)—against *Khephera*, the sacred scarab.
5. Murrain (plague) on Egyptian cattle—against *Apis*, the symbol of fertility represented by a

       bull, and *Hathor*, the mother and sky goddess, represented by a cow.

6. Boils on man and beast—against *Typhon*, the evil-eye god.
7. Hail—against *Shu*, the god of the atmosphere, and *Seth*, who manifests himself in wind and storms.
8. Locusts—against *Serapis*, the protector from locusts.
9. Darkness—against *Ra*, the sun god.
10. Death of the firstborn of man and beast—against *Ptah*, the god of life.

That morning, after the tenth plague, the roads were clogged with Hebrews carrying personal belongings, leading loaded donkeys, and herding their animals. From the distance the Egyptians saw the clouds of dust created by the Israelites on the move. They were on their way to freedom. Little did they know the price this freedom would exact.

BUT DID IT REALLY HAPPEN?

What a marvelous story, and it's been told to children all over the world for possibly four thousand years. But did it really happen, or is Rabbi Sherwin Wine right when he describes the story as "old legends and distorted memories"?

Even within the stories there are inconsistencies. For example, the biblical writer reports that all the "cattle" died with a disease that killed both man and beast. Yet apparently some survived, since Egyptian animals were later infected with boils, and even later Egyptians hurried their animals under shelter to avoid the hailstorm.

Overriding such details is the great question of whether any of it happened. And if it did happen, when did it happen? If such plagues ever occurred, there should be mention of them in Egyptian historical records, since these plagues impacted an entire nation.

Let's see if there is any evidence that suggests the plagues occurred.

First, it is important to determine when the plagues and the Exodus actually occurred. Scholars for various reasons have, for a long time, placed the end of the Exodus, marked by the entry of the Israelites into Canaan, at 1230–1220 B.C. This, of course, is forty years after they left Egypt and wandered in the wilderness for that amount of time.

The problem with these dates for the Exodus and Canaan entry is that they do not fit the archaeological evidence. There is nothing to suggest the Israelites were in the Sinai during this period. Nor do we find Canaanite cities that Joshua could have conquered on his entry into Canaan. In virtually every case the archaeological evidence is inconsistent with the biblical evidence, which actually places the Exodus at about 1460 B.C.

Archaeologists John J. Bimson and David Livingstone, using archaeological evidence, do an excellent job of refuting the 1230–1220 B.C. date for Israel's entry into Canaan in the September/October 1987 issue of *Biblical Archaeology Review*. They sum up by saying:

> About 1420 B.C. becomes the suggested date for the
> Israelite conquest of Canaan. The Exodus should be placed

forty years earlier, around 1460 B.C. This is in harmony with the biblical data.

But we also have other ways of more precisely documenting the plagues, the Exodus, and the entry into Canaan, according to chronologist Gene Faulstich of the Chronology-History Research Institute, located in Spencer, Iowa:

> The Exodus story is probably one of the easiest events of the Bible to date precisely, using astronomical computerized dating data in correlation with biblical information given on eclipses, moon phases, and star risings. Also following the Hebrew weekly day cycles and biblical chronology itself contribute and correlate to the further accuracy of dating the Exodus.
>
> We're able to precisely date 116 major events connected with this account. For instance, Moses sees the burning bush on September 27, 1462 B.C. The first plague in which the river turned to blood occurred on January 24, 1461 B.C., while the last plague, the death of the firstborn, occurred on March 27, 1461 B.C. Moses crossed the Red Sea on April 3, 1461 B.C. The Israelites first heard the Ten Commandments spoken verbally by the Lord from Mount Sinai on May 28, 1461 B.C. The Israelites enter Canaan in the fall of 1422 B.C. to April of 1421 B.C., depending on which Canaanite city conquest is used to mark the entry into Canaan, the latter date being the conquest of Jericho.

There also seems to be documentation of the Exodus in Egyptian historical literature. The best evidence that fits the fifteenth century B.C. chronology seems to be cuneiform letters found at Tell-el-Amarna in Egypt. Letters being exchanged between the pharaoh and other kings talk about epidemics and plagues. The severe economic repercussions are also reflected in one letter.

However, other historical Egyptian evidence that provides many more specific details of the plagues comes from "The Admonitions of Ipu-Wer," "The Prophecy of Nefer-Rohu," and the "Cannibal Hymn." The Nefer-Rohu talks about the ninth plague of darkness, while the Cannibal Hymn mentions the slaying of the firstborn—the final plague.

California archaeological researcher and writer Brad Sparks says:

> The Ipu-Wer papyrus recounts in eyewitness fashion the plagues of blood, cattle disease, strange fire phenomena, darkness and the slaying of the firstborn. All the events we previously thought we only knew about from the Bible, we can read about in the Egyptian records.

Just before the crossing of the Jordan River, Moses is reviewing God's intervention on behalf of the Israelites. In Deuteronomy 11:3 and 11:4, he provides supporting testimony to both the economic devastation of the plagues and the social upheaval caused by the death of the pharaoh and his whole army:

> The signs He performed and the things He did in the heart of Egypt, both to Pharaoh king of Egypt and to this whole country; what He did to the Egyptian army, to its horses and chariots, how He overwhelmed them with the waters of

the Red Sea as they were pursuing you, and how the Lord brought lasting ruin on them.

Spoken forty years after the event, this recitation of the devastating cultural and economic impact of God's actions only confirms what has been found in Egypt about the disintegration of the country.

Back in Egypt, Pharaoh and his officials soon realized they had been had. This was no mere three-day trip into the desert to worship the God of the Hebrews. Too much had happened for the Hebrews to stick to that initial request. As Egyptian officials looked around them at empty villages and stalled building projects, they said, "We made a mistake. What were we thinking when we let them go?" Pharaoh put his army on alert, called up the reserves, and set out in hot pursuit. His scouts had reported that the Hebrews were wandering aimlessly in the desert.

IMPENDING DANGER!

A large multi-roomed tent with hanging partitions stood in the blazing sun of the desert. Inside sat Moses and Aaron, in effect holding court. Joshua and two captains entered the tent, bowing as they approached Moses and Aaron.

"It worked!" Joshua reported. "The spies have returned from Egypt and report that Pharaoh has summoned his army and has begun their forced march to try and catch up with us."

Moses stroked his beard, paused for a moment, and

responded, "Just as God said, Pharaoh thinks we are wandering around in confusion."

"But what do we do now?" one of the captains asked impulsively. "We have no army to turn them back."

Moses paused as though mulling over a thought. "We must put the sea between them and our people," he said.

"Have your scouts found any place we can cross the sea?" asked Aaron.

"There is nothing to the north, or to the south. In a week we might be able to reach Horus Road to the north, but we'd all be slaves or dead by then," Joshua declared.

"Then we'd run into another danger as well," Moses responded. "The Philistines to the north would be tempted to come down and attack us."

"Do you have enough armed men to provide a diversionary tactic, to confuse and stall the Egyptians while we get away?" Aaron asked Joshua.

"There is not enough time for even that," Joshua said regretfully. "My inner guard is dispersed among the tribes, trying to make warriors out of farmers and brickmakers. Pharaoh's archers and chariots would make short work of them." The sound of people talking loudly, even shouting, drifted into the tent.

"What is the noise about?" Moses asked.

"There are troublemakers in the camp," said one of the captains. "They, too, have seen the approaching Egyptians and are stirring up the people against you."

Moses and Aaron arose and made their way out of the tent. Coming toward them was a group of several hundred men rapidly attracting others. Everyone seemed to be talking at once, though at the head of the group were three who were clearly the leaders.

Joshua and his captains were joined by others on guard duty around the tent.

When they were within hearing distance, the ringleader shouted, tauntingly, "What have you done to us, O mighty Moses! Do you not see the clouds of dust announcing the Egyptian army's advance?"

His partner joined in: "Were there not enough graves in Egypt that we have to die here in the desert like rats?"

"Didn't we tell you to leave us alone and in peace?" a third complained. "We told you to back off and forget about your harebrained scheme. Now we'll all die like dogs in the desert."

The ringleader stepped forward as the crowd came to a stop. "Make me your emissary. I will meet with Pharaoh and reason with him. I will beg him to let us return and be forgiven. They need us and will listen, I'm sure."

"Let me take care of them," Joshua said to Moses as he stepped forward, followed by the two captains. Then turning to the leader of the group he hissed, "I'll cleave you in two, you traitorous turnip of a goldsmith."

Moses put out his hand to stop him. "Let us hear them out."

The ringleader had backed up quickly at Joshua's hostile move, but he was not through. "You wouldn't listen to us in Egypt, but had to go ahead with your wild scheme," he charged. "Now you listen to us. We are not about to die like jackals and become vulture food." He turned to the crowd and shouted, "Do you want to die here? Do you want to be torn up by an Egyptian chariot? Face the shower of arrows from their bowmen? Or do you want to sue for peace?"

The roar of the crowd revealed they were with him.

Moses waited until they had spent their energy and then roared, "Still your tongues."

The crowd quieted noticeably.

"You must have faith in the God of Abraham, Isaac, and Jacob," Moses shouted. "Do you think he would bring you out of bondage to let you die on the shore of this sea? Fear not the Egyptians and their chariots. Did not the Lord already do many mighty deeds on our behalf in Egypt? God will deliver us!" His voice fell to a whisper as he spoke directly to the leader of the group. "You will yet see God's power," he said firmly.

UP TO HIS EYEBALLS IN TROUBLE

Leadership can be a tenuous thing. When Moses was promising freedom and a home in a land of milk and honey, he was the Hebrews' hero, but the moment danger loomed, the malcontents marshaled their supporters for an attack on his leadership. What would he do now, what would his God do, to save them from the advancing Egyptian military might?

The answer is one of the great mysteries of the Bible. The story of the crossing of the Red Sea has aroused cynics, skeptics, and vocal critics. The consensus is that, at best, the story is a legend, with details added as the story was retold.

But is it? Is there a way to demonstrate, effectively if

not conclusively, that the water could roll back and let the children of Israel cross on dry land?

You may be surprised at some of the answers and their source, when we remove some of the mystery surrounding this ancient secret in the next chapter.

11

A WIND-AIDED CROSSING OR A VOLCANIC PHENOMENON?

The idea that the Red Sea could have parted into two walls of water, as portrayed by Hollywood moviemakers like Cecil B. DeMille, is just not credible.

Dr. Robert Eisenman
Professor of Middle East Religions

I<small>F YOU HAD DOUBTS ABOUT THE PLAGUES IN EGYPT,</small> then we've got an even more unbelievable mystery for you. Commonly called the crossing of the Red Sea, this biblical miracle arouses extraordinarily strong criticism.

After all, what archaeological record was left by nomads traveling through the desert? Who took pictures of the walls of water? Who recorded the event on any kind of historical inscription? Missing all the usual written records, except the Bible, the vast majority of scholars have denounced the biblical miracle.

A typical reaction is that of Dr. Robert Eisenman, chairman of the Department of Religious Studies and professor of Middle East religions at California State University in Long Beach, who is quoted at the head of this chapter. "Just not credible" is one of his kinder criticisms.

Recent research by an oceanographer provides a striking new twist to our understanding of how the crossing of the Red Sea may have been accomplished. We will get to that . . . but first, let's return to the dilemma Moses and Aaron faced as we closed the previous chapter.

In front of them lay a significant body of water, usually identified as a narrow extension of the north end of the Gulf of Suez, where there is an underwater ridge. The consensus is that the width of the Red Sea at that place was probably between two and six miles at the time of the crossing. Some scholars see the crossing happening farther north in an area called the Reed Sea, largely based on what they consider a misspelling of the name Red Sea. And a few put the crossing at the northern end of what is today the Suez Canal.

This northern extension of the Red Sea is, then, where the Israelites were encamped when the pharaoh's army went in hot pursuit. The dust clouds of the rapidly approaching Pharaoh and his whole Egyptian army struck fear in the hearts of everyone in the Israelite encampment. Everyone except Moses, that is.

FACING RETURN OR DEATH

Leaving Joshua and his guards to deal with the malcontents, Moses and Aaron returned to the tent.

"I must commune with our God," Moses said to Aaron, lifting the curtain and going into an inner room.

"Lord God Almighty," he prayed, "the God of Abraham, Isaac, and Jacob, you have promised to bring us safely to the Promised Land. I believe you. But the army of Pharaoh is on our heels and the sea is before us. We need your intervention, and we need it now."

The reply was immediate and forceful: "Why are you crying out to me again? Do you not trust me? Raise your staff and stretch it over the sea to divide the water so the Israelites may go through it on dry land. I will harden the hearts of the pharaoh and his men so they will follow you. And I will gain glory through what will happen to them."

Moses worshiped the Lord God. Then he quickly arose and went out, signaling Aaron to join him. Night was already falling, with stars just beginning to twinkle in the darkening sky.

"Look," said Aaron, "the cloud that has been in front of us is moving. It's moving between us and the Egyptians. Look how bright it is, brighter than a full moon."

"We must move quickly," said Moses. "Joshua, collect the leaders. God is going to do a mighty act this night, and we need to be ready to move."

Joshua turned to his guard unit. "Hurry into the encampment and round up the leaders of all the tribes and their immediate subordinates," he said. "We have no time to lose."

The guards ran off on the double, catching many just getting ready for their evening meal. "Come quickly. Moses has a special message from God. God will yet save us from the Egyptians."

Wives and children looked questioningly at the men as they left, wondering what would happen next.

Stragglers were still arriving when Moses walked up a rise overlooking the sea. It seemed to run into the water as well.

"Now you will see what the Lord God will do for us. But you must be ready to begin to respond immediately, for we will cross the sea tonight," he said.

The men looked at each other quizzically, wondering what Moses would do now. With that he lifted his staff, stretching his arm over the water and pointing it at the other side.

A WIND FROM THE EAST

First it was just a sound, then the crowd could see the water beginning to be whipped up into waves. Then it hit them, a powerful blast of wind that tore at clothing and bent the bushes at the water's edge.

Tent door hangings began to flap in the wind. Ropes holding down the tents began to "sing." Mothers and children scrambled to catch belongings being picked up by the wind.

Messengers spread throughout the camp. "Moses says we will cross the sea tonight. He is confident that God will part the water. Pack your belongings so we can break camp as soon as the sea parts," they shouted above the noise of the wind.

Mothers began rolling up bedding that they had been preparing for the night. Fathers secured bundles for everyone to carry.

And still the wind blew.

At the edge of the sea several tribal and military leaders met to see what was happening.

"Look, the water is beginning to move to the right. You can see the beginning of what looks like a wall. I wonder what will happen now," one of the captains shouted at his friend over the noise of the wind.

"See the water starting to go down?" his friend shouted back, pointing to the slowly widening shoreline.

Some hours later they returned to check progress.

"Look, there's a ridge showing," one of them yelled. "And look at the wall of water beginning to really build on the right. It's a miracle! God is performing another miracle to save us from the Egyptians. We'll be able to cross on the ridge!"

The word spread like wildfire as the tribal and military leaders rushed back into the camp and spread the word. "We're moving on tonight!" they told their followers. "We will cross the sea on dry land and escape the Egyptians."

A young man rushed up to Moses as he was returning to his tent. "The Lord has performed another miracle," he said breathlessly. "The Egyptian side of the camp is in total darkness but the cloud is giving us light. They have started to make camp for the night because they are unable to see where we are and where they are going."

"The Lord be praised. Tell Joshua," Moses said, as the young man rushed off.

All over the camp, tents were being taken down. Household furnishings were being loaded onto donkeys or strapped onto the backs of men, women, and family members. As families finished packing up they were pointed toward the sea.

All night the light shone, showing the way onto the gravel-covered ridge, as thousands surged into what had been the sea and began the trek across it.

Dawn broke to reveal the last of the Israelites a third of the way across.

Scouts from the Egyptian army rushed to Pharaoh's tent. "The Hebrews are escaping! The camp is empty. They have escaped over a ridge in the sea."

Pharaoh immediately summoned his officers. "We must begin our pursuit immediately. They cannot escape."

Before the last of the Israelites reached the shore on the other side of the sea, the Egyptian army had begun to cross on the ridge in a broad formation.

The Israelite lookouts on the shore shouted, "Tell Moses the Egyptians are coming after us. They will cross just as we did." A captain of the guard arrived breathlessly at Moses' position. "The Egyptians are coming across the sea," he barked. "Almost all of them are already in the channel through the sea."

Moses took his staff and walked to the edge of the sea. He pointed it over the water at the Egyptian army. Suddenly the wind stopped, and the wall of water on the left began to move like a tidal wave. Seeing the advancing water, the Egyptians tried to turn around quickly to get back onto land.

In their haste, many charioteers tried to turn too quickly, breaking off wheels. Horses ran into the broken-down chariots. As horses neighed in terror and men screamed obscenities at horses and each other, the advancing wall of water inundated them. Soon there were only items of clothing floating on the water.

Cheering crowds of Israelites lined the shore as they watched the water advance on the Egyptians in their desperate attempt to escape.

"The Lord God of Israel is the victor again" became a refrain, picked up by one group after another. "The Lord God has destroyed our enemies."

WHO SAYS IT COULD HAPPEN THAT WAY?

As indicated earlier, the lack of any archaeological evidence, of even one clearly identifiable inscription from the period referring to an event of this magnitude in human history, appears to leave the field to the critics. They are quick to attack the historical credibility of the crossing of the Red Sea. One of the foremost critics is Rabbi Sherwin Wine, founder of Humanistic Judaism. He says simply:

> It never happened. The waters of the Red Sea never parted. The Israelites never passed through the water of the sea. And the story that you find in the Book of Exodus is primarily fiction.
>
> The idea that hundreds of thousands of Israelites passed through the Red Sea is crazy. The Bible says there were 600,000 males. That means over two million people passed through those waters. It most likely would have taken several weeks for all those people just to cross. The whole idea is ludicrous.

Dr. Robert Eisenman, whom we identified earlier, agrees:

> The idea that the Red Sea could have parted into two walls of water, as portrayed by Hollywood moviemakers like Cecil B. DeMille, is just not credible.
>
> The portrait we have has probably been worked upon by folk imagination and pious enthusiasm. The exaggeration we have is two walls of water, the Israelites going through

dryshod, and the chariots of Pharaoh being overwhelmed and drowned. This is the incredible part of the story.

NAPOLEON TRIED CROSSING

Will these eminent critics, and the millions who agree with them, have the final word? Is the idea of a wind moving massive amounts of water into walls and then releasing it suddenly nothing more than Hollywood stuff?

Not according to people who have seen the wind move large bodies of water at both the north end of the Suez Canal and the south end, where it enters the Gulf of Suez. And not according to an oceanographer we will introduce shortly.

In the description of the Red Sea in *The New International Dictionary of Biblical Archaeology*, we read about an area at the southern end of the Suez Canal, an area many scholars consider the most likely place for the crossing by the Israelites. It says:

This crossing may well have taken place just north of the present-day Bitter Lakes area. The digging of the Suez Canal has now drained this region considerably, resulting in some original marshland disappearing. When the Israelites crossed this area, the marshlands would have been more extensive than the present land would indicate and would have constituted a formidable military barrier. . . .

It has been observed that this area can be affected by an east wind in the same way as mentioned in Exodus 14. In 1882 Major-General Tulloch was engaged in military investigations relating to the Suez Canal. He noticed that the waters of Lake Menzaleh, about 1.5 to 1.8 meters [5 to 6 feet] in depth, had been affected by an easterly gale during one day. The water had receded for about 11 kilometers (7 miles). A similar phenomenon has been observed later (1945–46).[22]

Even earlier than that, according to Dwight Pryor, founder of the Center for Judaic-Christian Studies and editor of *Archaeology of the Land of the Bible,* the French emperor Napoleon tried to duplicate the crossing at the northern end of the extension of the Gulf of Suez. Pryor tells us:

In 1799 Napoleon's engineers discovered an underwater ridge some 600 feet wide that extended from shore to shore at the north end of the Gulf of Suez. His engineers calculated the exact time needed to cross this 5.3-mile-long land bridge when the east wind would blow to clear the sea bed of water. However, Napoleon barely escaped with his life when a sudden change in wind direction brought an onrush of water that covered the land bridge within a matter of minutes.

EXPERIMENT PROVES CROSSING POSSIBLE

These reports are certainly intriguing and indicate what might have happened, but they do not provide scientific

[22] *E. M. Blaiklock and R. K. Harrison, "Red Sea,"* New International Dictionary of Biblical Archaeology *(Grand Rapids, MI: Zondervan Publishing House, 1983), p. 386.*

evidence. Tackling a research project never tried before, two scientists, Dr. Doron Nof, a professor of oceanography at Florida State University, and Dr. Nathan Paldor, professor of meteorology at the University of Rhode Island, were able to demonstrate the feasibility of a steady wind drying up a ridge through the top of the Gulf of Suez.

As a result of their experiment, Dr. Nof states, "Based on recent developments in physical oceanography and meteorology, we can prove today that the crossing of the Red Sea would have been possible."

The results of their experiment were so dramatic, newspapers, radio, and television covered the experiment worldwide. Here is how Dr. Nof explains what they did:

Dr. Paldor and I developed what we in physical oceanography call a mathematical model of the part of the Red Sea where many people believe the crossing could have occurred. What is particular about the Red Sea is that it is very long and narrow. The Gulf of Suez, which is a branch of the Red Sea, is even narrower than the general Red Sea. It's about two hundred miles long, but it is only about ten to twelve miles broad at its greatest width.

Most of the Gulf of Suez is extremely shallow, only about one hundred feet deep. If you let the wind blow on this body of water for ten or twelve hours, especially if it blows from the northwest, you get the shoreline receding back from its normal position for about a mile. That would expose a strip of land about a mile wide and ten miles long that was previously covered with water.

The basic idea is that the Israelites possibly crossed when

the wind pushed that water away. Of course, after the wind relaxes, the water wants to come back to the position it had before. It does that via a giant wave, which we calculated moves at the speed of fifteen feet per second. No one could escape water moving at that speed.

PHYSICAL MODEL DEMONSTRATES THEORY

Drs. Paldor and Nof developed an actual physical model to represent conditions in the Red Sea and on the Gulf of Suez. Dr. Nof described their experiment as he operated his model for interested sleuths:

What we built is a physical model of the Red Sea. The deep part is supposed to represent the main part of the Red Sea, which is two thousand to three thousand feet deep. The shallow part is to represent the Gulf of Suez, which is much shallower, only about one hundred feet deep. In addition, we have introduced an artificial ridge that is supposed to represent perhaps the ridge where the Israelites crossed. The depth of the water over the ridge is only about ten feet deep.

As Dr. Nof turned on a fan that represented a wind over the Gulf of Suez, the water over the ridge gradually receded, building a "wall" of water beyond it. On the side from which the wind blew the water remained. This left the ridge exposed and quickly drying.

You need a wind of about forty knots per hour for ten to twelve hours to expose the ridge. So when the Israelites crossed on the ridge, they saw water on both sides. They saw the water on the left side of the ridge and on the right side.

Dr. Nof then quickly cut the wind, letting the water flow back at fifteen feet per second to cover the ridge. "The water coming back quickly after the wind died caught the Egyptian army and they drowned," he said.

This research adds credibility to earlier conclusions by a Hebrew University geographer, Menashe Har-El. In a book published in 1980, *The Stairway to Heaven*, noted author and linguist Zechariah Sitchin writes:

> It was against this newly understood background of the ancient Sinai that a Hebrew University biblical geographer, Menashe Har-El, offered a new theory *(Massa'ei Sinai)*. Reviewing all the arguments, he pointed out the submerged ridge which rises between the Great and Little Bitter Lakes. It is shallow enough to be crossed if a wind blows away the waters; it was there that the crossing had taken place.[23]

That a wind-aided crossing of the waterway between the boundary of Egypt and the Sinai Desert is possible has been established. Where exactly it happened is less clear.

Alternate theories for the destruction of the Egyptian army exist. One possibility is suggested by a leading Egyptologist, Dr. Hans Goedicke.

---

[23] *Zechariah Sitchin*, The Stairway to Heaven *(New York: Avon Books, 1980), p. 224.*

A VOLCANO AND A TSUNAMI WAVE?

According to Dr. Hans Goedicke, chairman of the Near Eastern Studies Department at Johns Hopkins University in Baltimore, Maryland, and one of the world's leading Egyptologists, the drowning of Pharaoh's army should be tied to a volcanic eruption on the island of Thera in the Aegean Sea.

Hershel Shenks, editor of *Biblical Archaeology Review,* in an article reviewing Dr. Goedicke's thesis, writes:

The most important volcano in the Mediterranean region is located on the island of Thera/Santoríni, thirty miles north of Crete. Seismologists have there established, on the basis of the tephra-structure, three major ancient eruptions, one about 1600 B.C., another about 1475 B.C., and a third in the twelfth century B.C.. . . . The volcanic eruption of Thera/ Santoríni about 1475 B.C. was important not only for the Exodus. On the basis of Egyptian sources, it has been established that the high Minoan civilization of Knossos on the island of Crete was destroyed about 1475 B.C., and archaeology has linked this destruction beyond doubt with an outbreak of the Thera volcano.

Such an eruption must have triggered a *tsunami,* a huge tidal-like wave, which simply drowned Knossos. This tsunami would have reached the Nile Delta and flooded it within three hours as it rolled through the southeastern Mediterranean. Then it passed through the shallow Lake Menzaleh and filled the plain south of the Pelusian branch of the Nile to the edge of the elevated desert plateau—

drowning the Egyptians waiting to confront the Israelites on Tell Hazzob.[24]

What this theory does not address is how the Israelites made it across the sea. Instead, its focus is on the destruction of the Egyptians. Yet scholars who doubt the miraculous element in the biblical story of the crossing of the Red Sea find theories like Dr. Goedicke's attractive.

In the absence of hard archaeological evidence, theories will continue to be advanced. The important issue is that the crossing of the Red Sea is not an outlandish story. There is conclusive meteorologic and oceanographic evidence that a wind blowing steadily all night could have exposed a land bridge through a section of the Red Sea, just as related in the Bible story.

MORE EVIDENCE FOR THE EXODUS

Beyond the arguments about the Hebrews crossing the Red Sea on dry land is the overarching criticism that the whole Exodus is a fictional story. Where, say the critics, is the evidence that the Israelites spent forty years in the wilderness? And why cannot the famous Mount Sinai, the place where Moses received the tablets, be identified with any certainty?

In 1985 Emmanuel Anati, an Egyptologist and

[24] Hershel Shenks, "The Exodus and the Crossing of the Red Sea, According to Hans Goedicke," Biblical Archaeology Review, September/ October 1981, p. 42.

archaeological writer who has spent thirty years excavating ruins in the Negev, the desert between Beersheba and the Gulf of Aqabah, startled the scholarly world with new evidence found at Har Karkom, a mountain located about halfway between Beersheba and the gulf. This mountain is 2,795 feet above sea level and clearly visible for great distances in all directions.

As early as 1955 Professor Anati reported finding rock engravings at this site, but in 1985 he presented an astounding new conclusion. He announced that he had found unmistakable indications of Hebrew presence at the mountain during the period when the Bible says they were in the desert after escaping Egypt.

Writing in the *Biblical Archaeology Review,* Professor Anati reports:

On the last day of our 1982 campaign—December 20 to be exact—I was climbing down the mountain as the sun was descending in the western sky. Every stone was etched in sharp shadows. Suddenly, I saw the silhouette of a strange sequence of standing stones beside one of the archaeological sites near our camp. Although I had visited the particular site several times before, I had never noticed it in this light.

I made a short detour to examine more closely this structure at the edge of . . . one of the Bronze Age campsites at the foot of the mountain. There was a group of twelve pillars or standing stones fixed vertically into the ground. Next to this group of *masseboth* were the remains of a structure that could not have been a dwelling place—it contained a platform and a courtyard. The surface finds did not indicate that it included any roofed rooms.

This group of twelve pillars and the platform nearby vaguely reminded me of a passage in the Bible. I went on to our camp and took out a Bible and found the passage: "And Moses . . . rose up early in the morning, and builded an altar under the hill, and twelve pillars, according to the twelve tribes of Israel." [Exodus 24:4]

FINDINGS CORROBORATE THE BIBLE

Professor Anati continues:

I asked some members of my team to go to the site with me and, standing there, I read them the passage from the Bible. We had a long discussion, and two additional items of interest came up, one relating to a cleft in the rock on the top of the mountain and the other to the small temple on the plateau of the mountain.

The cleft on the top of the mountain forms a small rock shelter that bears a striking correspondence to the cleft in the rock on the top of Mt. Sinai described in Exodus 33:21–22: "And the Lord said, Behold, there is a place by me, and thou shalt stand upon a rock; and it shall come to pass, while my glory passeth by, that I will put thee in the cleft of the rock, and will cover thee with my hand while I pass by." To find such a niche or cleft on the very summit of a mountain is geologically quite unusual. I know of only one other such cleft on the top of a mountain: the cave on Jerusalem's Temple Mount.

Professor Anati's reference is to a time in the Sinai Desert when Moses asked to see God. God explained that he could not be seen, but he would let his glory pass by so Moses would be reassured of the presence of God. God placed Moses in the "cleft of the rock," a cavelike formation, so he would not be exposed to the full glory of God and be destroyed.

Let's return to Professor Anati's report:

> The second item of interest that was raised in our discussion was the small Bronze Age temple at the center of the plateau of the mountain. . . . The Bible seems to make clear that Moses saw an old temple on Mount Sinai, which he later used as a model and prototype: "And look that they make them after their pattern, which was showed thee in the mount." [Exodus 25:40]

Professor Anati further suggests that the burial customs discovered on the mountain, in which the bones of the dead are preserved and eventually brought to be buried on hallowed ground, are similar to those practiced when the Israelites fled from Egypt carrying the bones of Joseph.

Professor Anati reports another intriguing find:

> . . . an engraving on a rectangular stone tablet with two ear-like shapes on top. Lines divided the tablet into ten squares. The Bible is not explicit as to what was engraved on the tablets containing the Ten Commandments. Nowhere are we told whether they were engraved with a script, either ancient Semitic or Egyptian, or with symbols, or with simple markings. Any script would probably have been unintelligible to the majority of the Israelites fleeing from Egyptian slavery. It is quite conceivable that the

Tablets of the Law were actually slabs of rocks engraved with symbols or markings not unlike those found along the paths and on the plateau of Har Karkom.[25]

EVIDENCE OF WATER RESERVOIRS

Another intriguing fact is that Moses led the people from Rephidim, which had no water, to an encampment at the foot of Sinai. Why should they go there? According to Professor Anati:

> There is an important water hole on the plateau. In addition, in the western valley at the foot of the mountain, there are several water holes located below the cliffs. The rock there is quite impermeable and only a little rain is needed for the precipices above to become actual waterfalls. Around these water holes are the remains of small artificial canals that must have been built to collect rainwater even more efficiently. . . .
>
> No doubt this desert region was able to provide sufficient drinking water for travelers through the entire year.[26]

Amazing what a little attention to the Bible will do to an archaeologist, isn't it? For thirty years Professor Anati was concerned about the more than thirty-five thousand rock engravings found in this particular region. They and

---

[25] *Emmanuel Anati, "Has Mt. Sinai Been Found?"* Biblical Archaeology Review, *July/August 1985, p. 54.*
[26] *Ibid., p. 56.*

the ruins of dwellings showed that the site had been used for religious purposes for several thousand years.

Professor Anati was not even thinking about the area as a possible stop for the Hebrews on their way from Egypt to Canaan until he saw the twelve stones, six upright, in keeping with the biblical story. Then he discovered the tablets with ten squares engraved on them. Finally, he saw a cleft in the mountain that proved strongly reminiscent of God's place for Moses while God revealed himself to him. His new perspective turned an archaeological dig into a Bible study, with astonishing results that may suggest Moses and the Hebrews may have stopped at Har Karkom for some time en route to Canaan.

In the past three chapters we have covered a remarkable sequence of miraculous events, each more incredible than the previous one:

- We have demonstrated that the burning bush out of which God spoke to Moses really could have burned without being consumed. Even today the desert has a bush that will burn without being consumed.
- We have discovered that the ten plagues God sent to persuade Pharaoh to release the Hebrews to serve their God are mentioned in Egyptian writings.
- We saw how God could create a bridge of dry land through the Red Sea by letting a steady wind blow through the night, letting the Hebrews escape the Egyptian army.

The biblical stories of Moses and the Exodus really happened—and they happened as the Bible says they did!

The person who accepts the Bible as historically accurate can meet the criticism of the skeptic on any issue.

12

DID THE ANCIENTS OF THE BIBLE KNOW ABOUT DINOSAURS?

The popular evolutionary myth that dinosaurs became extinct about seventy million years before man "evolved" is fallacious, both biblically and scientifically.

Dr. Henry Morris
Author, *The Remarkable Record of Job*

Two mysteries have kept dinosaur specialists digging up fossilized bones of dinosaurs. One is the strong disagreement on the kind of world in which the dinosaurs lived, and the other is the cause for their sudden extinction. Theories abound, but hard evidence has been difficult to find.

A third mystery has scientists scrambling and in strong disagreement. In recent decades the voices of those insisting that dinosaurs and man were contemporaries have grown remarkably stronger and more convincing.

Donald R. Patton, a geologist and excavator of dinosaur fossils, says:

> There is now evidence from Russia, Australia, and several sites in the United States that humans actually walked the earth with dinosaurs. In 1983 Russians found dinosaur and human prints together similar to the ones found at Glen Rose, Texas. There we found a human track superimposed on the dinosaur track. When we superimpose a footprint on the line drawing, we can see they (the humans) were actually stepping in the dinosaur's footprints.

Traditional scientific theories insist that dinosaurs roamed the earth from possibly two hundred million years ago to sixty-five million years ago, well before man appeared. Any memory of them among humans would be strictly folk legend. Pictographs in ancient caves depicting mammoths, saber-toothed tigers, humans, and dinosaurs together also do not represent reality, a living memory, but a collective consciousness that has come down through the ages, say many scientists.

Under that premise, for example, the Bible's Noah would not have had the privilege of inviting dinosaurs aboard the ark he built to escape the coming flood. They would have disappeared sixty-five million years before Noah's time.

Amazing discoveries of footprints and other human remains in conjunction with dinosaur footprints and bones are shaking this conventional scientific thinking about dinosaurs. These extraordinary discoveries in the United States, Australia, and Turkmenia in the former Soviet Union strongly indicate that man and dinosaur were contemporaries.

DOES THE BIBLE MENTION DINOSAURS?

Yet why even consider a topic as potentially controversial as the time when dinosaurs roamed the earth in a book on the Bible? Is it only a fun topic to add spice to the book, or do dinosaurs have relevance when considering the accuracy and truthfulness of the Bible?

If you are asking that question, then maybe you, like most readers, we suspect, are unaware that in the Book of Job in the Bible, God appears to describe a dinosaur. The description may be found in Job 40:15–20, in which God says to Job:

> Look at the behemoth, which I made along with you and which feeds on grass like an ox. What strength he has in his loins, what power in the muscles of his belly! His tail sways like a cedar; the sinews of his thighs are close-knit. His bones are tubes of bronze, his limbs like rods of iron. He ranks first among the works of God, yet his Maker can approach him with a sword.

Does that remind you of a dinosaur? If so, then you may be at odds with evolutionary scientific thinking. You see, God seems to be assuming in his conversation with Job that the "behemoth" lived, ate, and played in the presence of humans—and this as recently as possibly forty-five hundred years ago.

Dr. Duane Gish, professor of natural science, and author of books on dinosaurs, says:

> The biblical view put forth in Job 40 and 41 is that a behemoth (meaning gigantic beast), such as Diplodocus and Brachiosaurus, lived together with humans less than ten thousand years ago. Furthermore, at that time there were large marine reptiles, such as Plesiosaurus.

If the "behemoth" is a Brachiosaurus or Diplodocus, could the marine reptile Plesiosaurus be the "leviathan" God describes as well in Job?

Can you pull in the leviathan with a fishhook or tie down his tongue with a rope? Can you put a cord through his nose or pierce his jaw with a hook? Can you make a pet of him like a bird or put him on a leash for your girls? Can you fill his hide with harpoons or his head with fishing spears? If you lay a hand on him, you will remember the struggle and never do it again. [Job 41:1–2, 5–8]

Maybe some of those stories about human life in dinosaurland are not so farfetched after all, despite what evolutionary scientists say.

DINOSAURS ON THE ARK?

Yet accepting the biblical record about the mention of dinosaurs creates another problem. If ancient Job, who apparently was a contemporary of the patriarchs, or who may even have preceded them, was aware of both the Brachiosaurus and Plesiosaurus, that means they must have survived the worldwide flood described in Genesis, right?

Dr. Henry Morris, trained as a hydraulic engineer, writes in his book, *The Remarkable Record of Job:*

Although most of the earth's great fossil graveyards were formed by the flood, representatives of each animal "kind" in the dry land were preserved on Noah's ark to repopulate the world after the flood. (It can be shown that the ark could easily hold two of each known species of land animal, both living and extinct.)

Thus, Job and his contemporaries could easily have seen

many kinds of animals that later became extinct due to the earth's more rigorous climate and vastly depleted resources after the flood. The behemoth, however, was identified by the Lord as "the chief of the ways of God," indicating that he was the largest of all land animals. Almost certainly, therefore, God was speaking of a mighty dinosaur. The description does fit certain dinosaurs, but no other animals that we know of.

The popular evolutionary myth that dinosaurs became extinct about seventy million years before man "evolved" is fallacious, both biblically and scientifically. God made the behemoth with man, God assured Job.

But what about the leviathan mentioned by God in his discourse with Job, according to the Bible? Dr. Morris writes:

As the behemoth was the greatest terrestrial animal, the leviathan was the greatest aquatic animal. Like the behemoth, it seems to be extinct, although reports continue to persist of great sea serpents and plesiosaur-like animals in oceans and deep lakes around the world.

Most commentators . . . insist on calling the leviathan a crocodile. Once again, however, the awesome description in Job 41 does not fit at all. Whatever the leviathan may have been, it was not a crocodile! Neither was it a whale. . . .

What about the following description? "His snorting throws out flashes of light; his eyes are like the rays of dawn. Firebrands stream from his mouth; sparks of fire shoot out. Smoke pours from his nostrils as from a boiling pot over a fire of reeds. His breath sets coals ablaze, and flames dart from his mouth." [Job 41:18–21]

Dragons of various kinds were capable of breathing out fire—at least according to traditions from all parts of the world. Certain insects can, in effect, give out light or fire (e.g., the bombardier beetle and the firefly). Perhaps more to the point, dinosaur fossils have been excavated that show a strange protuberance, with internal cavity, on the top of the head. It is conceivable that this could have served as a sort of mixing chamber for combustible gases that would ignite when exhaled into the outside oxygen.[27]

DO DRAGON LEGENDS CONTAIN TRUTH?

Let's stop to consider the dragon. All of us grew up hearing stories of ancient dragons, but are these simply legends, or were they based on real creatures, like dinosaurs? Author Paul S. Taylor writes in *The Great Dinosaur Mystery and the Bible:*

The ancient, original "dragon" legends must have come from memories of dinosaurs. Scientists agree that legends are almost always based on facts, not just pure imagination. It cannot be an accident that so many separate peoples of the world tell such stories.

"Dragon" legends and pictures can be found in Africa, India, Europe, the Middle East, the Orient, and every other part of the world. Dinosaur-like animals have been

[27] *Henry M. Morris,* The Remarkable Record of Job *(Grand Rapids, MI: Baker Book House, 1988), pp. 115–118.*

drawn, written about and told about since the beginning of recorded history.[28]

The British had Saint George and the Dragon; the Babylonians had Gilgamesh, who encountered a huge reptile-like creature that ate trees and reeds; the Scandinavians had a reptile-like animal with a body about the size of a cow; in France the city of Nerluc was renamed in honor of the killing of a "dragon" there (it had long, sharp, pointed horns on its head like a Triceratops); an Italian scientist, Ulysses Aldrovandus, described a small "dragon" seen along a farm road that hissed at a farmer's oxen; in China they even had books about families that kept "dragons"; and an Irish writer described a beast with iron nails on its tail and with thick legs and strong claws like a Kentrosaurus.[29]

Recognizing that "dragons" are part of the world's folklore would seem to prove they were survivors of the flood, but how do you get hundred-ton dinosaurs into Noah's ark? After all, Noah had to depend on wood construction instead of steel and concrete. Logic would say that with the variety of dinosaurs in the world, there is no way a complete selection of all varieties could have entered Noah's ark.

Enter Dr. Carl Baugh, a Texas museum curator and dinosaur specialist who has found numerous dinosaur tracks in Glen Rose, Texas. He says:

[28] Paul S. Taylor, The Great Dinosaur Mystery and the Bible (Elgin, IL: David C. Cook Publishing, 1987), p. 36.
[29] Ibid., pp. 36–43.

The biblical record indicates very clearly that all land-based creatures, including creeping things, did go on the ark by twos and sevens. The optimal specimens would have been juveniles. Since reptiles reproduce their birth weight in size prolifically, a young dinosaur would have been of a relatively small stature.

Yet is there really scientific proof that dinosaurs and man roamed the world at the same time? Before we begin that discussion, let's first examine the dinosaur as a species. What are we really talking about when we use the word "dinosaur"?

A RATHER NEW IDENTIFICATION

In 1822 the wife of a British collector of fossils brought home an unusual stone she had found while on a walk. Mary Anne Mantell showed it to her husband, who discovered that the stone contained a tooth similar to, yet larger than, those of modern reptiles. Dr. Mantell concluded it belonged to a giant plant-eating reptile, which he named "Iguanodon." He began to aggressively popularize the age of reptiles.

Sir Richard Owen, the famous British paleontologist, in 1841 coined the word *dinosaur*, a Greek word meaning "terrible lizard."[30] It's a term that caught on, and in both evolutionary and popular culture identifies prehistoric reptile-like creatures.

[30] *Ken Ham, Andrew Snelling, Carl Wieland*, The Answers Book (*El Cajon, CA: Master Books, 1990*), p. 21.

VARIETIES OF DINOSAURS

Let's examine just a few of the hundred and fifty varieties of dinosaurs that have been identified by their bone deposits; then let's consider whether these giant beasts really could have coexisted peacefully with humans, based on solid, scientific evidence.

In the category of horned dinosaurs, Triceratops was a plant-eating dinosaur who was probably about twenty feet long and weighed almost ten tons. His only protection against the meat-eating dinosaurs was his collection of three horns on his head and the armor plate around the base of his neck.

Next to Triceratops, the two-ton, plant-eating Stegosaurus seemed like a baby. Though he walked on four legs like Triceratops, his front legs were half the size of his rear legs and he had armor plate all over his body.

Stegosaurus knew how to protect himself, for he had four spikes near the end of his tail that could wipe out most attackers in one swipe. Though his brain appears to have been very tiny, he had a second "command center" near his hips in the form of a knob that was twenty times as large as his brain. It served as a sort of computerized control center for his tail, hind legs, and rear quarters. This feature shows up on numerous other dinosaurs.

Ankylosaurus had a weapon of a different kind, a huge club on his tail. The top of his fifteen-foot body was covered with large, round knobs of bone.

You've heard of the duck-billed platypus, but have you seen a picture of Trachodon, with two thousand teeth in his duck-billed jaw? A mere thirty feet long, Trachodon stood eighteen feet tall. Three webbed toes on both front and back feet indicate he must have been a swimmer. What a sight he must have been in the lakes of Noah's day, with his head alone showing above the water line!

Many fossils of the duck-billed dinosaurs have been found next to the meat-eating Tyrannosaurus, who was fifty feet long and stood twenty feet tall. His huge head was five feet long and his teeth six inches long, so he could probably make short work of a weakened Triceratops.

One of the larger plant-eaters was the Diplodocus, who measured one hundred feet long and weighed twenty-five tons. Yet compared to the eighty-ton Brachiosaurus, with a head forty feet up in the air, the Diplodocus seemed a baby.

Although the giant marine reptiles appear to have become extinct as well, their fossil remains show they were reptiles, not fish. The Plesiosaurus had paddles, instead of feet and legs.

ARE THERE TRANSITIONAL FORMS?

The amazing fact about all of these dinosaurs is that they all seem to have just appeared. Despite the best efforts of evolutionary paleontologists and archaeologists, no one has ever found the remains, or fossils, of a creature that was an intermediate step between reptile and dinosaur.

Though in public statements, evolutionary scientists dispute the lack of evolutionary transitional fossils, like that between the reptile and dinosaur, they backtrack when pressed in interviews. For example, when interviewed on camera for the film *The Evolution Conspiracy*, Dr. Preston Cloud, director of geological science at University of California at Santa Barbara, said, "In fact, there are so many transitional forms between species that we must often fall back on statistical analysis to separate one from another."

Yet when pressed, Dr. Cloud admitted, "The problem of transitional forms is one that all honest paleontologists have a problem with. The geological record is incomplete."

The escape route Dr. Cloud took is a common one: "It's incomplete because of erosion."[31]

Though disconcerting to the evolutionist scientific community, the lack of an intermediate creature has given biblical creationists added ammunition.

Dr. Donald A. Chittick, whose doctorate is in physical chemistry and who has been a professor of chemistry at George Fox College, now lectures on science and the Bible. In a paper entitled, "The Puzzle of Ancient Man," Dr. Chittick writes:

> Fossil evidence provides no support for the idea that one type of animal has changed into another type of animal. For example, fish appear suddenly in the fossil record as fish. There is no evidence of their becoming fish. . . . How do we recognize a fish in the fossil record? Because it looks like a present-day fish.

[31] *Quoted by Caryl Matrisciana and Roger Oakland in* The Evolution Conspiracy *(Eugene, OR: Harvest House Publishers, 1991), pp. 97–98.*

Dr. Chittick's observations certainly are true of the dinosaur fossil record as well.

A VANISHING BREED?

Okay, the Bible may well indicate that dinosaurs and giant marine reptiles were still around during the years before Abraham more than four thousand years ago. However, if they survived the flood, what happened to them during the thousands of years since the flood? And is there any contemporary evidence that dinosaurs or giant sea reptiles may still be around?

To understand what happened, we first need to recognize the rather significant differences between the world's atmosphere before the flood and after it, for that difference may well hold the secret to the giant size of the dinosaurs as well. Earlier we introduced Dr. Carl Baugh, who has also made a study of atmospheric conditions. Dr. Baugh writes:

> We've been doing extensive research into the ancient atmosphere, the one that produced the fossil record. Our research indicates that essentially everything was larger in the past. For instance, the club mosses which today reach sixteen to eighteen inches often approach two hundred feet in the fossil record. The great dinosaurs, with their relatively small lung capacity, reached tremendous stature. Seismosaurus could reach his head almost seventy feet in the air. Something has to explain this anomaly in terms of today's atmosphere.

The difference, Dr. Baugh explains, may well be in the atmospheric pressure:

> In today's atmosphere we have 14.7 pounds atmospheric pressure per square inch at sea level. But to oxygenate the deep cell tissue of these great dinosaurs we need much greater atmospheric pressure. Research has shown that when you approach two times today's atmospheric pressure, the entire blood plasma is saturated with oxygen. Now this matches the pre-flood context of the Bible.
>
> The biblical record states clearly that there was a firmamental canopy made up of elements of water surrounding the earth in Noah's day. Our research indicates there was about 27 pounds per square inch of atmospheric pressure. That would beautifully solve a problem even paleontologists admit exists.
>
> In addition, the oxygen supply in the fossil record has been found to be 30 percent oxygen compared to 20 percent today. Ancient air bubbles trapped in amber have been analyzed and revealed this heavier concentration of oxygen. If we had those conditions today, we could run two hundred miles without fatigue.
>
> But there are added benefits. Water, because of its physical nature, filters out ultraviolet radiation, one of our major problems today, increasing the incidence of cancer and charging the atmosphere with free radical charges that violate the very nature of chemistry.

UNUSUAL CONDITIONS FOR PLANT GROWTH

Dr. Baugh continues:

> Under the above conditions we would have an unusual condition for plant growth. In addition to the charged hydrogen in the water vapor, the water canopy of crystalline content would glow with a magenta color we know as pink. This is the exact wavelength that encourages the growth of photocells in plants. This means that under the pre-flood conditions, plants had no choice but to grow and flourish abundantly. Add the increased oxygen in the atmosphere, and we have the conditions for the increased length of the biota.

Dr. Baugh reports that a Japanese experiment simulating some of these conditions resulted in a cherry tomato plant that in two years grew sixteen feet tall, with 903 tomatoes on it!

What happened after the flood? The water canopy was gone, the ultraviolet rays could get through, the oxygen was gradually reduced to 20 percent of the atmosphere. As Dr. Baugh puts it, "The biblical model indicates that the atmospheric pressure would not have lost all of its pressure after the flood. But it would have tapered off exponentially. That means dinosaurs could have survived for several centuries after the flood."

Paul S. Taylor writes about post-flood conditions in *The Great Dinosaur Mystery and the Bible:*

Temperatures had become extreme. Some parts of the world got much hotter after the Flood. This eventually dried up all the water and left great deserts. In other places, snow began to fall for the first time because of freezing cold. A short ice "age" followed the Flood in some parts of the world. . . . After the Flood many parts of the world became too harsh for dinosaurs. No longer did the earth have the same great forests of huge, nutritious plants. It would have been hard for the dinosaurs to locate enough food as they got bigger and bigger.[32]

All this information is predicated on the biblically based assumption that the dinosaur and man lived in the same pre-flood and post-flood environment. Yet is there any genuine scientific evidence that man and the dinosaur lived on the earth at the same time?

MODERN SURVIVORS POINT TO COEXISTENCE

Outside the legends of dragons, is there hard evidence of dinosaurs or giant sea reptiles surviving until today?

For starters, let's join a Japanese fishing ship off the coast of Christchurch, New Zealand, on April 10, 1977. The crew of the *Zuiyo Maru* is pulling in a net from nine hundred feet underwater. Suddenly the fishermen's eyes open wide. There suspended in the net is a huge, decaying underwater creature.

They measured and weighed this huge creature, dis-

[32] *Taylor*, The Great Dinosaur Mystery and the Bible, *pp. 34–35.*

covering it was thirty-two feet long and weighed two tons. It had four fins, each about three feet long. All the evidence, including tissue samples, indicate it was one of the great marine reptiles of ancient times, the Plesiosaurus.

Dr. Duane Gish, professor of natural science and author, comments, "So important was this find that the Japanese honored it with a postage stamp." The Plesiosaurus was also used as the official emblem for the 1977 National Exhibition in Japan, which celebrated one hundred years of scientific discovery.

The Navy ship *USS Stein* tangled with such a creature on its way to track submarines near South America. When its sonar equipment suddenly stopped working, the captain headed the ship back for repairs at the Long Beach Naval Shipyard. When the tough underwater sonar dome was examined in dry dock, the crew found the rubber covering torn and battered with dozens of big gouges. Hundreds of sharp, hollow teeth (or claws) were left embedded in the covering. Some were longer than an inch.

For all the world it looked like a giant sea creature had been attracted to the underwater sounds of the sonar and tried to bite it and break it. After months of examination, scientists at the Naval Oceans Center announced, "The animal must have been extremely large and of a species still unknown to science."

One of the most famous giant sea reptiles is the Loch Ness monster in Scotland. The first reported sightings go back to 565 A.D., when Saint Columba is supposed to have seen it.

Since then there have been numerous reported sightings and some pictures taken. The existing pictures and descriptions match that of an ancient sea reptile.

A GIANT CREATURE IN AFRICA

Reports of a giant creature the Africans call Mokele-Mmembe that lives in a remote section of the Congo were investigated in the early 1980s. Scientist Roy Mackal of the University of Chicago investigated the reports personally, showing various pictures to the Africans in the area. Only when he showed them pictures of the sauropods and of the Brontosaurus did they identify its shape.[33]

Writing about the efforts to determine whether the reports from the Africans were accurate, Dr. Baugh says:

Reports have surfaced over the last two centuries, and then, in 1959, "pygmies allegedly killed one that was disturbing their fishing on Lake Tele."

Another report was by A.P. [Associated Press] science writer Robert Locke, dated 11 June, 1981. The creature had been described by the natives as brownish-grey, with short, thick legs, weighing probably about nine to fifteen tons, and being about thirty-five feet from its small head to its tail. It was vegetarian, and though it had killed fishermen, it had not eaten them. . . .

In a later report, reporter Dick Donovan informed the world that two (not one) independent scientific expeditions

[33] *Carl E. Baugh with Clifford A. Wilson,* Dinosaur *(Orange, CA: Promise Publishing, 1991), p. 132.*

had offered solid proof that huge, terrifying dinosaurs still prowl the Earth. He stated, "Space Scientist Herman Regusters astounded the world by announcing he saw a gigantic dinosaur when his expedition probed the jungles of Africa." . . .

Regusters's reported sighting was a creature that raised its head out of the water and traveled for a quarter of a mile, then dived beneath the surface. They sighted it again four hours later.[34]

All these sightings have taken place after these giant sea creatures were supposed to have died out 65 million years ago! Yet where is the fossil and archaeological evidence that man and the dinosaur actually lived at the same time before the flood?

FOSSIL EVIDENCE OF MAN AND DINOSAUR?

Probably the most intense work in trying to determine if dinosaurs and humans walked the same trails some thousands of years ago has been done at Glen Rose, Texas, by a team headed by Dr. Carl Baugh, author of *Dinosaur*, and lecturer on archaeology and paleoanthropology. Commenting on their work at Glen Rose, Dr. Baugh says:

Here on the McFall Ledge near Glen Rose we have been excavating for more than a decade. During the course of these excavations we discovered a large Acrocanthosaurus

[34] *Ibid.*, p. 133.

dinosaur. We have identified 203 dinosaur footprints. Among these 203 dinosaur footprints we have excavated 57 human footprints. Seven of those human footprints have been up to fourteen inches long.

Anthropologically and physiologically there is no doubt that these are human footprints. There is also no doubt we have excavated them under original deposition. The features of these footprints are the great toe, unique to mankind, third and fourth little toe, the ball, flange, metatarsal arch, medial section of the longitudinal arch, lateral section of the longitudinal arch, and the heel section. These human footprints have been excavated under deposits of limestone.

Not only are the physiological features in these footprints very distinctive, but the size of these footprints is also distinctive. We have excavated some that were as small as five inches, others that were as long as sixteen inches. Those would be for an individual more than seven feet tall.

Now having found these series of footprints in connection with, and on the same layer as, the dinosaur footprints, it is obvious that these were giant-sized individuals, genetically superior.

HUMAN TRACKS KNOWN TO LOCALS

In actual fact, these human footprints in conjunction with dinosaur tracks were known to local residents for at least sixty years before scientists became interested. Robert Summers, the Texas Sesquicentennial Artist in 1986 when Texas celebrated the 150th anniversary of its founding, reports:

As a young teenager I used to come to this area often with friends and family to picnic here. I'd show them the dinosaur tracks. One day we were walking along and one of my friends looked down and said, "What are these tracks down there?"

I replied, "Oh, these are just human tracks. There's not much to those. You can see those tracks every day at the river or at the swimming pool. But look at those dinosaur tracks." Little did I realize the significance of what I was seeing, and what those tracks meant.

As a professional sculptor today I have no doubt that what I was looking at were human footprints. After all, the study of anatomy is one of the prerequisites for being an artist and sculptor. I have no doubt they were human prints, and I think there are still some out there today. Some have undoubtedly eroded over the forty years since I first came here. Many were also removed when they sent a whole set of tracks from here to the New York Museum of Natural History.

For Dr. Carl Baugh and his associates, items found in connection with the footprints of dinosaurs and humans are equally valuable:

Also found in the same limestone layer was a confirmed fossilized human finger. In adjacent areas, in the same Cretaceous layer of sandstone, we discovered a man-made artifact, an ancient hammer. This ancient artifact was, according to our calculations, made by a man who lived contemporaneous with dinosaurs.

I took this artifact to the Batelle Laboratories in Columbus, Ohio, the same laboratory that analyzed the moonstones. The elemental analysis shows that the hammerhead is 96.6 percent iron, 0.74 percent sulphur, and 2.6 percent chlorine. Physicists tell us that under today's atmospheric conditions you cannot compound chlorine with metallic iron. Yet here it is.

ANCIENT HAMMER DATES TO DINOSAUR DAYS

Dr. Baugh concludes:

Research indicates that this ancient man-made hammer would have been made during the generations of Tubal-Cain and Noah in the Bible. Therefore, it would have been deposited sedimentarily in the worldwide flood of Noah's day. This leads us to the conclusion that man and the dinosaur did live contemporaneously.

Carbon dating of carbonized wood found in the same Cretaceous layers also revealed that the fossils were between twelve thousand and forty-five thousand years old. Similar dating of fossils in dinosaur beds in Colorado and Russia indicate the fossils were an average of twenty-five thousand to thirty-five thousand years old. In other words, the dinosaur fossils are one thousand times younger than scientists have steadfastly insisted for many years.

Recent findings, incidentally, indicate that radiocarbon dating is accurate up to what is called Carbon 14's half-life, or 5,730 years. Because of different atmospheric conditions before the flood, a "radiocarbon year" would not correspond to an actual year. Thus, even the readings of twenty-five thousand to thirty-five thousand years may actually be much less because of the pre-flood conditions.

The findings of Dr. Baugh and many other scientists actively uncovering dinosaur prints and related human prints have been verified by similar human/dinosaur print combinations in Australia and in Turkmenia, in what was the Soviet Union. Correspondent Alexander Romashko of the *Moscow News* reported in 1983:

I stood only a step away from a smooth clearing receding up the slope. I stepped forward and found myself in the Mesozoic Era; i.e., nearly 150 million years in the past. A chain of dinosaur tracks started at my feet. It looked as if the huge prehistoric beasts passed by here very recently, leaving imprints of massive paws every 1.5 meters.

Paleontologists explained to me later that with this long stride, the reptiles had to be 8–12 meters tall. All of a sudden we saw, next to the three-fingered track of a dinosaur, a not very clear but quite discernible track looking very much like a human footprint. Anyway, all those who saw it first thought so. Since I'm no scholar, I ventured to come forth with an assumption: "Who knows but maybe our very far-removed ancestors did mingle with dinosaurs?"

"Science might possibly answer that in the affirmative in the future," said Professor Kurban Amanniyazov, head of the expedition, corresponding member of the Turkmen SSR Academy of Sciences and director of the Institute of Geology. "Here at present we don't have enough grounds to say this. We've imprints resembling human footprints, but to date have failed to determine, with scientific veracity, whom they belong to. After all, if we could prove that they do belong to a humanoid, then it would create a revolution in the science of man."[35]

All of the evidence at these various sites points to man and the dinosaur living side by side in a semitropical environment. The fact that in almost every case man and dinosaur tracks indicate a pattern of flight would tend to prove they were attempting to escape a catastrophe. That catastrophe, some believe, was the worldwide flood of Noah's day.

Scientists will obviously be following up many discoveries, attempting to determine the validity of initial scientific analysis. Enough has been presented to spark a lively debate, whether you are an evolutionist or a creationist.

By the way, next time you go to South America, see if you can verify the sightings by U.S. Air Force officers of a giant bird the size of prehistoric flying reptiles. They were in an airplane looking for drug smugglers when they saw this huge flying creature. There may be another contemporary dinosaur-type bird to confound the evolutionary scientists insisting dinosaurs died out sixty-five million years ago.

And speaking of flights, we hope we didn't take you too far from Moses and Joshua. The Bible has an interesting story to tell about one of the world's most sought-after artifacts—a story critics love to debunk. Since we enjoy debunking the critics, you'll want to stay with us.

[35] *Baugh and Wilson*, Dinosaur, *pp. 140–145.*

13

THE ISRAELITES'
MOST SACRED OBJECT

There never was an ark of the covenant. It's as fictional as the search for it by Indiana Jones in Raiders of the Lost Ark.

Jordan Maxwell
University Mythology Educator

WHAT IS THE MOST SACRED OBJECT IN YOUR HOME? In the church you attend? In your state or country? Many of us have objects that are special and, yes, even sacred to us, because they represent a significant religious or personal experience.

Of all the ceremonial and sacred objects in the Bible, the most argued about is the ark of the covenant. Arguments rage about whether it really existed, what significance it had, why it disappeared, and where it might be hidden. During the twentieth century, people have spent decades and small fortunes looking for the mysterious ark of the covenant.

This object so revered is a wooden chest covered with beaten gold and inlaid with gold. According to the Bible, it became the center of all religious ceremonial practices of the Hebrews while they were still in the desert on their way to Canaan, possibly thirty-five hundred years ago. Many doubt it ever existed. If it did, it apparently disappeared forever more than twenty-five hundred years ago. Yet the mystery continues to fascinate people of many faiths.

The critics do not mince words.

> There never was an ark of the covenant. It's as fictional as
> the search for it by Indiana Jones in *Raiders of the Lost
> Ark*. As serious scholars, we can all stop looking for that
> lost ark of the covenant and leave it to Hollywood, because
> that's where it belongs, in the realm of fantasy.

So says Jordan Maxwell, author and guest lecturer at
the University of Southern California.

Providing a quick rebuttal is Canadian Grant Jeffrey,
author of *Armageddon Revisited: Appointment with
Destiny* and archaeological researcher in Israel, who
says, "There is ample archaeological and historical proof
that the ark of the covenant still exists exactly as described in the Book of Exodus in the Bible."

There is much more to the argument than that, of
course, but before we pursue it further, let's revisit
Moses and the Israelites encamped in the desert at
Mount Sinai.

ENHANCED SKILLS FOR A
SPECIAL PROJECT

Thousands of goatskin tents dot the sloping plain, arranged in twelve orderly camps. Men sit in groups and
talk, while women take care of household duties. Older
teenagers under the watchful eye of veteran shepherds
keep an eye on goats and sheep grazing on the slopes
beyond the tents. In the background a rocky mountain
keeps silent vigil. Even the cloud that had covered it for
so long was gone.

In front of one of the tents a small forge is heating a

clay pot with metal in it. Two men are busy with molds to receive the metal when it can be poured.

"I hear Moses has come back down the mountain with another set of stone tablets containing the law of God," commented Oholiab to Bezalel, deftly moving the pot so it was better centered over the fire. "He was at the top of the mountain with God a long time."

"This time Aaron and Joshua kept the people focused on worshipping God," Bezalel said, setting up another mold. "It was sad to see so many die because of the golden calf Aaron had made."

"I'm so glad he did not approach me to make that golden calf. I don't know what I would have said to Aaron, our leader, since I worship only the Lord God," said Oholiab.

At that moment a messenger approached them. "Moses has asked me to invite you to join him in his tent. He has a special message for you, and says you will need to make extensive notes."

Oholiab looked quizzically at Bezalel, took the metal off the fire, and began pouring it into the molds. "Tell our great leader Moses that we'll do his bidding as soon as we have completed this task," Oholiab said.

"I wonder what he wants now," said Bezalel as he and Oholiab carefully filled the molds. "There is so much work to do now that we are starting all over again. There is no shortage of gold and jewelry, nor of household vessels, but it seems we are busier than we were in Egypt with all these special projects."

When they reached Moses' tent, the guard lifted the flap and let them in. They touched their foreheads and bowed as they entered.

"Be seated. We have much to talk about," said Moses. "God has given me special plans for a Tent of Meeting that will be His dwelling place. He has also given me instructions for all the ceremonial utensils and fixtures," he continued. "This new Tent of Meeting will be a magnificent structure to replace the tent where He has been meeting with me."

Aaron nodded approvingly. Moses had already shared with him some of the exciting details of the new Tent of Meeting.

CRAFTSMEN SPECIALLY GIFTED BY GOD

"Your fame as skilled artisans has caught the eye of the Lord, whom you worship so faithfully," Moses said to the two men. "You have been selected by the Lord to be the leaders of the teams of craftsmen we will need to do all the work. Your own special skills will be necessary for the fine detail work needed on the altars and the ark of the covenant, the place where God will speak to us."

"We are but simple workers, lord. We are not as skilled as the great architects and craftsmen of Egypt," said Bezalel, bowing again.

"Do not be concerned," Aaron said, smiling gently. "God does not ask more of us than we are able."

GOD-GIVEN SPECIAL SKILLS

Moses bent forward, his eyes burning with enthusiasm. "God has promised to fill you with His Spirit and give you extra skill, ability, and knowledge, even in crafts that you know little about. And the people you will choose to help you will also be filled with the Spirit of God for work in gold, silver, and copper, to cut and set stones, to work in wood, and to make the curtains and coverings. You will be surprised at what you can do because the Lord has called you."

"We are the servants of the Lord God," said Oholiab, bowing again.

"We will announce to all the people that God has chosen you to lead the skilled craftsmen," said Moses. "There will be no shortage of people to help you."

"But where will we get all the materials needed?" asked Bezalel.

"We will be asking all the people to give an offering of gold, silver, and bronze; blue, purple, and scarlet yarn and fine linen, goat hair, ram skins dyed red, and hides of sea cows. Also, acacia wood, olive oil, spices, onyx stones, and other gems," replied Moses. "The Lord blessed us abundantly when we left Egypt. Now let's begin with the plans for the Tent of Meeting, the tabernacle of God; then I'll share God's plans for the ark of the covenant, the table, golden lamp stand, altars, and utensils." Moses leaned back as though lost in thought for a moment.

Over the next two hours Moses described in detail the plans for the tabernacle itself and the various pieces to go into it. As he wound up, he turned to Bezalel.

BEZALEL'S SPECIAL ASSIGNMENT

"Bezalel, your skills are so special I'm asking you to make the ark of the covenant yourself. Make it of acacia wood, two and a half cubits long, a cubit and a half wide, and a cubit and a half high. Overlay it with gold inside and out. Make a gold molding around the top of it."

As Moses continued to describe it, Bezalel could see it taking shape in his mind's eye. A lid covered with beaten gold, two cherubim with outstretched wings on top, gold rings on the lower side for the gold-covered poles. He knew it would be a lot of work, but he was so eager to get started he could hardly wait for Moses to end his description.

The next day the leaders of the twelve tribes and the seventy elders were summoned into the presence of Moses. They were told what God wanted the people to contribute toward the tabernacle. They moved out among the people, informing them of the special plans for the tabernacle of God and what the craftsmen would need to finish their special assignment.

All day men and women came from every direction in the camp with their contributions. The containers overflowed with gold earrings, arm bracelets, necklaces, specially woven materials, and precious stones.

"Tell Moses we have enough. We cannot handle anymore. The people are too generous," Bezalel told Oholiab, who rushed to Moses' tent to give him the exciting news.

Moses called Joshua. "Send word to all the elders to

tell the people their generosity is much appreciated, but the craftsmen have enough."

WHY BUILD AN ARK?

Why the special attention to this ark of the covenant? After all, the Israelites were already building a beautiful tabernacle according to specific instructions from God.

The Bible reports that God himself invested this box of acacia wood covered with gold with special significance. After God gave Moses detailed instructions, the Bible reveals, God promised, "There, above the cover between the two cherubim that are over the ark of the Testimony, I will meet with you and give you all my commandments for the Israelites." [Exodus 25:22]

According to Doug Wead, David Lewis, and Hal Donaldson, the authors of *Where Is the Lost Ark?*, the ark of the covenant "became a symbol of the pledge of God's presence, an instrument from which He audibly communicated His laws and directions."[36]

Its direct participation in key events in Israel's history verifies that the Israelites did not only consider it a symbol of God, but as bringing the presence of God with it. Comments Roy Lee DeWitt in *Teaching from the Tabernacle:*

> This is verified by Israeli history, which points to the ark as being synonymous with God. For this reason, the ark led the way in the wilderness wanderings and was taken into

[36] Doug Wead, David Lewis, and Hal Donaldson, Where Is the Lost Ark? (Minneapolis: Bethany House Publishers, 1982), p. 14.

battle often. When Israel brought the ark into their camp after their defeat by the Philistines, Israel's shouts were understood by the Philistines to mean that the ark was with them. The Philistines' reply was, "God is come into the camp." [1 Samuel 4:7-8]

The mercy seat also, like the ark, was thought of as representing God. [1 Samuel 4:4; Psalm 80:1] From between the two cherubim on the mercy seat, God spoke to the nation through the high priest.[37]

Religious leaders in Israel who are committed to the eventual restoration of the temple on Temple Mount in Jerusalem and its worship ceremonies even today focus on the spiritual significance of the ark of the covenant. Rabbi Chaim Richman, executive director of the Temple Institute in Jerusalem, says:

The temple is seen by Judaism as the sole vehicle for the spiritual rectification of the relationship between God and man. I think this is best symbolized by the position of the ark in the Holy of Holies in the temple. God spoke to Moses that through the ark would be the manifestation of God, the Shekinah glory, the presence of God. This Shekinah glory can only rest among humanity in the temple. That presence is symbolized by the ark.

---

[37] *Roy Lee DeWitt,* Teaching from the Tabernacle *(Grand Rapids, MI: Baker Book House, 1986), p. 180.*

AN ARK BASED ON EGYPTIAN MODELS?

Yet was the ark an original design or a copy of Egyptian and Babylonian religious arks? Is it really possible for a people just released from slavery to have the skilled craftsmen described in the Book of Exodus? Was the technology available for the fine metalwork, for the fine linen, for the precious stones cut for the ephod on the high priest's garments?

Not according to the critics!

"The Jewish people actually adopted the Egyptian theology and copied it, using it as they went to Israel," says Jordan Maxwell, a southern California mythology educator and co-author of *The Book Your Church Doesn't Want You to Read*. Even the name *Israel*, he says, originated in Egypt. Maxwell continues:

IS was the personification of Isis, the feminine wisdom. RA was for the Sun, and EL was for God. So they inculcated these religious movements and used the ark of the covenant for religious ceremony only in the story and only for morality.

The story of the ark is a very ancient story in the Semitic world. It goes all the way back to the Babylonians, the Assyrians, the Persians, the Greeks, the Egyptians. All of those ancient Semitic cultures had a story of an ark of the covenant. The Egyptians had the most important ark, for that is where the Hebrew ark is borrowed from.

These criticisms are not easy to counteract. They represent a major segment of scholars of Near Eastern studies. Dr. J. Randall Price, a man who has spent many years studying the ark of the covenant, its purposes, and where it might be today, provides a clear response. The author of *Ready to Rebuild* and professor of biblical studies at the Central Texas Bible Institute says:

As to the question of whether the ark really existed, there are many nonbiblical references to support this fact.

The technology also existed to build the ark of the covenant. Similar gold-plated shrines existed in Egypt long before the time of Moses.

To the Israelites, the ark was undoubtedly their most sacred religious object, for it served as the footstool of the true God, and the divine presence was once visible there. Within the ark of the covenant were contained the two tablets upon which were written the Ten Commandments, Aaron's rod that had budded, and the pot of manna that was once used to feed the Israelites on their long wilderness journey.

Writing in his book, *In Search of the Lost Ark,* Bible teacher Don Stewart reveals that there were indeed arks in other cultures, but they do not have the same origin or significance:

Ancient analogies to the ark have been sought in model temples, tent-shrines, chariots for gods, squared thrones, and even coffins for the gods. Therefore, it is argued, there is nothing unique or supernatural about the ark, since it was one of many such objects.

There are three basic problems with the view that Israel's ark was one of many such "arks" in the ancient world.

First, the references to the arklike objects in other cultures have only a superficial resemblance. . . . Second, many of the similar structures were built after the ark of the covenant. If any borrowing was done, it was probably from the ark of the covenant, not the reverse.

Finally, and by far the most important, the history of the ark shows that it was not some ancient pagan box devoid of power. Supernatural events took place around the Ark.[38]

Agreeing with that assessment is author Grant Jeffrey:

The ark of the covenant was the most important object in ancient history. Yet it mysteriously disappeared thousands of years ago. In my opinion, there is ample archaeological and historical proof that the ark of the covenant still exists exactly as described in the Book of Exodus in the Bible.

We will explore what happened to the ark of the covenant and why it is still missing in the next chapter. But first let's look in on a festival that revealed how special the ark of the covenant was to the Israelites and to God.

A SURPRISE ENDING TO A PARADE

The procession had begun early in the morning at the home of Abinadab. King David had decided to bring the

---

[38] *Don Stewart,* In Search of the Lost Ark *(Orange, CA: Dart Press, 1992), pp. 69, 71.*

ark of the covenant into the tabernacle in the city of Jerusalem after it had stayed in Abinadab's home outside the city for some years.

"I'm so glad King David decided to bring the ark of the covenant to the tabernacle," Zadok said, turning to his fellow priest Ahimelech as they walked in the parade. "That's where it belongs, according to our ancestor Aaron. Yet it's been fifteen years since it was brought back by the Philistines and placed in the home of Abinadab."

The music of the orchestra accompanying the procession almost drowned out his words. Musicians ahead of them with harps, lyres, tambourines, sistrums, and cymbals seemed in ecstasy as they played their hearts out.

Ahimelech looked back. "This seems like a military procession, for all I can see are King David's warriors. The ark certainly did not need an army to protect it after it was captured by the Philistines in battle," he commented.

"That's for sure. They did not keep the ark very long after their god, Dagon, mysteriously fell over onto his face in front of the ark," Zadok said.

Ahimelech listened to the music for a minute. He could see David playing his harp with the best of them.

"No wonder David is bringing the ark to the tabernacle on a new wagon pulled by oxen. That's how the Philistines brought it back safely," he added, almost as an afterthought. Turning to Zadok he said, "But if he had asked me, I would have told him that the law says it must be carried on poles by priests."

Zadok's arm shot out. "Look, the ark is going to fall off the cart!" he shouted.

Ahimelech and Zadok could see one of the sons of Abinadab, who had been appointed by his father to accompany the ark, reach out to steady it. In that frozen moment of time between the cart starting to tip and Uzzah reaching to steady it, a streak of blazing light hit Uzzah and knocked him to the ground.

The sound of music stopped instantly. Confusion reigned as people crowded around the prone Uzzah. King David hurried over as well. After checking to make sure that Uzzah could not be revived, he moved quickly to Uzzah's father, Abinadab, expressing his dismay and sorrow at the turn of events.

King David sent the priests and people home while he arranged for the ark to be temporarily stored in the nearby house of Obed-edom. Before he moved the ark again, he had to come to terms with why God had so dramatically interrupted the triumphal procession. After all, his intentions had been good.

Once King David had dealt with his initial anger at God, he called in Zadok and Ahimelech and sought their counsel.

"The Book of Numbers gives clear directions that the ark of the covenant is to be carried on poles by priests steadying the weight on their shoulders. The poles were designed specifically for that purpose," Zadok and Ahimelech told him.

Three months later King David set out again. This time the ark of the covenant was safely carried by its poles on the shoulders of priests until it rested in the tabernacle of God.

THE ISRAELITES' SECRET OF POWER

What made the ark of the covenant such an important national symbol that King David insisted on it being brought to the tabernacle? Beyond the fact that God had said to Moses that he would speak to him from it, why was it so revered?

God's cloud indicating his presence with the Israelites in the Sinai Desert had moved over and into the tabernacle and over the ark of the covenant. Moses "took the Testimony and placed it in the ark, attached the poles to the ark and put the atonement cover over it. Then he brought the ark into the tabernacle and hung the shielding curtain and shielded the ark of the Testimony, as the Lord commanded him." [Exodus 40:20–21]

Once all the ceremonial altars and objects had been placed in the tabernacle, God moved in:

> Then the cloud covered the Tent of Meeting, and the glory of the Lord filled the tabernacle. Moses could not enter the Tent of Meeting because the cloud had settled upon it, and the glory of the Lord filled the tabernacle. In all the travels of the Israelites, whenever the cloud lifted from above the tabernacle, they would set out; but if the cloud did not lift, they did not set out—until the day it lifted. So the cloud of the Lord was over the tabernacle by day, and fire was in the cloud by night, in the sight of all the house of Israel during all their travels. [Exodus 40:34–38]

This experience made the ark of the covenant a special indication of God's presence. When Joshua and the

Israelites approached the Jordan River, Joshua's officers told the people, "When you see the ark of the covenant of the Lord your God, and the priests, who are Levites, carrying it, you are to move out from your positions and follow it." [Joshua 3:3]

As the priests' feet touched the Jordan River, it parted. The priests moved into the middle of the Jordan and waited there until all the people had crossed. The Bible reports, "The priests who carried the ark of the covenant of the Lord stood firm on dry ground in the middle of the Jordan, while all Israel passed by until the whole nation had completed the crossing on dry ground." [Joshua 3:17]

According to the Book of Joshua, chapter 6, the ark of the covenant was carried all the way around the city of Jericho right behind the priests blowing the rams' horns, representing the presence and power of God.

WHEN THE ARK BROUGHT DEATH

When the Philistines captured the ark of the covenant in King Saul's day, they returned the ark after disaster upon disaster hit them. They reached the conclusion that the god of the ark was punishing them for keeping it. When they returned it, they left it on a rock at Beth-shemesh. After Levites sacrificed before it, curiosity got the better of some of the residents. Seventy men, the Bible reports in 1 Samuel 6:19, died because they opened the lid and looked into the ark of the covenant.

God not only judged Uzzah and the people at Beth-shemesh when they touched the ark, he also blessed the household of Obed-edom. In fact, the blessing was so obvious, King David got jealous—and moved it on into the tabernacle he had built specially for it.

When King Solomon brought the ark of the covenant into the Holy of Holies in the new temple he had built in Jerusalem, the Bible reveals:

> The priests brought the ark of the Lord's covenant to its place in the inner sanctuary of the temple, the Most Holy Place, and put it beneath the wings of the cherubim. . . . When the priests withdrew from the Holy Place, the cloud filled the temple of the Lord. And the priests could not perform their service because of the cloud, for the glory of the Lord filled his temple. [1 Kings 8:6, 10–11]

The retelling of stories like this clearly gave the ark of the covenant exalted status as the object that brought God's presence into their midst. Thus, it is indeed surprising that there is no mention of the ark after King Solomon brought it into his temple. No subsequent kings ever took it into battle again or used it to bring God into their activity.

The evident power connected with the ark of the covenant has intrigued even leaders like Mussolini of Italy and Adolf Hitler of Germany. According to Jordan Maxwell, writer and television host:

> Indiana Jones was not the only one looking for the lost ark in the movie *Raiders of the Lost Ark*. They had Nazis there, too.
> The reason Indiana Jones and Adolf Hitler were both looking for the lost ark was because it has a very significant

connection to the occult world. There is a mystical quality about the ark. And Adolf Hitler and the Nazis truly believed the ark would give them supernatural powers over mankind.

Before World War II, one of the aims of Mussolini's Fascist army was to capture the ark, said to be kept in Aksum, Ethiopia. He captured Ethiopia in 1936 and retained control until 1941, but the ark eluded him.

What happened to the ark of the covenant? Was it secretly spirited away by disgruntled priests during Solomon's day . . . or during the reign of later kings who did not worship the Lord? Did it survive until Nebuchadnezzar broke into the city and plundered the temple?

The mystery of the missing ark of the covenant continues to intrigue both Christians and Jews, scientists and fundamentalists alike. Coming up, we'll examine this ongoing mystery in more detail. There are those who say they know precisely where the ark of the covenant is today, perhaps even *two* arks.

14

HAS THE ARK OF THE COVENANT BEEN FOUND?

There is absolutely no reason to imagine that the ark survived in any way, shape, or form. To believe that is to be in a script in Hollywood.

Rabbi Sherwin Wine
Birmingham Temple, Michigan

THE LOST ARK OF THE COVENANT. IT'S LIKE THE Crusaders' search for the Holy Grail. There's something about it that attracts enthusiasts generation after generation.

Bible scholars and Jewish specialists dream about the possibility of finding it as they clamber through caves, underground tunnels, and cisterns. For the rabbis in Israel, discovering the ark of the covenant is, of course, intimately tied to the third rebuilding of the temple, which they consider essential to the practice of their faith.

One of the spokesmen emphasizing the importance of the ark in relation to restoring the temple is Rabbi Chaim Richman, director of public affairs of the Temple Institute, who says:

> The goal of the Temple Institute is really to raise the consciousness both of the Jewish people and the entire world to the realization that our spiritual vacuum can only be fulfilled by the holy temple.
>
> The Jews have 613 commandments that they are obliged to fulfill—fully one-third of them are completely contingent on the existence of the temple for their fulfillment. This means actually producing, restoring, creating, the vessels

that can be used in the temple. Of the ninety-three basic categories of vessels that are described in the holy sources, we have so far created almost sixty vessels made of gold, copper, and silver, according to the complicated nuances and requirements of Jewish law. And they are so accurate they can be used in the temple.

In addition to the work on restoring the vessels, we are also engaged in ongoing science and research related to projects like the weaving of priestly garments. These are all geared toward the principle of doing as much as possible to prepare for the temple itself.

The temple is universal and is seen by Judaism as the sole vehicle for the spiritual rectification of the relationship between God and man. This is best summarized by the position of the ark in the Holy of Holies in the temple. God spoke to Moses through the ark, the divine glory, the manifestation of the presence of God. In other words, the presence of God can rest amongst humanity only through the temple. That is why our activity includes many of the vessels described in holy sources for use in the temple.

The ark is one item that is not on our schedule for recreation, because we are aware of the location of the original ark.

Yet do the rabbis really know where the original ark of the covenant is today? Not if you talk to the Ethiopians, who insist they have the original ark of the covenant, but won't show it.

"If you love a mystery, well, this is where it starts," says Marvin Luckerman, publisher of *Catastophism and Ancient History* and a specialist in the history of the Middle East. "There is no mention again of the ark in any active sense after Solomon. But of legends and stories there are more than enough."

The first consideration is to try to determine when the ark of the covenant vanished. That probably is as difficult as finding the lost ark!

Some scholars believe the ark of the covenant was taken from the temple by an Egyptian pharaoh not too many years after the death of King Solomon. Consider the following scenario.

THE EGYPTIAN CONNECTION

"How quickly our people have been corrupted," the old temple priest complained as he accompanied another priest to daily temple ritual. "King Solomon started well, but his many foreign wives introduced their gods into our ruling class, and the corruption spread quickly."

His companion nodded. "Now look what is happening on all the hills around Jerusalem," he said. "They've set up shrines to Astarte with sacred stones and are worshiping the gods that the old Canaanites worshiped before we conquered the land."

"I'm convinced God is going to punish us for forgetting him and running after foreign gods," the old priest said.

His companion responded, "Maybe that judgment is closer than we think. The Egyptians are at the walls of the city. I hear they will attack at any time. Shishak, king of Egypt, can't wait to defeat the grandson of King David and son of great King Solomon—and get his hands on the gold accumulated by Solomon."

That night battering rams broke through the wall,

and Egyptian mercenaries poured through the breach. Pharaoh (King) Shishak personally led an elite unit to plunder King Solomon's magnificent palace and temple. They took home the golden shields, golden utensils, and anything else of value only five years after the death of King Solomon in 925 B.C.

The amount of gold taken can be imagined from an event that took place four years later in Egypt. In 921 B.C., Pharaoh Shishak's son, Osorkon I, gave to the gods and goddesses of Egypt an astonishing 383 tons of gold and silver, according to cuneiform pillars left behind. But there was still plenty left over to meet the needs of the pharaoh's court.

The priests in Jerusalem could not be consoled after the Egyptian army left.

"They have taken all of our temple treasures, the golden candlestick, the laver of brass, the table of shewbread," the old priest mourned. "How can we worship God when his sacred objects are no longer with us?"

"We can make copies, just like God gave Moses a new set of the tablets of the law when Moses broke the first set," his companion replied hopefully. "Maybe God will inhabit the temple again when we show our devotion by restoring the treasures used in our worship."

MAYBE NOT ALL TREASURES WERE TAKEN

The Bible seems to indicate clearly that all of the temple treasures were taken, for we read:

> In the fifth year of King Rehoboam, Shishak, king of Egypt,
> attacked Jerusalem. He carried off the treasures of the
> temple of the Lord and the treasures of the royal palace.
> He took everything, including all the gold shields Solomon
> had made. [1 Kings 14:25–26]

There is a mystery here, however, for it would appear from a later incident that not all the treasures were taken. King Abijah of Judah, King Rehoboam's son and King Solomon's grandson, seems to have been a faithful worshiper of the Lord. Facing a battle with the breakaway ten tribes who had rebelled under King Jeroboam, King Abijah climbed a hill and insisted God was on their side. Among the reasons he gave was their devotion to God:

> The priests who serve the Lord are sons of Aaron, and the
> Levites assist them. Every morning and evening they
> present burnt offerings and fragrant incense to the Lord.
> They set out the bread on the ceremonially clean table and
> light the lamps on the gold lamp stand every evening. [2
> Chronicles 13:10–11]

Gold lamp stand? Didn't Pharaoh Shishak of Egypt take away all the temple treasures?

There are those who suspect he did not. The collaborators on *Where Is the Lost Ark?*—Doug Wead, onetime presidential public liaison adviser to President George Bush; David Lewis, chairman of the National Christian Leadership Conference for Israel; and Hal Donaldson, editor of *On* magazine—suggest:

The lamp stand was made of pure gold [Exodus 37:17], weighing over fifty pounds. [Exodus 37:24] The Egyptians certainly would have taken it if they had been able to find it. This leads one to believe that the ark and the more valuable temple furnishings were successfully hidden from the Egyptians.[39]

But then the Babylonians came. King Zedekiah had been installed by King Nebuchadnezzar of Babylon, the Chaldeans, as the Bible calls them. Zedekiah remained a loyal vassal until he thought he saw an opportunity with the increasing military might of Egypt, so he revolted in 588 B.C.

The great King Nebuchadnezzar of Babylon, the most successful Babylonian king ever, was not amused. After all, he had made three armed raids on Judah on his way to do battle with the Egyptians, and had conquered Jerusalem nine years earlier. He had carried off the young King Jehoiachim and installed Zedekiah as king of Judah in Jerusalem. Now the king he installed was rebelling—again because Egypt seemed to be regaining strength. He laid siege against Jerusalem in earnest, sealing the city so no one could come in or leave for more than eighteen months.

DID THE PRIESTS HIDE THEM?

"There is no food left in the market," Esther said as she placed a thin soup before her husband. "I hear of terri-

---

[39] Doug Wead, David Lewis, and Hal Donaldson, Where Is the Lost Ark? (Minneapolis: Bethany House Publishers, 1982), p. 44.

ble things going on in the city. People are eating rats and mice. There is even a report of a child being killed and eaten. When will King Zedekiah surrender to Nebuchadnezzar?"

"Never, is the rumor. But never may be now. I hear the Babylonians are about to breach the wall and enter the city," Jephthah, one of the temple priests, replied. "I wish he would have listened to the prophet Jeremiah. We could have avoided all this suffering."

"Why have we been able to survive the siege of more than two years?" Esther asked, chewing on a dry crust of bread.

"Our good King Hezekiah years ago built such a large water storage system, with cisterns and connecting tunnels, that we still have not run out of water," Jephthah answered. "King Zedekiah knows that if he surrenders he will probably be put to death. Certainly he will be dragged off to Babylon as a slave. He'd rather die in the city than become a slave to Nebuchadnezzar."

"I'm afraid the mighty Nebuchadnezzar is so angry we'll all be slaves and dragged to Babylon, just like the prophet has said." Esther shook her head sorrowfully as she cleared the table.

The priest watched her movements, slowed by a starvation diet. "My biggest concern is the vessels and sacred treasures in the temple. We have a plan to hide them in a vault, but we cannot appear to be indicating lack of support for the king, so we have to be ready to act as soon as the wall is breached," he said.

"But who will help you?" Esther asked.

"We have two loyal young priests committed to spiriting the sacred vessels and the ark of the covenant into an underground vault. They will be helped by four older priests. We have developed a communication system that will give us the time to notify everyone when anyone hears the wall has been breached," Jephthah said as he prepared to go back to the temple. "They are ready to rush to the temple and remove the sacred objects."

At that moment someone pounded on the door. Jephthah opened it, and a young man burst in. "The wall has been breached," he said breathlessly. "The soldiers are flooding into the city."

"Thank you! Run to Abiathar's dwelling nearby and tell him I sent you," Jephthah said, sighing deeply.

In minutes hooded figures approached the temple's entrance for priests, slipping in quickly. They had rehearsed what they had to do and immediately set about the task of hiding the great treasures of the temple.

AN UNLIKELY SCENARIO?

According to Rabbi Sherwin Wine of Humanistic Judaism:

> There is absolutely no reason to imagine that the ark, which
> was in the temple in Jerusalem in 586 B.C. when that
> temple was destroyed by Nebuchadnezzar, survived in any
> way, shape, or form.

Again, ark-of-the-covenant critic Jordan Maxwell is equally convinced the furor over the ark is misplaced:

> The ark or chest described in the Bible, if it existed at all,
> disappeared in Solomon's time, probably dismantled for the

gold said to be part of it . . . and there is serious doubt as
to whether even Solomon existed. Solomon's time itself is
probably a myth.

A highly qualified defender of the biblical account is
Dr. J. Randall Price, whose doctorate is in Hebrew studies, and who has done graduate work at the Hebrew
University in Jerusalem in ancient Jewish history and
archaeology. Dr. Price has spent years researching the
possibility of a third temple in Jerusalem. He says:

> As serious historians we can accept the historical accuracy
> of the Bible and the general reliability of the Jewish
> traditional sources. There is documentary and
> archaeological evidence to support the existence of the
> Israelite King Solomon and the renowned ark of the
> covenant.

Solomon's reign was indeed remarkable, as archaeological evidence unearthed in the past sixty years demonstrates. For example, Nelson Glueck, a member of the
famous American School of Oriental Research, in 1937
discovered Solomon's copper smelters and seaport at
Ezion-geber. The smelters were the most sophisticated
in the world at that time, and author Werner Keller suggests that Ezion-geber was the "Pittsburgh" of Solomon's day.[40]
In addition, a Phoenician priest, Sanchuniathon, describes how Hiram of Tyre provided Solomon with lum-

[40] *Werner Keller,* The Bible As History *(New York: William Morrow and
Company, 1956), pp. 193–197.*

ber for building the ships at Ezion-geber. He even names the "shipmen with knowledge of the sea" sent to help the Israelites, who had no knowledge of shipbuilding or of manning the ships.[41]

Excavations at ancient Megiddo in northern Israel and in Jerusalem revealed large horse stables from Solomon's day.

With archaeological discoveries validating the Bible's story of King Solomon, it is not difficult to accept the biblical account of him bringing the ark of the covenant into the temple built for it.

Yet if the ark of the covenant really did exist, what happened to it? The mystery really deepens when we consider the legend that places the ark of the covenant in Ethiopia. This legend involves one of the most mysterious personalities in the Old Testament, the Queen of Sheba, and a son she is supposed to have had with King Solomon.

THE ETHIOPIAN CONNECTION: QUEEN OF SHEBA

The Bible reports that the Queen of Sheba traveled many miles to visit King Solomon in Jerusalem. Though she came from an advanced civilization with great architectural achievements, she was greatly impressed with the wisdom of King Solomon.

Yet who was this Queen of Sheba? Where was the kingdom of Sheba? According to *The New International Dictionary of Biblical Archaeology:*

[41] *Ibid., p. 198.*

Sheba was the home of the Sabeans, originally a nomadic group which by the Israelite monarchy period had settled in the East in the area of what is now known as Yemen. They traded in precious metals, jewels, spices, and odoriferous resins, and once their commercial activities developed, they appear to have founded colonies farther to the north. The original capital of Sheba was Sirwah, but this was replaced subsequently by Marib (Mahram Bilquis), where outstanding examples of Sabean architecture, flood control dams and pagan temples have been discovered.

While priest-kings (mukarribs) generally ruled Sheba in the first half of the first millennium B.C., cuneiform inscriptions have been recovered which show that, particularly in North Arabia, tribal confederacies were sometimes governed by queens during the period of the ninth to the seventh centuries B.C.[42]

In about 1000 B.C., the Sabeans crossed the Red Sea and conquered the Hamites of Ethiopia. By the first century A.D., the victors had established the kingdom of Aksum, which was ruled by the Solomonic dynasty, so called because the kings claimed direct descent from the biblical King Solomon and the Queen of Sheba. In the fifth century Syrian migrants led Aksum's Emperor Ezana to accept Christianity, though Ethiopian tradition traces the Ethiopian church's founding to the Ethiopian eunuch baptized by Philip in Acts 8:26–39.

About four hundred years after the reign of the

[42] E. M. Blaiklock and R. K. Harrison, The New International Dictionary of Biblical Archaeology (Grand Rapids, MI: Zondervan Publishing House, 1983), pp. 409–410.

Queen of Sheba, in 542 B.C., the gigantic dam that blocked the Adhanat River in Sheba broke. It destroyed the very prosperous spice industry, leaving the desert to creep over the irrigated fertile lands.

TRADE AGREEMENTS MOTIVATED QUEEN OF SHEBA?

The Sabeans are credited with domesticating the camel so that the fifteen-hundred-mile run up to Jerusalem on the old Arabian Incense Road became a fast and profitable route for moving incense, spices, gold, and precious stones. Thus, the real reason for the Queen of Sheba coming to see King Solomon probably was to strike trade agreements to let her country's merchant camel caravans export to Israel and to pass through Israel en route to Egypt, Phoenicia, and Syria without being overtaxed.

In 1957 a southern Arabian cuneiform clay seal was discovered dating back to 900 B.C., the time of the Queen of Sheba, clearly establishing that hers was a literate civilization. Also, the Ethiopian national history, known as the Royal Chronicles of Ethiopia, incorporating the *Kebra Nagast* (*The Book of the Glory of the Kings*), indicates that the Queen of Sheba also became the Queen of Ethiopia.

Ancient Hebrew tradition is that King Solomon married the Queen of Sheba, just as he had married seven hundred other royal foreign wives for political reasons. The biblical basis for this tradition is that before she left, King Solomon gave the Queen of Sheba the "desire of her heart."

The tradition reports that they had a son. This is

where the Ethiopian connection becomes really fascinating.

Grant R. Jeffrey, host of the TV show *Appointment with Destiny,* has made researching the Ethiopian connection a special focus. He says:

> The official national epic of Ethiopia tells us that the ancient Ethiopian monarchy is descended from King Solomon. The late Emperor Haile Selassie claimed he was the Lion of Judah and was descended from King Solomon through the Queen of Sheba and Prince Menelik I.

A REPLICA MADE OF THE ARK?

Grant Jeffrey reports:

> The Royal Chronicles of Ethiopia make a very amazing statement. They claim that when Prince Menelik was nineteen years old he wanted to leave Jerusalem and his father, King Solomon, to become the king of Ethiopia. King Solomon had his craftsmen make a perfect replica of the ark of the covenant. This ark of the covenant, looking exactly like the real one, was, according to the Ethiopians, mysteriously switched.

The Ethiopians claim some of the priests literally substituted the new replica into the Holy of Holies. The next day when King Solomon and the Israelites thought that Prince Menelik was leaving for Ethiopia with the replica, he took the real one.

Is this possible? There is an unbroken historical tradition in the Royal Chronicles of Ethiopia that they have the ark of the covenant. There is an underground temple in the northern Ethiopian city of Aksum. This underground temple is underneath the church today called the Church of Zion of Mary. Many heads of state have come to visit this temple because it claims to contain the true ark of the covenant.

Jeffrey reveals some of the reasons why he believes the story:

Is there any historical or nonbiblical evidence that would support the Ethiopian history outside of their Royal Chronicles? I have a photo of a mural in Addis Ababa, the capital of Ethiopia, which shows the marriage of the Queen of Sheba to King Solomon. It also shows the ark being taken to Ethiopia, where it was left.

ETHIOPIANS CERTAINLY BELIEVE THEY HAVE THE ARK

Jeffrey continues:

Over the last several years I have interviewed Prince Stephen Mengesha of Ethiopia, Ephraim Lufemarian, a deacon from the church in Aksum in Ethiopia, plus over one hundred Ethiopians who have approached me or written to me. All, without exception, have told me that they believe they have the ark of the covenant.

What I can say as a researcher is that they do have an object that looks like the ark. They believe it is the ark, and they have a continuous unbroken historical record, with some proof behind it, that they have an object that is arklike. Could it be the real one, or is it a replica? We won't know until it is brought forth.

Based on an interview with Prince Stephen Mengesha, Jeffrey explains:

Prince Stephen Mengesha, the great-grandson of Emperor Haile Selassie, is one of the few survivors of the Selassie monarchy alive today. He was out of the country when the Communist coup occurred in 1974. Visiting in Toronto, he said, "The ark of the covenant is in the basement chambers of the Church of Zion of Mary in ancient Aksum for safekeeping. The ark guardian never leaves. A boy is selected at the age of seven to be the guardian of the ark for the rest of his life in the underground temple. The boy never leaves the ark until his death, when he is replaced by another boy. This has gone on without interruption for three thousand years.

"The ark guardian, the priests, my father, and Emperor Selassie told me it's the real ark. I know of several famous people who have visited the church to see it, including Queen Elizabeth and Prince Philip in 1965. Israeli agents repeatedly asked the emperor about the ark and suggested it was time to return it to Israel. My father's grandfather, the emperor, told them, 'I agree that the ark should be returned to the temple, but the correct time has not yet come.' "

Not all Bible scholars agree with Jeffrey in his conclusion that the ark of the covenant is most likely in Ethiopian hands. That is certainly the case with Jewish rabbis in Jerusalem, who have made their own claims about the location of the ark of the covenant, which we'll now investigate.

FOUND BY JEWISH RABBIS?

According to several contemporary Jewish rabbis, the ark of the covenant was hidden in a secret vault under the Holy of Holies in King Solomon's temple. The Holy of Holies is the innermost sacred room in the temple where the ark of the covenant had been kept. Using a variety of measurements, they have pinpointed to their satisfaction the exact location where the Holy of Holies would have been. They insist it is far enough away from the Dome of the Rock to permit the construction of another temple without interfering with the Muslim holy place.

As a result of an archaeological dig penetrating under the Temple Mount in Jerusalem in 1982, three Jewish rabbis insist they found the sacred temple treasures, including the ark of the covenant. The excavation activities nearly touched off a holy war between the Arabs and the Jews, so they had to stop the dig. They say they have been unable to resume excavation because of the Israeli government's reluctance to provoke further outbreaks between Muslims and Jews.

The main purpose for the dig was to discover original stones of the Solomonic temple in the Western Wall, according to Rabbi Yehuda Getz, chief rabbi of the Western Wall, who said:

> We were excavating fifty-seven feet underground when one
> of the workers moved a stone, and a huge amount of water

came out, and they saw a big room, an arch and a beautiful hall. This big vault was one of the main entrances to the first temple. Through this passageway they discovered the ark of the covenant.

We know exactly where the utensils are, including the lamps, ark of the covenant, possibly tablets and the manna tin, and the budding rod of Aaron.

Here's how Rabbi Shlomo Goren, former chief rabbi of the Israeli Defense Forces, describes the astounding discovery deep within that passageway under the temple mount:

I started digging just beneath the Temple Mount from the outside. We were very close to the place on the Temple Mount where the Holy of the Holies was located. We were very close, beneath the Holy of Holies.

We believe that the holy ark made by Moses, and the table from the temple, and the candelabra made by Moses, along with other very important items, are hidden very deep underneath the Holy of Holies. We started digging and we came close to the place; we were not more than thirty or forty yards away.

But unfortunately, when we came so close, the Arabs started rioting and disturbing us, and the government became afraid. And they stopped us and built a wall, and we had to stop digging. But I am sure if we could keep on digging, we would find tremendous results from the items from the temple.[43]

---

[43] *Interview with Schlomo Goren (by Jimmy DeYoung), July 22, 1991.*

Author Don Stewart reports as well on this tunnel-digging activity:

> Bible prophecy specialist David Lewis tells of a
> conversation with Rabbi Hacohen, one of the Jewish
> activists engaged in preparation for building a third temple.
> Speaking to Dr. Lewis and his tour group, Hacohen told
> about some of the excavations made underneath the
> Temple Mount.
>
> Lewis tells Hacohen's story: He told how he was working
> late at night with Rabbi Getz, a group of archaeologists,
> and rabbinical scholars . . . Hacohen told of how they
> were excavating along the lower level of the Western Wall.
> Passing through this doorway, the crew entered a fairly long
> tunnel. At the end of the tunnel, Rabbi Hacohen said, "I
> saw the golden ark that once stood in the holy place of the
> temple of the Almighty. It was covered with old, dried
> animal skins of some kind. However, one gold, gleaming
> end of the ark was visible." He could see the loops of gold
> through which the poles of acacia wood could be thrust so
> that the ark could be properly carried by the dedicated
> Levites.
>
> Hacohen and his friends went immediately to the home
> of then Chief Rabbi Shlomo Goren. The sleeping rabbi was
> awakened to hear the news that the holy ark of the
> covenant had been discovered! Goren told the excited
> group that preparations had already been made for such an
> event. The ark would be carried out in triumph, by
> members of the tribe of Levi, the very next morning. But
> the next morning brought a shock to the group as they
> went to the tunnel!
>
> Lewis explains: "They found that during the night, the

Muslims had erected a wooden frame and prepared a concrete wall, sealing off the tunnel that would give access to the ark of the covenant."[44]

That particular wall was clearly built to prevent access to whatever might be in the tunnel and its secret vault, for finding it could increase the Jewish claim on the Temple Mount.

Grant Jeffrey provides a reason why the Jewish rabbis believe the ark is in a secret vault under the temple area.

The possibility is that the ark of the covenant has been under the Temple Mount during this whole period. There is a passage in the Bible in 1 Chronicles, chapter 35, that suggests that King Josiah was involved in moving the ark of the covenant underneath the temple. There is a tradition in the Mishna Torah that this ark was placed under the wood chamber in the original place where the temple stood.

Exuding the same assurance that the ark of the covenant has been found is J. David Davis, leader of B'nai Noah Community in Athens, Tennessee, who has been researching Christian origins for twenty-five years and did archaeological work in Israel from 1986 to 1991:

As an official representative of the Temple Institute in Jerusalem, I am not aware of any plans to rebuild the ark

---

[44] Don Stewart, In Search of the Lost Ark (Orange, CA: Dart Press, 1992), p. 259.

of the covenant. The question would be why. The answer is that they know where the ark is now.

In *Ready to Rebuild,* Thomas Ice and Dr. J. Randall Price write:

> Rabbi Getz still says to this day that he knows exactly where the ark is located. He does not want to reveal the precise location for fear that the Muslims would steal or destroy the ark and other temple treasures. He has confirmed that the ark's supposed hiding place is known to the Israeli government, but that it decided the issue was too politically volatile and closed the case, allowing Arab authorities to block the entrance. The announcement would eventually cause worldwide media attention to be focused on the already sensitive Temple Mount area and could provoke "premature" action by fringe groups wanting to build the temple.[45]

After the initial interviews and media exposure, the rabbis have significantly backed off on their claim of having found the sacred pieces from the temple, including the ark of the covenant. Are they experiencing some doubts about what they have found? Have the Israeli authorities muzzled them?

We have examined the evidence for the ark of the covenant and how it might have disappeared. Here's what we have discovered:

---

[45] *Thomas Ice and J. Randall Price,* Ready to Rebuild *(Eugene, OR: Harvest House Publishers, 1992), p. 147.*

- The Israelites had the technical skills to make a sophisticated, gold-covered ark of the covenant during their wanderings in the Sinai Desert, after escaping from Egypt.
- The ark of the covenant was still a revered object during King David and King Solomon's time, with the historical validity of their rule archaeologically established.
- Israeli rabbis insist they have seen the ark in an area underneath the ancient site for the temple's Holy of Holies on the Temple Mount.
- Ethiopian sources report the ark was brought to Ethiopia by Prince Menelik, son of King Solomon and the Queen of Sheba. Today, Ethiopians say, it is in a special room under the Church of Zion in Aksum.

Yet what does it mean if the original ark of the covenant does surface again?

WHAT IMPACT, IF FOUND?

The ark of the covenant is not only a symbol of God's presence. It represents the glorious religious heritage of the Jewish people. And for Christians it represents a link in God's plan of redemption, the atonement by blood. If it were found, what might the repercussions be?

For Christians, it would be another proof of the validity of the biblical record. As such, it would confirm their faith in the Bible. But it could also signal that the third temple was about to be built.

Author and chairman of the 1992 Annual Temple

Conference in Jerusalem, Bible scholar Chuck Missler says:

> Biblical scholars who take the Bible seriously have been looking for a critical series of events:
>
> 1. Israel to be reestablished in the land. Since May 14, 1948, this has been under way.
> 2. Israel to regain biblical Jerusalem. This was a result of the Six-Day War, June 7, 1967.
> 3. The temple to be rebuilt. Their preparations have begun.

For the Jews awaiting the rebuilding of the temple and the coming of the Messiah, it would give tremendous impetus to find a way to rebuild the temple so that, according to their teaching, the Messiah could come.

The Arab Muslims in Jerusalem and throughout the Middle East, on the other hand, fear that finding the lost ark would dramatically reduce their claim on the Temple Mount. After all, the Dome of the Rock, one of their most holy mosques, is located on the Temple Mount. Any attempt to rebuild the temple on the Mount could result in another outbreak of hostilities, possibly even a holy war.

Will the lost ark of the covenant be found in our lifetime? Who will open it if it is found? Will that person be struck dead like Uzzah was in King David's day? What will be found in it? How will what is found change each one of us? More mysteries to ponder. . . .

From a hidden room under the earth to a spaceship on the moon, the Bible continues to fascinate and excite our imagination. According to some, science is the downfall of the Bible; others contend the Bible is the source of important scientific considerations. We'll look at this seeming contradiction.

15

AN OBSTACLE
THAT BECAME A MIRACLE

*The idea that the Jordan River stopped flowing
to let Joshua and the Israelites cross on dry
land is one reason to question the entire book
of Joshua.*

William B. Lindley
Editor, *Truth Seeker*

ONE OF THE TRULY ASTONISHING MYSTERIES OF the Bible, and totally unverifiable by on-site digging, is the Bible's account of the crossing of the Jordan River on dry land by the Israelite nation.

Even before that crossing story we have another mystery—how desert nomads who had lived off the land for forty years were transformed into a disciplined army. These nomads, the Bible says, first developed the military muscle to defeat entrenched forces in cities in the Negev Desert south of Canaan. Then these campaign-hardened troops overran established cities in Canaan. Many consider these military victories as great a miracle as the walls of Jericho collapsing after a shout.

No wonder critics have been sniping at this series of biblical episodes for centuries. Typical of the skeptics is William B. Lindley, contributing editor of *Truth Seeker* magazine, a publication that examines unexplained phenomena. He has a masters degree in physics from California Institute of Technology. As quoted earlier, Mr. Lindley states, "The idea that the Jordan River stopped flowing to let Joshua and the Israelites cross on dry land is one reason to question the entire book of Joshua."

Another approach is that taken by Fred Acquistapace, author of *Miracles That Never Were.* He writes:

> There are several natural ways the river could have stopped flowing. . . . At the city of Adam, sixteen miles upstream, there are clay banks on the sides of the river. These banks are about forty feet high and are subject to landslides. During flood season, the water was known to undercut the banks, collapsing into the river and blocking the flow. . . .
>
> In Joshua 1:10–11 I see a plan to send men upstream, undercut the clay banks, and block the river long enough for the people to cross to Jericho. . . . I think the river was blocked on purpose so the people could cross, and they were probably unaware that Joshua had planned the whole thing. Joshua was a good leader, so he prepared the people, and when the flow stopped, the people made their move. Moses and Joshua sent spies into Canaan, and they learned about the clay banks at Adam. Joshua used this information to impress and inspire his people. Perfect timing was necessary, and Joshua was well prepared to handle the job.[46]

From the perspective of logic, the positions of Lindley and Acquistapace are not unusual. Yet Dr. Amos Nur, chairman of the department of geophysics at Stanford University in California, has information that should catch even the attention of critics:

> Normally the Jordan River flows far too swiftly to permit a crossing, but during the aftermath of an earthquake, the

---

[46] Fred Acquistapace, Miracles That Never Were *(Santa Rosa, CA: Eye-Opener Books, 1991), p. 82.*

river has stopped flowing many times. In 1906 it stopped for two full days. There is no doubt in my mind that the Jordan's flow stopping in Joshua's day was due to an earthquake.

Before we get in deeper with critics and defenders, we must tackle some unfinished business. We left Moses communicating with God from the mercy seat of the ark of the covenant—and following the cloud, the visible manifestation of God's presence, from oasis to oasis in the desert. There must have been other tribal groups living on oases and in cities on the route to Canaan. Did they simply provide the Israelites safe passage through their territory, or did they resist the intrusions into their territory?

Let's join Moses, Aaron, and Joshua as they might have prepared to face their first military crisis since crossing the Red Sea.

THE BATTLE IS JOINED

Moses and Aaron were sitting in their pavilion, with Joshua standing next to them, when a young man rushed up to the guard and whispered in his ear. The guard opened the tent flap and let the young man in. He bowed to Moses and Aaron and said, "The Amalekites are preparing for battle. We saw them assembling their army. They will be ready to attack us in no more than two days." He paused to catch his breath.

"Good work, Dan. I knew I could depend on you and Samuel to keep an eye on them," Joshua said. "How big is their army, do you think?"

"They will outnumber our trained men," Dan responded, "but the Lord is on our side."

"Thank you for your report. You may go now." Joshua dismissed him with a wave of his hand.

Moses looked at Joshua. "What progress have you made in training the men for battle?" he asked.

"The men are eager to learn, but only a few of them served in the Egyptian army," Joshua replied. "Using those with experience as unit leaders, we have been teaching the rest how to use the sword and other defensive weapons. This will be their first test."

"Go and organize your men to repulse the attack by the Amalekites," Moses ordered. "I will go to the top of the hill in the morning and hold the staff out over the field of battle. With God's help you will defeat the Amalekites."

"Yes, my Lord, we will!" Joshua bowed and left the pavilion.

The next morning it quickly became evident that the green troops led by Joshua had their hands full. They were making progress in repulsing the Amalekites when suddenly the battle turned and the Israelites began giving ground.

Aaron quickly saw what was happening. "Moses, the tide turned against our brave men as soon as you let your arms and the staff down," he cried. "Put your arms up again."

As soon as Moses raised his arms, the battle lines shifted remarkably, with the Israelites again getting the upper hand.

"Amazing!" Aaron said. "Now we've got to find a way

to keep your arms up. Why don't you sit down on that large rock? Hur and I can prop up your arms."

Moses moved over to the rock and sat down. Aaron and Hur sat beside him and held up his arms. By evening the Amalekites were in full flight and the Israelites had captured those unable to run.

TRAINING AND EXPERIENCE PAY OFF

Miracle or motivation? That's the question in respect to Moses' arms being held up while Joshua's army fought the Amalekites. Austin Miles, noted author and Bible critic, writes:

> As for Moses' rod that he held in the air, this cannot be substantiated in any reliable literature or written reports. . . . Moses represented stability and strength. As long as they could see him standing on the hilltop with his arms upraised, they felt secure, the adrenaline flowed, strength flowed through them and they prevailed.
>
> The rod he held was symbolic of God's mystical power, and the people reacted. It probably was not necessary for the rod to send forth magical power. God was able to use the natural strength of the people, maximize it with mental stimulation, and see them victorious.

That naturalistic explanation overlooks the biblical record, for in Exodus 17:16 we read, "He [Moses] said, 'For hands were lifted up to the throne of the Lord. The Lord will be at war against the Amalekites from generation to generation.' " Over the next nearly forty years in the desert and on the plains of Moab opposite Jericho, Joshua's training and the experience fighting the Amalekites paid off, according to the biblical account. They defeated one tribal king after another as they made their way to Canaan.

In time they arrived on the plains on the other side of the River Jordan from Jericho, adjacent to the kingdom of Moab, which was inhabited by Midianites. Hearing of the relentless march of the Israelites and their conquest of one tribal king after another, Balak, the Midianite king of Moab, feared for his kingdom.

A CURSE BECOMES A PROMISE

Balak wiped perspiration from his brow. He looked deeply troubled as he shifted restlessly on his throne. His military commanders stood in front of him, waiting for the king to speak.

"Does any one of you have a military defense that will thwart any Israelite attack, now that they have arrived at our border? Your scouting reports indicate they are a much larger group than I had anticipated. Their sheep and goats will quickly overgraze the area where they are, and that dramatically increases the potential for a border incursion."

"Your Excellency, we have studied the reports of their defeat of King Sihon and King Og and their forces. They are the most potent armed force to approach our borders in our memory. And they fight like men possessed," replied Jared. "We need the help of the gods if we are to go into battle against them, or they will overwhelm us."

"What kind of help do you suggest?" Balak asked.

One of the other commanders responded. "We have an idea, Your Excellency. Our intelligence reports that there is a sorcerer named Balaam who has a remarkable record. When he curses someone, that person is cursed, and when he blesses someone, that one is blessed. We recommend you send for Balaam, reward him handsomely, and have him curse the Hebrews. Maybe then we could defeat them in battle."

"Great idea. I'll send for him immediately," Balak said.

The next evening the messengers arrived at the home of Balaam. He greeted them cordially, set out food, and entertained them hospitably.

"Your reputation as a great sorcerer has reached the ears of King Balak," said the leader of the emissaries. "Our king has sent us to you because an extraordinarily large group of people have come out of Egypt and settled next to our kingdom. They have defeated every king who has attempted to halt their progress. Without your help, they will be too powerful for us. King Balak will reward you handsomely if you will come and put a curse on them."

Balaam bowed and said, "I need time to talk to the Lord. Stay for the night, and tomorrow morning I will give you the answer I receive from the Lord."

The next morning Balaam reported, "I cannot go with you. I must do what my God tells me, and he has told me not to curse the Israelites."

Disappointed, the emissaries returned to Balak, who sent back an even more powerful group of emissaries, including several princes. This time the Lord agreed that

Balaam could return with the men, but only on condition that he "do only what I tell you."

The next day Balaam mounted his donkey, and accompanied by servants, set out to meet the king of Moab. He had not gone far when his donkey veered to the left and headed into a field. Chagrined, Balaam beat her and guided her back to the road. A little later they were going through a vineyard with walls on both sides, when the donkey again veered to the left, crushing Balaam's foot against a wall. Now Balaam was angry, and beat the donkey unmercifully.

Sometime later, they were riding through an even narrower passageway when the donkey lay down. Balaam in another fit of anger beat the donkey. His staff was raised when he heard the donkey say, "What have I done to make you beat me three times?"

Balaam was so angry that he exploded, "You have made a fool of me. If I had a sword, I would have killed you."

"But, sir, am I not your faithful donkey? Have I been in the habit of doing this before?" the donkey inquired.

"No," said Balaam, by now puzzled by the turn of events. As he said that, the Lord opened his eyes, and he saw the angel of the Lord standing in the road with a drawn sword. Balaam fell on his face.

"Why have you beaten your donkey three times? I have come to oppose you because you are on a reckless and dangerous mission," the angel said. "If the donkey had not turned aside, I would have killed you by now."

Balaam acknowledged his sin, inquiring if he should return. The angel gave him permission to go on, but again warned Balaam to speak only the words God gave him.

True to his word, despite repeated blandishments from King Balak, the man of God spoke only blessing on Israel. [Numbers, chapters 23 and 24] In one of his oracles he even forecast the coming of the Messiah through Israel. [Numbers 24:17] Yet the Bible later indicates Balaam suggested that Moabite women seduce Hebrew men and thus bring God's judgment on them. [Numbers 31:15–16] This proved extremely effective, with God's judgment resulting in the death of twenty-four thousand Hebrew men.

Sometime later Moses urged Joshua and his men to attack the Midianites living in Moab. A new generation born in the desert had learned desert warfare from their fathers. They not only thoroughly defeated the Midianites inhabiting Moab, they also killed Balaam, who had clearly accepted a rich reward from King Balak.

So the Joshua-led Israelite forces represented vigorous young men who had distinguished themselves in desert warfare. The report of their battle successes had preceded them and sent waves of fear into the cities on the west side of the Jordan, including Jericho. Joshua's men fully expected to march triumphantly into the land promised them through Moses.

Then the unexpected happened.

A NEW LEADER IS APPOINTED

"Moses," God said in one of his periodic communications with the leader of the Israelites, "you are not permitted to cross the Jordan into the Promised Land because of your disobedience. When you had no water at Kadesh in the Desert of Zin, I asked you to speak to the rock. Instead, you struck the rock with your staff. Water gushed out and everyone drank because of my love for you."

Moses bowed his head in extreme disappointment. The severity of the punishment for that one disobedience stunned him. After a minute or two, he asked, "But please, may I at least see the land for which I have given my last forty years?"

"You will do that, but first you must appoint a successor. I want you to take Joshua to Eleazer and in the presence of the people anoint him to succeed you," God said.

Though he was extremely disappointed he could not enter Canaan, Moses took courage from the selection of the man he had trained for leadership. Joshua had proved he could not only lead an army, he had the faith in the God of Israel that would help him make the transition after Moses was gone.

As one of his final acts of leadership, Moses wrote a song that he and Joshua recited for the people. Then he extended his arms and blessed all the tribes in the name of the Lord. He left the camp to climb Mount Nebo, from where God showed him the land of Canaan. The Bible says God buried him in Moab, with no one there to determine exactly where.

FABRICATED STORIES
OF ENEMIES?

Yet were the enemies described in the Bible really inhabitants of the Sinai and the Negev—present-day Saudi Arabia? What proof do we have that the Amorites, Midianites, Amalekites, and all the others mentioned in the Bible were really desert dwellers?

Dr. Gerald Larue, emeritus professor of biblical history at the University of Southern California, doesn't think so. Dr. Larue says:

> It's important to remember that the Joshua story is temple literature. It was written by priests for use in the temple. The archaeologists like Kathleen Kenyon, who investigated the site, found absolutely nothing that indicates that the Hebrews invaded Canaan.

Many archaeologists, following the lead of the famous British archaeologist Dame Kathleen Kenyon, agree. However, in the next chapter we will examine in some detail the latest discoveries by Syro-Palestinian archaeologist Dr. Bryant Wood, which throw some new light on the subject. But first we must investigate the mysterious crossing of the Jordan on dry land at the time of the year when the Jordan was a swiftly flowing river.

A NARROW ESCAPE

As preparations continued for the expected attack on Jericho, Joshua remembered his days as a spy in Canaan forty years earlier.

At that time he was concerned only about getting himself and a couple of companions across the Jordan River. Now he was faced with moving the entire Israeli nation across and, as if that weren't enough, mounting an attack on the well-fortified city of Jericho shortly thereafter. It would indeed require a flawless plan—and a miracle from God.

A light breeze wafted the sounds of children at play into the open tent where Joshua was meeting with his military leaders. "The time for us to cross the Jordan River has come. But before we do that, we must send a couple of our men to Jericho to reconnoiter the city. Whom do you suggest?" Joshua asked.

"I'm convinced that Issachar and Ephraim can do that for us," Caleb replied. "They are extremely intelligent, brave men who have already distinguished themselves as spies in our desert warfare."

"Bring them to me," Joshua ordered.

A messenger tracked down Ephraim and Issachar and brought them to Joshua.

"Your assignment is to get into Jericho undetected, mingle with the people in the marketplace, and discover what their mood is," Joshua said. "Keep a sharp eye out for special defensive installations that we need to be aware of when we breach the city walls. And find out if there are any weak areas that could be attacked successfully."

The men left for their tents. Since it was harvest time they decided to disguise themselves as local farmers bringing grain into the city. They slipped into Jericho easily enough with the other farmers, and when nightfall came they found lodging with Rahab, a prostitute. A suspicious merchant, however, sent word to the king of Jericho.

"I encountered two men today who are clearly up to no good. Based on their accent, I suspect they are spies sent by the Hebrews encamped on the other side of the Jordan River. I had one of my servants follow them, and they are spending the night at the prostitute Rahab's house," he reported.

The king immediately called in one of his officers. "I want these men brought to me at once," he ordered.

Half an hour later the officer was banging on Rahab's door. When she opened it he pushed his way inside.

"Where are the men who have taken lodging in your house? I am to bring them to the king, since they are clearly spies sent by the Hebrews." His eyes searched every corner of the room.

"Oh, yes, two men did come here for a bite to eat," Rahab responded, "but I did not bother to ask them from where they came. They left at dusk to get out of the city before the gates closed."

The officer searched the house, but found no one. Disappointed, he returned to the king, who immediately dispatched a patrol to try to catch up with the men on the road to the river. Then the city gate was closed.

Meanwhile, Rahab rushed to the roof of the house, where she had hidden the men under stalks of flax. "They are after you," she told them, "but I know that the Lord is with you. We have all heard the reports of your progress from Egypt to the River Jordan, how you have defeated every king en route. Our hearts melted with fear when your people arrived on the other side of the Jordan River. I know that the God of Heaven will give you the victory and you will destroy this city as well. But, please, do me a favor, save me and my family in return for my hiding you."

"Indeed we will," said Ephraim. "All we ask is that when you see us attack the city you hang a scarlet cord from your window. If you will do that, we will spare you and everyone in your house."

"Thank you! And now you must go," Rahab said urgently. "I will let you down on a rope through my window in the wall. Head for the hills and stay low for three days. That will give the king's patrol time to search the area and return to the city."

Ephraim and Issachar did as instructed, safely fording the Jordan River. After three days they reported to Joshua.

"The Lord has most assuredly given us the whole land," they reported. "Morale of enemy troops is at an extremely low point because they have heard of our success against other kings and cities. Their lack of confidence will be in our favor when we attack the inhabitants of Canaan."

Yet how would they get across the river? After all, they had been desert dwellers for forty years, with no experience in crossing water barriers, except for that of Joshua and Caleb. They were the only ones who had personally seen how God had helped them go through the Red Sea on dry land.

NEITHER BRIDGE NOR BOAT?

Joshua and his leadership team were on a knoll overlooking the swollen Jordan River.

"Just look at that raging torrent," Caleb said. "The spies have come back with a positive report, but it looks as if we'll have to wait many months before we can cross the Jordan."

"I don't see the women and children getting across even if we form a human line through it. The spies were good swimmers, but we'd lose too many household goods in those waters," Eleazer added.

"The Lord has given us a plan," said Joshua. Everyone turned to him expectantly.

"The priests are to walk into the Jordan carrying the ark of the covenant. One thousand yards behind them we will send the advance party of troops. They will be followed by the rest of the people. The Lord has assured me that when the soles of the priests carrying the ark of the covenant touch the water, the Jordan will pile up in a heap to the north of us. Everyone will cross without incident."

"But the river is running so strongly. There's no way it will just stop flowing," Eleazar interjected.

"We must trust the Lord. God has assured me that just as he was with Moses when we crossed the Red Sea, so he will be with us now," Joshua responded.

The men shook their heads and looked at each other in disbelief. "But you still have not told us how we will cross the river!"

"Our first step is to move our camp," Joshua replied. "We are too far from the river to act quickly enough when God opens up the way for us. Once encamped right up against the river, I will let you know God's plan."

The next day the whole encampment broke up and

moved to the area next to the River Jordan. Everyone could now see that the river was running strongly.

A DOUBTER IN EVERY CAMP

"I cannot understand you men. It's as though you've taken leave of your senses," Hannah grumbled to her husband as she set up her cooking utensils. "We were doing fine at Shittim, with an abundant supply of water from the wells and pasture for our sheep and goats. Now you've let Joshua and his visionaries drag us here on the pretext that we will cross that river. I can't believe none of you has the guts to stand up to Joshua and make him see reality!"

"When God speaks to Joshua, Hannah, we must listen," her husband responded gently. "I have yet to see us go wrong when we followed Joshua's instructions."

Three days later messengers spread out through the camp with orders from Joshua: "We break camp again tomorrow and leave as quickly as possible after the day begins. As soon as you see the Levites carrying the ark of the Lord toward the River Jordan, begin to fall into line, tribe by tribe. Be sure to leave about a thousand yards between you and the priests carrying the ark. In the meantime, have everyone go through ceremonial purification tonight so you will be consecrated to the Lord and ready for him to act."

The next morning Joshua met with the Levites charged with carrying the ark of the covenant.

"You will lead the way to the river," he told them. "The Lord has told me that when your feet touch the waters of the Jordan River, the flow will stop, and you will be able to go down into the center of the river bottom. I want you to stop when you get there and let the people pass by you. You are to be the last to leave the river, for it will resume its flow after you are on the other side."

Then Joshua called together the leaders of the twelve tribes.

"Today you will see what the Lord will do for you." Joshua's instructions were very clear: "When you cross the Jordan River you will know that God will drive out the tribes now occupying the land of Canaan. Select one man from each tribe to pick up a large rock from the river bottom and deposit it on a pile on the other side as a memorial."

Their tribal position put Hannah and her husband in the first group behind the Levites carrying the ark of the covenant.

"We might as well have walked off into the desert, for all the good this will do," she asserted caustically. "That river won't give way to a bunch of priests even if they are carrying the sacred ark."

Her husband had learned not to argue, so he just kept moving with his family. Suddenly a shout went up and every eye focused on the river. The Levites were now at the edge of the river with the ark of the covenant held high.

"Look, the river is going down . . . I can't believe it," one of the people ahead of Hannah and her husband shouted. Everyone started running, hoping to see what was happening.

"It's like someone pulled a plug in the river . . . it's

draining away so quickly," one of the first at the bank of the river exclaimed.

Hannah refused to be stampeded. Her husband reluctantly stayed with her despite all the excitement up ahead.

"Just wait. It will all come back," Hannah insisted. "I won't believe it until my feet go up the other side."

An hour later Hannah and her husband were doing just that.

"Didn't I tell you that when God speaks to Joshua, he gives us the victory? I just know we are going to conquer all of the land ahead of us," her husband said, triumphantly, as they made their way to their new encampment in the land God had promised them.

WHAT STOPPED THE WATER?

Another fanciful priest story, or an event based on reality? Is there a natural phenomenon that could have caused the Jordan River to suddenly stop flowing?

In an article in *New Scientist*, Dr. Amos Nur writes:

During the 1927 quake, chunks of mud slid into the River Jordan near Damiya, about forty kilometers north of Jericho, and caused lesser damage that was remarkably similar to the damage inferred from historical descriptions of past earthquakes. There have been about thirty earthquakes with a similar destruction pattern in this area during the past two thousand years or so.[47]

[47] Amos Nur, "And the Walls Came Tumbling Down," New Scientist, *July 8, 1991, p. 46.*

Though the particular earthquake that may have dammed up the Jordan River cannot be identified, the frequency of quakes on this fault line makes Dr. Nur's suggestion plausible. It confirms that what the Bible records as history certainly could have happened.

Help for dating the crossing of the Jordan comes from another source, however. Gene Faulstich, director of Chronology-History Research Institute, says:

Astronomy is an exact science. Astronomers have been used to help historians date events, especially when ancient people tied that event to something like a solar eclipse. Present-day scientists can reconstruct the sky on computer screens so they can tell precisely to the minute when the event took place.

For some reason historians have not employed astronomers to help them in the evaluation of the dates in the Bible, even though the Bible has more events dated by astronomy than any other ancient history. Every Jewish date is based on the position of the sun and moon, and many of them are also tied to one of several Sabbath cycles of the Bible. Moses required ancient Israel to keep a count on every seventh day, and every seventh seventh year, called a Jubilee year. They also had to rotate their twenty-four sections of temple priests every week.

A straightforward reading of the Bible dating gives us 1461 B.C. for the date of the Exodus from Egypt, and 1421 B.C. for the crossing of the Jordan and the conquest of Jericho.

That the Israelites crossed the River Jordan is clear. Accepting the history of earthquakes repeatedly damming up the Jordan River helps us understand how it might have happened. Placing the event in real time by the dates provided by Gene Faulstich helps confirm that the event really happened.

Yet now that the Israelites have crossed the Jordan, another danger confronts the Hebrews. How will they attack Jericho, the gateway to Canaan and the oldest and most fortified city in all of Canaan?

The secret of the destruction of the walls of Jericho certainly merits a closer look!

16

THE SHOUT
THAT DESTROYED A CITY

All the shouting and trumpet blowing in the world will not cause fifteen-foot-thick walls to collapse.

Dr. Gerald Larue
Senior Editor, *Free Inquiry*

R<small>EPEATED</small> <small>AND</small> <small>EXTENSIVE</small> <small>ARCHAEOLOGICAL</small> <small>AC-</small>
tivity on the site of Jericho has convinced scholars that it
is man's oldest inhabited city. Yet none of the chapters in
its extended history intrigues man as much as one seven-
day period described in the Bible.

Truly one of the most debated mysteries of all time is
how a strategy whose final act was a shout succeeded in
breaking down the walls of Jericho. Only rubble covering the ancient site of Jericho, which has been repeatedly excavated by archaeologists, holds the clues to what
might have happened.

Skeptics find the story of the collapse of Jericho's
walls totally unbelievable on a variety of counts. They
agree with Dr. Gerald Larue (quoted above), emeritus
professor of biblical history at the University of Southern
California at Los Angeles, when he says, "All the shouting and trumpet blowing in the world will not cause
fifteen-foot-thick walls to collapse. The whole Joshua/
Jericho account is just a religious legend."

Not shaken by such criticism, Dr. Amos M. Nur,
world-renowned earthquake specialist and professor of
geophysics at Stanford University, Berkeley, California,
responds, "We have a great deal of evidence, scientific

evidence, that the walls of Jericho collapsed because of an earthquake exactly as the Bible describes it."

We'll examine some of that evidence more closely, later! But right now, let's take a look at what it must have been like to be part of the army of the Israelites when they faced the monumental task of attacking the fortress Jericho. The city was, after all, one of the most stoutly fortified and well defended cities in what was then the known world. At least some of the Israelites must have had some doubts about their chances of defeating it.

WHO WILL ATTACK WALLED JERICHO?

Three men emerged from a tent in the newly relocated encampment. In the distance the fortress of Jericho was clearly visible. There was no doubt it represented the gateway into Canaan.

"We have put ourselves into a terrible position," Zebulon said as he and two other men walked away from the tent. "Now we have the river at our back, with all of the armed cities of Canaan before us."

"You're right," Abner responded. "We are fair game for the armed men in Jericho. My counselors are suggesting we move south, that we begin with a smaller campaign. As we begin to win territory from the Canaanites, they will begin to panic. That way we can outflank Jericho, rob its leaders of their support from other kings in the region."

"If Joshua insists on attacking Jericho, we will waste the flower of our army on those walls. And it could take years before we starve them into submission. Better we attack less formidable positions than this one first," added Lothel.

"We need to hurry. Joshua is waiting," said Zebulon, picking up the pace at which he was walking. They joined the circle of other leaders already around Joshua.

"Good news, generals," was Joshua's welcoming comment. "Further intelligence confirms what the spies reported. The Amorite bastion of Jericho is ripe for assault."

He looked around at his men and could see skepticism.

STRANGE TACTICS INDEED

"By the first of the new moon, brave Zebulon—" Joshua started again, only to be interrupted by Masilah.

"That is a mere seven days away, sir."

"God made the entire universe in less than that," Joshua replied. "Let me say it again . . . in seven days Jericho will be ours." Joshua was firm in his intent.

"Do you have some news from the city that they are willing to give in without a fight, to sign a covenant with us?" Lothel asked, his tone of voice a mixture of challenge and mockery.

Joshua looked at Lothel, recognizing that Lothel spoke for many others.

"They scorn us and our presence," Joshua said matter-of-factly, "and they are as strong and well-supplied as we had imagined. The harvest is in, and they could withstand a siege for several years."

"Then how do we make this pagan fortress ours? Surely not by throwing ourselves against those high and remorseless walls?" Zebulon's voice took on a harder edge.

"With faith, my able and worried commanders." Joshua smiled as he looked each of them in the eye. "Our Lord God has spoken to me, and I will tell you of the plans . . . for we begin when the dawn comes up in the morning."

Joshua's generals looked at each other quizzically.

"By your leave, mighty Joshua," Lothel said deferentially, "we have less than twenty percent of our men ready to fight. It will take weeks before we can have the army up to full strength for such an assault."

"I understand the logic of your argument, Lothel, but this victory will not come by the strength of our arms, but through the power of our Lord God. That is why there will be no prizes taken, no looting, not one single omer of grain."

"No prizes, no rewards?" burst out Zebulon. "If the city is full of grain, it would feed our people for months!"

"Nothing is to be taken, my generals. Nothing," Joshua emphasized, his voice taking on a hard edge. "Under pain of death . . . nothing! Our only purpose is to destroy this abomination with the sword and with fire."

"But my lord," another general chimed in, "if we kill all the people, you will not be able to stop the looters. If our soldiers don't take the provisions, the gold and silver, the hangers-on that we have accumulated or those living in the region will. After all, we've been in tents in the desert for forty years and need to prepare to live in cities."

Joshua remained unpersuaded. "The people kept the booty from the Midianites, the Amalekites, and the Amorites," he said evenly. "They have enough to start over in Canaan. God wants to make Jericho an example for all time, so there will be no spoils taken. Is that clear?"

The gathering fell silent, but the exchange of glances between the generals revealed they remained unconvinced. Only Masilah seemed to sense the spirit permeating Joshua's warning.

"Perhaps we might know how the Lord would have us do this thing?" he asked.

Joshua signaled for all of them to draw closer. "The plan our Lord God has given me is most unusual, so listen carefully. We will start by marching around the city. Units of the army will be in front. The ark of the covenant will be put in the center of the march, carried by the Levites. Seven priests with rams' horns will be in front of the ark. The rest of our army will follow the ark of the covenant.

"For six days we will walk around the city of Jericho once each day. You must insist that everyone keep quiet. There will be no taunting of those watching from the walls, no response to their taunts, either. The only sound will be that of the rams' horns and the shuffle of feet and rattle of swords."

The men looked baffled. Finally Masilah asked, "But Joshua, how do we keep our armed forces muzzled for six days when they are being jeered at and taunted by the residents of Jericho on the wall?"

"You must tell them that on the seventh day they will have their chance," responded Joshua. "On the seventh day we will walk around the city seven times. After we have completed the seventh turn around the city, the rams' horns will sound for the last time, signaling that everyone is to shout as loudly as possible. The Lord will give us the city."

The preparations were completed just as Joshua ordered. For six days the line of march went silently around the great walls, except for the sounding of the rams' horn trumpets by the priests. The trumpets helped to drown out the jeers and taunts from those on the wall.

Inside the city of Jericho there was a lot less bravado than that displayed by the rabble on the wall. Though most of the residents carried on normal business and household duties, the atmosphere was tense. When Rahab went into the marketplace on the fifth day to get supplies for meals, she heard the chatter, the fears expressed by ordinary citizens.

"Can you believe what is going on? My husband says the Hebrews have been marching around the city silently for five days. I wonder what their god will do for them next!"

"The word is that their god stopped up the Jordan River and let them walk across it," said one woman as she picked over a display of grapes.

"My husband says the king is half frightened to death because the Hebrews have been so successful thus far. Nothing seems to stop them. But this is downright eerie," her friend added.

Rahab only smiled, for even though she did not know what would happen, she knew she and her family would be saved.

On the seventh day, the Israelites made seven circuits around the city. At the end of the seventh, the trumpets blared and the people shouted mightily. Suddenly there was a rumble. The earth started shaking. Feeling the earth moving under their feet, the armed men sensed something momentous was happening. Soon they saw buildings collapsing, bricks flying in every direction. Ramps of bricks appeared at regular intervals along the lower wall. With a shout of victory, the Israelite army stormed up the ramps into the city, killing everyone in sight, setting fires throughout the city.

Ephraim and Issachar had gained permission from Joshua to set up a special detachment of troops so they could enter the city near the window with the scarlet cord hanging in it. They clambered up the brick ramp near Rahab's house and quickly made their way to it. They banged on the door, and Rahab opened it.

"Ephraim! Issachar! I'm so glad you came," she exclaimed. "I've gathered my father and mother, my brothers and sisters and their families. Will you take care of all of us?"

"Indeed we will, for we promised that everyone in this house would be saved if the scarlet cord was in the window. Now let's collect everyone so we can accompany them back to the camp while the rest of our men press the attack," said Ephraim.

SCIENTIFIC EXPLANATION?

That's the essence of the biblical story. Can science shed any light on the mystery of how it might have happened? And can it tell us when it may have happened? Are there any secular records, in Egypt, for example, indicating an Israelite presence in Canaan after the destruction of Jericho, Ai, and other cities?

Earlier we quoted Dr. Larue, a scholar who is not ready to accept the biblical account as valid history. He insists:

> The temple literature attempted to explain why these walls fell down and related it to a person we know very little about, whom they call Joshua. You must remember that when you have a temple legend or myth, it is always reenacted.
>
> The temple ritual gave the basis for the reenactment of this particular event. You can almost see the priests carrying the ark of the covenant in the temple courtyard, preceded by men blowing the shofar and passing between the great lavers of water, as they reenacted this legend during the month of April, just before the Passover. So this becomes a teaching story.

Many scholars would agree with Dr. Larue. The story of the capture of Jericho is just too fantastic to be believed. Yet archaeological spadework and painstaking comparisons of materials and pottery found at the site of what is commonly accepted as Jericho give us new insights into what may have happened.

Dr. Bryant G. Wood, who gained his doctorate in Syro-Phoenician studies and has been a visiting professor in the Department of Near Eastern studies at the University of Toronto, is the author of *The Sociology of Pottery in Ancient Palestine*. He has made a special study of what the various archaeologists found at the Jericho site. Dr. Wood says:

> For many years scholars thought the story of Jericho was a mythical legend. When the archaeological evidence is properly interpreted, however, we find that it agrees with the biblical story in an amazing way.
>
> Even though Jericho is one of the oldest cities in the world, and there are many towns built one on another, we can still very precisely date the one that was destroyed by fire as described in the Bible.
>
> Jericho was a very well-fortified city, with two mud-brick walls surrounding it. The archaeological evidence indicates that those walls collapsed because of an earthquake. And, in fact, there are parts of the mud-brick wall still intact today.
>
> Imagine the city surrounded first by an outer stone wall about twelve feet high. On top of that was an inner mud-brick wall about eighteen feet high. Behind those walls was a sloping massive earthen embankment that surrounded the entire city. At the top of that embankment was another mud-brick wall about fifteen feet high. On the embankment below that top wall were houses where Jericho's outcasts, like Rahab the prostitute, lived. This is what the Israelites faced as they marched around the city.
>
> When archaeologists excavated at the base of the outer wall, they found piles of collapsed brick . . . ample evidence that the biblical record is entirely correct, for the Bible tells us that the walls fell flat.

GRAIN INDICATES SHORT SIEGE

Dr. Wood further reports:

Within the city they found a great quantity of grain, indicating there was a very short siege of the city. When armies laid siege to cities, they usually waited until just before the harvest, when supplies were at their lowest and the least amount of food was available. So it is very unusual to find large amounts of grain in ancient sites. In Jericho, however, we found great jars of grain in almost every building.

In addition, armies entering a city would usually plunder any grain still left after the siege. Yet the Bible tells us that the Israelites were forbidden to plunder the city, that anything valuable was to be offered up to God. That helps explain the great jars of grain still left in the city. This, of course, again supports the accuracy of the biblical account.

Within the city there is also much evidence of a great fire. The Bible tells us that when the Israelites went into the city, they set it on fire. Now even though these mud-brick walls had collapsed, the stone wall is still there today. How did the Israelites get over that? Well, the way the mud-bricks fell, they formed a ramp so the Israelites could merely go over the wall on these ramps and set the city on fire. Every detail that archaeologists have found agrees precisely with the biblical narrative.

Dr. Wood's statements are based on his extensive personal evaluation of reports on what was found at the site. But his dating of the final destruction of Jericho to the period when Joshua and the Israelites arrived in Canaan is based on his analysis of pottery unearthed by the various teams digging on the site. He has been particularly concerned about Kathleen Kenyon dating the destruction of Jericho well before the Israelites could have entered Canaan, a dating widely accepted by skeptics and critics of the conquest of Jericho. Dr. Wood writes:

> Based on Kenyon's conclusions, Jericho has become the parade example of the difficulties encountered in attempting to correlate the findings of archaeology with the biblical account of a military conquest of Canaan. Scholars by and large have written off the biblical records as so much folklore and religious rhetoric.
>
> Kenyon died in 1978 without living to see the final publication of her excavation of the site. Her conclusions were reported only in a popular book, published the year before she completed her fieldwork, in a series of preliminary reports, and in scattered articles.
>
> The detailed evidence, however, was never supplied. This became available only in 1982 and 1983 when two volumes on pottery excavated from the tell were published.[48]

And what does this detailed description of the pottery show? According to Dr. Wood, Kathleen Kenyon's opinion that Jericho had been destroyed before the Israelites arrived was based almost exclusively on the absence of pottery imported from Cyprus and common to the Late Bronze I period. To make matters worse, she

[48] Bryant G. Wood, "Did the Israelites Conquer Jericho?" Biblical Archaeology Review, March/April 1990, p. 49.

also based her conclusions on a very limited excavation area—two 26-foot-by-26-foot squares.

Dr. Wood concludes, "She based her dating on the fact that she failed to find expensive, imported pottery in a small excavation area in an impoverished part of a city located far from major trade routes!"[49]

FOUR TYPES OF EVIDENCE

Four types of evidence have convinced Dr. Wood that the Bible's account of the conquest of Jericho is indeed accurate:

- First and foremost is the ceramic data, which Dr. Wood now concludes validates a date of around 1400 to 1450 B.C., when he believes Joshua and the Israelites arrived at Jericho.
- A second consideration are the many layers of reconstruction after destruction by attackers, one on top of the other. The careful excavation work of Kathleen Kenyon identified twenty architectural phases, with three major and twelve minor destructions from Phase 32 to the end of the city. A fortification tower was rebuilt four times and repaired once, followed by areas of habitation rebuilt seven times. It is Dr. Wood's contention that all of this activity could not have been compressed into the one hundred years of the period earlier suggested, the Middle Bronze III period.

[49] *Ibid., p. 50.*

- Third, there is the scarab series discovered by an earlier archaeologist, John Garstang. Scarabs are small Egyptian amulets shaped like a beetle with an inscription, sometimes the name of a pharaoh, on the bottom. These scarabs can be dated right up to a pharaoh who died in 1349 B.C., indicating there were still people living there.
- Fourth, a carbon-14 sample from material at the site has been dated to 1410 B.C., plus or minus forty years.[50]

Dr. Wood concludes that "the correlation between the archaeological evidence and the Biblical narrative is substantial."

Earlier we mentioned Dr. Amos M. Nur's personal conviction that an earthquake caused the Jordan River to be dammed so the Israelites could cross. Dr. Nur says:

This same series of quakes did serious damage to the city of Jericho. You see, since 31 B.C. to the present, sixty-four earthquakes in the magnitude of the 6.8 range have been historically recorded. With modern instruments we are able to determine the magnitude of these ancient quakes. There is evidence that a big quake, one as strong as the 1906 San Francisco earthquake, a magnitude of 8.0, struck in that area during the 1400 B.C. time frame. I believe this was the Jericho quake in Joshua's day.

[50] *Ibid., p. 51.*

A CASE FOR SOUND VIBRATIONS?

Both Dr. Nur and Dr. Wood indicate an earthquake was probably responsible for weakening or cracking the city walls. Then why were the Israelites ordered to shout and blow their trumpets at the end of the seventh circuit of the city? Could the sheer volume of sound have caused enough vibration to cause the upper brick walls to collapse? Is it possible, as some scholars believe, that the earthquake so loosened the bricks that the sound vibration brought them tumbling down?

This shouting technique is not new. Talking too loudly on Mount Ararat, where Noah's ark came to rest in eastern Turkey, for example, caused rock slides and avalanches. And we have all seen the television commercial in which a singer breaks a glass by hitting a high note. Consider the following examples of the use of sound vibration:

- *The World's Last Mysteries,* a Reader's Digest book, reports about Tiahuanaco: "Soon after the Spaniards discovered the city, a Jesuit wrote that 'the great stones one sees at Tiahuanaco were carried through the air to the sound of a trumpet.' "[51]
- In the book *Cycles of Heaven* there is a description of a Swedish aircraft designer, Henry Kjellson, who observed Tibetan monks moving large

[51] The World's Last Mysteries *(Pleasantville, NY: Reader's Digest, 1981),* p. 138.

stone objects up the side of a mountain in a religious ceremony involving the use of trumpets and drums.[52]

- In the November 1980 issue of *Omni* magazine, there is a report that NASA scientists were experimenting with moving small particles by a procedure called "acoustic levitation."

Since the Israelites surrounded the city with a "mighty shout," accompanied by rams' horn trumpets, it is quite possible that the decibel level was high enough to make the mud-bricks in the upper walls vibrate enough to fall into a heap.

Still one more question remains. Are there any contemporary historical notes that the Israelites actually occupied Canaan during this time?

OTHER EVIDENCE FOR ISRAELITE OCCUPATION?

Egyptian history contains numerous mentions of Canaan. At various periods Egypt controlled the whole area. Yet not until the Merneptah stele was discovered in Egypt in 1896 did there appear to be any indication of Israelite settlement in Canaan after the period of the Exodus. The stele changed all that.

Frank J. Yurco describes the stele in an article in the *Biblical Archaeology Review* as follows:

[52] *Guy L. Playfair and Scott Hill*, Cycles of Heaven (*New York: St. Martin's Press, 1978*), p. 38.

The Merneptah stele, in the Cairo Museum, bears the oldest known written reference to Israel. Engraved with its current text in 1207 B.C.E., the 7.5-foot-high, black granite monolith was discovered in the ruins of Merneptah's funerary temple in western Thebes in 1896. Most of its hieroglyphic text celebrates Merneptah's defeat of the Libyans and their Sea Peoples allies in his fifth regnal year.

The text's last two lines, however, briefly mention an earlier, successful campaign into Canaan, including four victories that seem to be depicted on the Karnak wall: "Ashkelon has been overcome. Gezer has been captured. Yano'am was made nonexistent. Israel is laid waste, (and) his seed is not."[53]

The reference to the "four victories that seem to be depicted on the Karnak wall" refers to Dr. Yurco's careful work in restoring the original artwork and hieroglyphics on an ancient wall in Karnak, Egypt. The four battle scenes he uncovered clearly depict action against the Israelite cities. Because they match the names of the cities mentioned on the stele, they corroborate each other.

Dr. Nancy Heidebrecht, whose doctoral studies were in ancient Near Eastern languages and who has been a frequent guest lecturer in Israel, has been deeply involved in archaeological excavations. Based on her studies of the pottery of ancient Canaan, she says:

[53] *Frank J. Yurco, "3,200-Year-Old Picture of Israelites Found in Egypt,"* Biblical Archaeology Review, *September/October 1990, p. 27.*

There are certain hallmark pieces of pottery that we look for when we are trying to trace the Exodus event and the migration of Israelite peoples into Canaan.

One of these pieces is a little pilgrim flask, heavily painted and with a specialized shape. It comes from Cyprus and must have been used to ship some kind of product. When you find it in excavations when looking at the migrations of people into the land, it gives us a time frame for dating the migration.

Another piece is a Philistine beer mug. The Philistines were great beer drinkers. They fermented the beer right in the jug and then poured it out through a sieve. The Philistine pottery is very nicely painted. When we find a Philistine jug next to a poor reproduction, we know we have an Israelite copy, meaning the Israelites were present. More and more of these hallmark pottery pieces are being found. More evidence is being excavated daily that indicates the migration of the Israelites into the land of Canaan really happened.

The evidence is mounting. There is clear evidence in Egyptian writings that Israelites occupied Canaan when the Bible says they were there. The earlier date for the conquest presented in Chapter 15 of this book, page 315 —1421 B.C.—also fits with evidence of nomadic invaders destroying cities in Canaan at that time. The identification of an 8.0 magnitude earthquake as taking place that year supports both the damming up of the Jordan River and the destruction of the walls of Jericho.

Summing up, Dr. Wood demonstrates how archaeological evidence at the Jericho site correlates to the biblical story:

1. The city was strongly fortified. [Joshua 2:5, 7, 15; 6:5, 20]
2. The attack occurred just after harvest time in the late spring. [Joshua 2:6; 3:15; 5:10]
3. The inhabitants had no opportunity to flee with their foodstuffs. [Joshua 6:1]
4. The siege was short. [Joshua 6:15]
5. The walls were leveled, possibly by an earthquake. [Joshua 6:20][54]

Even now the evidence for the conquest of Canaan by Joshua and his army is growing by leaps and bounds. The fact that the Jordan River has been dammed up several times because of an earthquake certainly appears to make the Israelite crossing credible. The evidence for the walls of Jericho crumbling, as well as for a fire, is believable. The newest research and discoveries we have reported keep renewing our trust in the Bible as truly reliable.

[54] Wood, "Did the Israelites Conquer Jericho?" p. 51.

17

THE BIBLE—
A SCIENCE ALMANAC?

W<small>HEN</small> <small>COLONEL</small> <small>JAMES</small> <small>IRWIN</small> <small>QUOTED</small> <small>THE</small>
Bible from the moon, he was not the first member of the
scientific fraternity to tie the Bible to scientific achieve-
ment. In fact, for most scientists before Charles Darwin
and his theory of evolution, the Bible represented truth
they could rely on—and for some it triggered extraordinarily important discoveries.

The overwhelming majority of scientists today, however, consider the Bible totally out of touch with scientific fact. For them, the Bible is an out-of-date document
not worth bothering with. According to them, the discoveries of science have outpaced the elemental and allegedly faulty information in the Bible.

Yet even today an amazing number of leading scientists find the Bible's scientific information as current as
today's weather news. Read thoughtfully, the Bible provides an astonishing array of tips and insights on a wide
variety of technical and scientific subjects—information
that in some cases is thousands of years ahead of its
time.

THE EARTH—A SPHERE

Contrary to the general scientific opinion of the day, when Columbus sailed west across the Atlantic he believed the earth to be round. A Bible student who believed God had called him on a mission of discovery, Columbus was tipped off on what he would discover by verses like the one in Isaiah 40:22: "He sits enthroned above the circle of the earth, and its people are like grasshoppers. He stretches out the heavens like a canopy, and spreads them out like a tent to live in."

Commenting on this verse, Dr. Hugh Ross, an astrophysicist and author of *The Fingerprint of God,* says:

> In Isaiah 40:22 we are told that God looks down on the circle of the orb of the earth. Only a spherical earth would appear to be circular from above. This was not discovered or acknowledged until 2,200 years later when Columbus sailed the world, making the biblical prophet 2,200 years ahead of the science of his day.
>
> Other biblical astronomy statements that were not confirmed until this century are that the number of stars exceeds the billions [Jeremiah 33:22], that each star is different [1 Corinthians 15:41], that the earth floats in space [Isaiah 40:22], and that light is in motion. [Job 38:19–20]

Similarly, science educator Dr. Richard Bliss, author of twenty-five scientific articles and several books, including *Voyage to the Stars* and *Origin of Life,* comments:

It seems that the authors of this book [Isaiah] had a clear understanding of what the shape of the earth must be. Interestingly, they speak of the circle of the earth and the puny nature of its inhabitants. It seems as though the writer had a clear space platform from which to make his observations.

The key biblical reference regarding the earth in space is Job 26:7, where Job tells his friends, "He spreads the northern skies over empty space, he suspends the earth over nothing."

Paul A. Bartz, editor of *Bible-Science News* and managing editor of the nine-volume *Our Science Readers' Books* series, comments on this pronouncement by Job:

The earth floats in space, attached to nothing, surrounded by a thin layer of air. The word translated "firmament" in the King James Bible comes from a Hebrew root word which refers to the process of making a statue. In making a statue, the ancient artisan would take a soft metal-like gold and begin to pound thin sheets of it carefully onto a wooden form of the statue until the wood was completely covered by a thin, form-fitted layer of gold. The use of this word [firmament] puzzled many people until the earth was first viewed from space. Then we saw it—the earth suspended on nothing in space, surrounded by a thin, form-fitted layer—our atmosphere.[55]

---

[55] *Paul A. Bartz,* Letting God Create Your Day *(Minneapolis: ColorSong Productions, 1991), p. 138.*

AN EXPANDING UNIVERSE

Today we are involved in space exploration of the planet Venus and beyond. Our space vehicles take many years to reach even these planets in our solar system, giving us a little feeling for the vastness of the solar system. Yet before man even dreamed of solar systems beyond ours, the Bible indicated the vastness of the heavens. Job responds to one of his "miserable comforters" by describing the Creator God in action in the solar system: "He alone stretches out the heavens. . . . He is the Maker of the Bear and Orion, the Pleiades and the constellation of the south." [Job 9:8–9]

Walter H. G. Lang, founder of the Genesis Institute and Bible-Science Association, writes:

> The word for spread ("stretches" in NIV [New International Version of the Bible]) is in an imperfect tense in Hebrew, representing continued action. . . . In applying this to the statement in Job 9:8–9, it means that God is continually stretching out the heavens. There is no end. The heavens are continually expanding.[56]

According to Dr. Hugh Ross, whom we mentioned previously, "In Genesis and Hebrews we are told that the stars are uncountable. The Hebrews were capable of counting up into the billions, so that establishes that they believed the stars must be more numerous than tens of billions. And for thousands of years people were saying that there were only six thousand stars!"

[56] *Walter H. G. Lang, "Bible Science Relationships from the Book of Job," a paper presented at the Twin Cities Creation Conference.*

What Job and other biblical writers seem to have already known, we are still discovering. Writing on "The Largest Structures in the Universe," David and Linda Harris, international lecturers on scientific subjects, comment on recent discoveries of the size of the universe by astronomers: "Structures have been found lately that are larger than anything ever imagined by scientists. Many astronomers are finding it difficult to cope with such findings."[57]

EARTH'S WEATHER PATTERNS

Equally astonishing is the ancient Hebrews' knowledge of weather and rain patterns. Consider the way winds blow in cyclonic patterns. The writer of Ecclesiastes described it in chapter 1, verse 6: "The wind blows to the south and turns to the north; round and round it goes, ever returning on its course."

Larry Vardiman, professor of atmospheric science at the Institute for Creation Research in San Diego, comments:

> Ecclesiastes 1:6 tells us that winds blow in cyclonic patterns, something not confirmed until the late 1700s by none other than Benjamin Franklin. This cyclonic wind pattern is now easily seen in today's satellite photos.

Couple this with what the Bible reveals about the rain-evaporation cycle in Job's conversation with his

---

[57] *David and Linda Harris, "The Largest Structures in the Universe," an unpublished article.*

friends. Elihu, who is talking "on God's behalf," says to Job, "He draws up the drops of water, which distill as rain to the streams; the clouds pour down their moisture and abundant showers fall on mankind." [Job 36:27–28]

Responding to criticism, Job tells his friends, "He wraps up the waters in his clouds, yet the clouds do not burst under their weight." [Job 26:8] Ancient Job again responds to his friends:

> God understands the way to it, and he alone knows where it dwells, for he views the ends of the earth and sees everything under the heavens. When he established the force of the wind and measured out the waters, when he made a decree for the rain and a path for the thunderstorm. [Job 28:23–26]

Who would have imagined that ancient man would even think about the stress that would be extended upon a cloud to hold the rain within itself, the issue of wind velocity in relation to water flow, and how a thunderstorm moved on the face of the earth?

"This whole hydrologic cycle was not correctly understood until the late sixteen hundreds, when Edmund Halley, the famous astronomer, discussed it conceptually," says Dr. Vardiman. "The full mathematical explanation of the rain cycle was not developed until the late eighteen hundreds."

Add to that the ancients' references to hail, frost, and snow. Both Job's friend Elihu and the psalmist describe these weather phenomena. We read in the Psalms, "He spreads the snow like wool and scatters the frost like ashes. He hurls down his hail like pebbles." [Psalm

147:16, 17] Job's friend asks, "Have you entered the storehouses of the snow or seen the storehouses of the hail?" [Job 38:22]

Though they lived in an area we think of as hot and dry, these writers are clearly commenting from personal observation of the phenomena of rain, snow, and hail. Today we know a lot more about the beauty and geometry of snowflakes, but there is much more to learn.

THE BIBLE AIDS ARCHAEOLOGICAL DISCOVERY

Many dispute the accuracy of biblical information. Yet when the Bible is read carefully, it often leads to new discoveries.

Archaeologists, for example, had no idea about the extent of the tunnel system under Jerusalem. Yet the Bible led them to Hezekiah's secret water tunnels that kept the city supplied with water during a siege.

Dr. Nancy Heidebrecht, a professor at Southern California College and field archaeologist on several Holy Land excavations, says:

Second Kings 20:20 reports that in about 711 B.C. King Hezekiah of Jerusalem built a secret tunnel under the city to bring water into the city during a siege he was expecting from King Sennacherib of Assyria. Based on this brief mention in the Bible, archaeologists in 1880 discovered the 1,700-foot tunnel cut through the rocks.

Hezekiah's Tunnel, as it is known, is a remarkable engineering feat on a scale unknown in the rest of the world of Hezekiah's day. It took all the water from the Gihon Spring outside the city to an already fortified reservoir on the other side of the city through a 1,700-foot tunnel. According to archaeologist Dr. Amihai Mazar:

> This tunnel runs under the ridge of the City of David in extraordinary S-shaped curves. The hewing was carried out by two groups of laborers working from opposite ends until they met at a point which is easily discerned.
>
> Unlike most later water tunnels [in the Hellenistic and Roman periods], the almost 600-meter-long Hezekiah's Tunnel was cut without vertical shafts, making the work exceedingly difficult. . . . The dramatic moment in which the two groups met was perpetuated in the Siloam inscription, incised on the tunnel's wall close to its end. Written in poetic style, it is one of the longest and most important monumental Hebrew texts from the period of the Monarchy.[58]

INSIDE TRACK ON OCEAN CURRENTS

Worldwide shipping owes a great debt of gratitude to a young naval officer in the U.S. Navy who believed the Bible contained facts worth following up.

In 1839 Matthew Fontaine Maury was laid up because of a stagecoach accident. During this time his son frequently read to him out of the Bible. One afternoon the son read Psalms, chapter 8. When he came to verse

[58] Amihai Mazar, Archaeology of the Land of the Bible (New York: Doubleday, 1990), p. 483.

8, his father interrupted him, saying "Read that again." His son read, "The fowl of the air, and the fish of the sea, and whatsoever passeth through the paths of the sea."

"It is enough," said Maury. "If the Word of God says there are paths in the sea, they must be there, and I am going to find them."

Up to that time sailors had not yet charted ocean currents, nor had they discovered the advantage of using ocean currents to navigate. Maury knew from personal experience that it was important to discover these paths. Maury described his search as "nothing less than to blaze a way through the winds of the sea by which the navigator may find the best paths at all seasons."

An outgrowth of this research was the landmark book *The Physical Geography of the Sea,* published in 1855. It is considered a milestone in the beginning of the science of oceanography. Today Maury is considered the dean of all physical geographers and a great contributor to the science of meteorology. He has been called "the pathfinder of the seas." His dream to perpetuate oceanographic knowledge brought into existence the famous U.S. Naval Academy at Annapolis, Maryland.

All of this happened in the life of Matthew Fontaine Maury because he took the Bible seriously and determined to discover the reality of what it suggested in the scientific field.

A BOOK OF MEDICINE?

When Moses handed down the day-to-day rules for cleanliness in connection with handling ill people or dead bodies, God gave him instructions that could have saved possibly millions of lives through the ages if they had been implemented universally. God through Moses told the Israelites:

> For the unclean person, put some ashes from the burned purification offering into a jar and pour fresh water over them. Then a man who is ceremonially clean is to take some hyssop, dip it in the water, and sprinkle the tent and all the furnishings and the people who were there. He must also sprinkle anyone who has touched a human bone or a grave or someone who has been killed or someone who has died a natural death. . . . The person being cleansed must wash his clothes and bathe with water, and that evening he will be clean. [Numbers 19:17–19]

What Moses taught was that those who made contact with "unclean" people and dead people had to wash themselves thoroughly. The water used contained a mild solution of lye, and the hyssop they used to sprinkle it contained a powerful antibacterial and antifungal agent.

Approximately 3,400 years later in 1847, Dr. Ignaz Semmelweis, a Hungarian physician, was disturbed that one out of every eight women died in childbirth of what was called "child bed fever." His research revealed that doctors were not cleaning their hands or instruments between patients. When Dr. Semmelweis instituted a policy requiring clean hands and instruments for each patient, the mortality rates immediately dropped to near zero. Medicine finally caught up with the Bible!

THE AMAZING EYE

Long before modern ophthalmologists discovered the extraordinary features of the eye, Jesus indicated the remarkable nature of the eye when he said, "The eye is the lamp of the body. If your eyes are good, your whole body will be full of light. But if your eyes are bad, your whole body will be full of darkness." [Matthew 6:22–23]

Only recently have we begun to understand the complex functions of the eye and how it "lights up" the body. Dr. Paul A. Bartz in *Letting God Create Your Day* writes:

> Computer scientists have learned that before one single image is ever sent to your brain, each cell of your retina must perform a huge number of calculations. Each second every cell of your retina performs ten billion calculations! Dr. Joseph Calkins, professor of ophthalmology at Johns Hopkins University, estimates that the fastest Cray supercomputer in the world would require many hundreds of years to do what the cells in your retina do each second.[59]

FOUNDATION SOCKETS FOR THE EARTH?

It has taken geologists many years to discover what Job learned from God possibly four thousand years ago. When God was quizzing Job about his knowledge of nature and the universe, he asked:

---

[59] *Bartz,* Letting God Create Your Day, *p. 183.*

Where were you when I laid the earth's foundation? Tell
me, if you understand. Who marked off its dimensions?
Surely you know! Who stretched a measuring line across it?
On what were its footings set, or who laid its cornerstone?
[Job 38:4–6]

Again according to Walter H. G. Lang, founder of
the Genesis Institute:

The Hebrew word there is *edeenah*. This is not the regular
word for foundation. . . . Mostly it is used for the sockets
which held the staves of the tabernacle in place. . . . In
[the Book of] Songs [or Song of Solomon] 5:15 [the "Love
Song" of the Old Testament], it is used for the sockets of
the legs of the ideal king. Down through the centuries
commentators have claimed this has no scientific meaning.
They felt it was part of the remarkable poetry of Job, but
no more than that.

In 1964, when the great Alaskan earthquake hit on Good
Friday, with 8.6 violence on the Richter scale, seismographs
were going all over the world. When the people who
manned and studied these instruments compared notes,
they came to the conclusion more than ever that mantle
rock [the layer of hard rock surrounding the core of molten
rock] is the foundation rock of the earth. . . .

When the *Glomar* drilling ship drilled in the Atlantic
Ocean in 1969, five years later, they hit mantle rock for the
first time. Their seismographs showed that under the
continents this mantle rock is three hundred miles deep,
indicating a virtual socket of mantle rock under each of the

seven continents. This is a remarkable confirmation of a truth found in the Bible.[60]

EVEN INSECT INFORMATION

For centuries the ant has been presented as a superb example of the importance of diligent work habits. But Proverbs 6:6–8 also mentions another kind of activity: "Go to the ant, you sluggard; consider its ways and be wise! It has no commander, no overseer or ruler, yet it stores its provisions in summer and gathers its food at harvest."

Skeptics of the Bible scoffed at that verse, saying there were no ants that gathered and stored food. Now entomologists have discovered three species of ants that do gather and store food—and two of the three species are native to Israel, where the Bible was written.

Scientists who accept that the Bible contains valid information continue to be amazed at the unique information unearthed by careful study. When they compare this information with what they have discovered in their scientific studies, their faith in the Bible is repeatedly validated.

In a unique turn of events, the Bible is confirming scientific discoveries about our earth and its environment, as well as often opening the door to new discoveries in a variety of scientific fields.

Still other discoveries await us as we pursue ancient

[60] Lang, "Bible Science Relationships," p. 4.

secrets of the Bible. Some of them have to do with marrying the biblical record with new scientific discoveries. In the next chapter we will overcome another of these barriers.

EPILOGUE

IS THE BIBLE AN ACCURATE HISTORY?

WHERE WERE YOU ON THE CONTINUUM OF FAITH when you started reading this book? You may have been a true skeptic, an "I need to be convinced" Christian, or a true believer who enjoys reading about secrets and mysteries that confirm your faith. Your personal assessment of the evidence for the accuracy of biblical history may also vary based on any number of factors.

On one fact we can all agree: Mysteries, biblical or not, normally remain somewhat mysterious despite our best efforts to explain them. That is, of course, especially true of biblical mysteries, since they typically have a strong element of miraculous activity involved.

The fact is, even contemporary mysteries have a similar element of the mysterious that defies explanation. For example, why are some people healed when they pray, while others are not? Why are some people rescued at sea after weeks under a broiling sun, while others disappear? Can we believe people who insist they met a person who, after some conversation or special help, disappeared abruptly? Was it an angel who took on human form for a special assignment?

How much more truth do we expect when we are investigating mysteries of antiquity? The Bible certainly has its share! The question is, can the biblical stories of extraordinary achievements, of citywide or even nation-wide destruction, be examined and verified as accurate by scientists and archaeologists? We've tackled several of these biblical mysteries, believing they would provide not only interesting reading, but also a firmer foundation in the Bible as an accurate document.

Yet being able to scientifically explain a mysterious biblical event does not take away the miraculous nature of the event. Rather, it clarifies it in terms of how God might have performed such a miracle. Investigating and clarifying the miracles of controversial Bible stories not only shows the hand of God at work, but strengthens our faith in these accounts as well as the overall message of the Bible.

So let's ask the question again: Can the Bible be trusted when we read its historical sections?

The answer is, it really depends on your criteria for proof. Let's take a quick tour of the evidence for solving the biblical mysteries we highlighted in this book.

SODOM AND GOMORRAH

The destruction of the cities of Sodom and Gomorrah in tandem with the story surrounding that famous pair, Abraham and Lot, are no longer a major mystery with the discovery of at least fifty thousand bodies in archaeo-logical sites like Bab edh-Dhra (Sodom) and Numeira (Gomorrah) opposite the Dead Sea. The heavy layer of ash everywhere indicates fire fell from heaven. In addi-tion, the 4,500-year-old *Eblaite Geographic Atlas* quite clearly demonstrates that a merchant from Ebla stopped at Sodom on his way to the Gulf of Aqabah. Finally, there is ample evidence that the region was indeed richly endowed with grass and trees and a wide variety of wildlife at the time of Abraham.

TOWER OF BABEL

What evidence is there for the existence of the Tower of Babel, the confusion of languages, and the dispersion of the races throughout the world? We discovered that ziggurats all over the world are similar in purpose to the Tower of Babel; that archaeologists have discovered the Tower of Babel at Babylon in Iraq; that modern linguists are convinced the original language, the proto-language, came from that region; and that cultural anthropologists are able to trace the migration of people throughout the world as having started in this biblical area of the Middle East. Examined critically and from a population-growth standpoint, the rapid expansion of languages is also possible.

Most intriguing of all in this section was the question of whether Saddam Hussein will duplicate the feat of Nimrod and expand his rule well beyond the borders of Iraq. He could become a most significant figure in the future, if biblical prophecy is any indicator of what is to come.

EXODUS—RED SEA CROSSING

The ten plagues God sent in support of Moses' plea to Pharaoh to let the Hebrews leave have been documented in Egypt's own historical writings. The disruption of Egyptian society by the departure of so many slaves plus the death of Pharaoh's army have also been noted in Egyptian records. Modern scientists have duplicated the wind blowing back the Red Sea to create a crossing area, demonstrating scientifically that this event mentioned in the Bible has validity.

ARK OF THE COVENANT

When Moses received the instructions to build the ark of the covenant it was the beginning of yet another mystery —the disappearance of the ark after its placement in the temple by Solomon. We discovered that, yes, the Israelites had the technical skills to build the ark. But we also examined the mystery of its use and ultimate disappearance, examining two traditional stories: that Menelik, the son of King Solomon and the Queen of Sheba, took it back to Ethiopia—where it is now kept in a secret underground church; or that Levite priests hid the ark in a secret temple vault when King Nebuchadnezzar broke into the city—and that it has been seen during recent excavations by Jewish rabbis.

WALL OF JERICHO
FALLING DOWN

The mystery of Joshua and the Israelites crossing the Jordan River without the aid of boats or a bridge may be explained by the presence of an upstream earthquake damming up the river. Recent archaeological work at the ancient site of Jericho indicates the city walls did collapse after a very short siege, providing ramps for the

Israelites to enter the city and burn it. And a layer of ash does in fact indicate destruction by fire—just as the Bible states! An earthquake may also be the logical explanation as a contributing factor for the collapse of the wall, though sound waves from the trumpet-blowing and shouting Israelites could have helped in toppling these earthquake damaged walls, as well.

DINOSAUR AND MAN— CONTEMPORARIES

Along the way we also considered remarkable evidence that dinosaurs and man were contemporaries, as the Bible seems to reveal. In fact, young dinosaurs may well have been on Noah's ark. Footprints of dinosaurs with human prints embedded in them or beside them have been found in several areas throughout the world, providing evidence for this biblical claim.

THE BIBLE—A SCIENCE BOOK

The Bible appears to be a remarkably accurate source of scientific information. A careful reading proves we can trust biblical statements on both science and health.

If you have approached this book with an open mind, the evidence is overwhelming that those who wrote the Bible, under the inspiration of God, had a clear understanding of many scientific and health principles not generally accepted or even noticed for centuries. It took Columbus, for example, to prove what God told Job two thousand years earlier—that the earth was an "orb."

With all of that settled, we can read the Bible for its message of God's love. After all, even the critics agree that the Bible contains an incredible message of hope for a happier and more fulfilling life.

INDEX